How to Read the Bible Well

How to Read the Bible Well

What It Is, What It Isn't, and How To Love It (Again)

Stephen Burnhope

Foreword by Jason Swan Clark

 CASCADE *Books* · Eugene, Oregon

Cascade Books
An Imprint of Wipf and Stock Publishers
199 W. 8th Ave., Suite 3
Eugene, OR 97401

www.wipfandstock.com

PAPERBACK ISBN: 978-1-7252-8142-4
HARDCOVER ISBN: 978-1-7252-8141-7
EBOOK ISBN: 978-1-7252-8143-1

Cataloguing-in-Publication data:

Names: Burnhope, Stephen, author. | Clark, Jason Swan, foreword writer.

Title: How to read the Bible well : what it is, what is isn't, and how to love it (again) / Stephen Burnhope.

Description: Eugene, OR: Cascade Books, 2021 | Includes bibliographical references.

Identifiers: ISBN 978-1-7252-8142-4 (paperback) | ISBN 978-1-7252-8141-7 (hardcover) | ISBN 978-1-7252-8143-1 (ebook)

Subjects: LCSH: Bible—Hermeneutics | Bible—Study and teaching | Biblical studies | Bible—Criticism, interpretations, etc.

Classification: BS476 B87 2021 (print) | BS476 (ebook)

04/21/21

Contents

Foreword

Jesus loves me this I know
for the Bible tells me so

ANNA BARTLETT WARNER, 1860

These wonderful words, a poem written for a dying child to hear, were set to a tune—with the chorus added: "Yes, Jesus loves me, Yes, Jesus loves me"—by William Bradbury. It became and still is one of the most popular hymns in the world. This song reminds us of how clearly and profoundly the Bible speaks to individuals. Many of us have made the amazing discovery that we can read the Bible on our own and God will speak to us through it. Indeed, one of the gifts of the Protestant Reformation was to place the Bible in the hands of ordinary people, for them to read, reflect, and meditate on before God. We now have apps that break the Bible down into daily chunks, so we might read all the way through it, again and again.

The truth is this: Christians need no permission in order to read God's Word. God delights in speaking to his followers, as they read his Word. But there is another truth. We can also be very bad at reading the Bible. At times even the most seemingly clear of things from the Bible, that Jesus loves us, is not "read" by others. Instead, they declare that the simple and plain reading of God's Word is that we are objects of God's wrath and judgment.

Then there are parts of the Bible we ignore, as we stick to the bits we like and understand. If we are honest, we think we know what some parts say only because other people have told us that's what they say. Then some parts are straightforward and clear, but we choose to ignore them because we do not like what we read, the challenges therein too much for us to entertain.

So we can all read the Bible on our own with God, but reading it *well* is not straightforward. The title of this book presumes and responds directly to this problem—that there are ways of reading the Bible that are not good. And there are indeed ways of hearing things from the Bible that God never intended. Most of us can likely bring to mind someone quoting the Bible to justify something we consider to be awful. Then there are the less-awful but also strange things people believe and claim are in the Bible. You might at times wonder if you have been reading the same Bible as others.

We may have already discovered some ways to read the Bible better. We realized opening it at random for God to speak to us has more in common with reading horoscopes. When we learn the Bible is a collection of sixty-six books, of different genres, our way of reading immediately opens up into something better. We discover that Genesis was not and is not a science account in chronological order. We don't have to force Genesis to fit scientific accounts. Or we find out something about the Greek and Hebrew behind the English translations of our Bible that helps us read what we could not understand before.

So perhaps like me you love the Bible, know it is God's Word, and want to read it better. But in our quest to read better, we can move from a mode of "simply" reading the Bible to a place where we might feel like we can never understand it unless we have a PhD in biblical studies. And even then, we know biblical scholars disagree with each other. Reading well can seem like harder and harder work. So too often, we default back to how we read it before, trying to keep it simple but knowing we are missing out on things.

So how on earth are you and I ever going to be able to read the Bible well? In your hands, you have the key to solving that problem. This book speaks to and responds to this most enormous of challenges. How to let the Bible speak by itself and directly, but how we might also better navigate it with an understanding that we cannot obtain on our own. We need a guide and this book will give us the tools to understand how to understand the Bible. Like a key and a compass, it will unlock things for us and show the direction to go, without being prescriptive.

No offence to the wonderful academics we have (and Steve himself has a PhD in theology), but this is not a book by an academic at some distance from daily life and the church. Instead, it is by a world expert in biblical theology, who did his theology while spending decades in work that was not pastoring. Steve came to full-time pastoral ministry later in life. He has been an exceptional pastor. So why does all that matter? Because it means Steve's teaching and training is filtered through all that life and ministry experience. There is an attention to reading the Bible well for everyday life that is uniquely present with Steve.

Not long ago, I encouraged Steve to record some of his teachings on how to read the Bible. After sitting in on those recordings, I experienced a few things. First, it inspired me and got me excited about reading my Bible. Second, I thought I want everyone in my church to hear this for their engagement with the Bible. Third, I realized this was so significant that others needed the opportunity to have this resource. So I suggested Steve write this book. When Steve asked me to write the foreword for it, I jumped at the chance.

This book will help you learn some easy-to-remember ways to approach Scripture better, but then leave you free to read unencumbered. It also offers some examples of how to read the Bible against some of the critical issues and challenges we face today. Whether you are a new Christian or a seasoned one, this book is a must-read for anyone wanting to read their Bibles well.

Jason Swan Clark, PhD
Senior Pastor, Sutton Vineyard Church, London, UK
Lead Mentor, D.Min LGP, Portland Seminary
June 2020

Preface

I've wanted to write a book on the Bible for a long time. Not a Bible study book as such, but more a book about what the Bible is and how we should relate to it. And, by the same token, what the Bible isn't and how we shouldn't be relating to it, which is just as important.

As a Christian who approaches the Bible with the highest regard for its standing as the Word of God, I wanted to write a book for people who start from the same standpoint but still struggle with what that phrase means in practice. This book is aiming to ask (and hopefully to answer) the kinds of questions that ordinary thinking Christians have about the Bible, posed in the kinds of ways that they ask them.

I also wanted to be writing for those who may have already lost faith in the Bible—and, most likely, in Christianity along the way—but who still maintain a belief in God and are open and interested to hear whether their problems with what they've been told are soluble. Whether, in other words, there are better answers out there.

There are plenty of academic books around that address the kinds of things I want to cover. Many of them are excellent. I love them. They dominate my bookshelves. The problem is, they're *academic* books. They're not accessible for most Christians. There are not so many books around that are written from an academic perspective, in a non-academic way, for ordinary readers. Our local Christian bookstore has different rooms for academic books versus so-called "popular" books (as academics call them—perhaps without realizing the irony) written by non-academics. You can almost see the panic in the eyes of the unsuspecting shopper who accidently wanders into the academic section by mistake.

So here, I'm aiming to cross the divide, to bridge the two. I want the book to be helpful for the ordinary Christian who loves God and loves the Bible, but wants to understand both more deeply. To make it as readable as possible is part of that. The academic reader may think that some of my treatment of some of the subjects covered is a bit shallow, or fails to address additional aspects that could or indeed should be included. That will almost certainly be the case; but again, that will mostly be by design, to better achieve its primary objectives.

As a pastor as well as a theologian I have always wanted to make good theological thinking more accessible in the church at large. I've found there's a big demand for it. People have a thirst to understand their faith beyond the boundaries of the standard inspirational weekly sermon—especially when it comes to some of the big questions of life and the big questions they have about God and the Bible. (Not that there's anything wrong with inspirational sermons—surely they should all be inspirational!)

If you've just picked this up browsing in a bookshop and don't know me from Adam, you may be wondering at this point whether I'm sound—which of course somewhat depends on what we mean by "sound." Generally, that's someone who thinks like we do! To try to put any worries to rest, I don't consider myself a "liberal," except insofar as Jesus was. He seems to me to have been both liberal and conservative, in the very best senses of each. Actually, I don't think either of those words is particularly helpful nowadays, because of the variety of things people mean when they use them (the words carry a lot of baggage), so generally we'll avoid them.

The end goal for this book is that readers will find a new lease of life to love the Bible (again), with a fresh confidence and enthusiasm in relating to it as the Word of God. A better understanding of the Bible will lead to a better understanding of the nature and character of the God who is its central character. The purpose of the Bible has never been to draw us into a relationship with the Bible, but to draw us into a relationship with *God*. Read well, the Bible will surely always do that and through it we will discover a fresh confidence and enthusiasm in our relationship with him.

To get the most out of the book, I recommend reading it in chapter order. It might be tempting to go straight to a chapter later in the book that sounds more enticing, but it will mean missing some of the groundwork that's laid in the earlier chapters, because the ideas "build" as they go along. I have no vested interest in you doing it that way (you've probably already bought the book by now!), so I say that only because I think you'll get more out of it if you do. That said, there is a small amount of repetition of key points as we go along, simply in order to enable chapters to stand-alone where you may wish to refer people to them.

Finally, I want to express my thanks and appreciation to a number of people. This is always risky because of the danger of leaving people out, but they do say it's better to have tried and failed than to have never tried at all! Firstly, to my wife Lyn, whose own studies led me into the world of theology, averting what might otherwise have been a mid-life faith crisis! Secondly, to our wonderful friends within the Vineyard movement and wider Christian world—in the US, the UK, and further afield—pastors and theologians, we love you so much! Special mention must go to our great friend Dr. Jason Clark, not least for his constant encouragement (aka hassling me) to write this book. Thirdly, to all our friends at Aylesbury Vineyard Church, especially the staff team and leadership team, for all your love and encouragement. I can't name all of you, but you know who you are! Fourthly, to Dr. Graham McFarlane at the London School of Theology, who continually challenged my closeted thinking, devoted great time and patience to supervising my Masters' dissertation and then provoked me in the nicest possible way to pursue a PhD. Fifthly, my wonderful PhD supervisors at King's College London, Dr. Susannah Ticciati and Professor Ben Quash. And then finally, last but not least, to my brilliant editor the Revd. Dr. Robin Parry, who I've so enjoyed engaging with, and his colleagues at Wipf and Stock Publishers. I am grateful for all of their support and contributions.

It remains only to say that, surrounded by such a great cloud of witnesses (Hebrews 12:1), any shortcomings in the end product are entirely down to me.

Introduction

For Christians, the Bible is the "Word of God"—which obviously sets it apart, in a category all of its own, compared to any other book. What's not immediately obvious from that phrase, though, is *how* exactly it's the Word of God. In *what way* it's the Word of God. What that actually *means* in practice. To believe that the Bible is the Word of God is only the start. What each of us, personally, thinks that means will determine the place that we give to it in our life.

If the Bible is the Word of God, featuring in some way *the words* of God, then presumably God has given it to us so that in some way he "speaks" to us through it. Notice already, the number of times I'm needing to say "in *some* way . . . ." Each of these statements needs to be explored, in terms of what we mean by it.

How God features in his Word, why and how he gave it to us, and, most importantly, how God speaks to us through it are really important questions for any Christian who starts from the perspective of being "Bible-believing" and sees the Bible as a vital part of their relationship with God. And that's because, ultimately, our interest is not so much the Bible itself as what it tells us about the God behind the Bible and how it "works" in communicating the things of God to us.

We need to know what "believing" the Bible looks like in practice and what we believe the Bible to "be" is an important starting point. We can't defend the Bible against its critics unless we know what we're defending, so we can be sure that we're defending the right things. The kinds of things that people have found difficult include:

- Whether Adam and Eve are to be taken literally;
- Whether, if the Bible wasn't exactly "dictated" by God, it was "as good as" dictated;

- Whether the Bible is "inerrant" and "infallible"—as the "of God" bit of Word *of God* might imply—since, if God is those things and it's "his" Word, then surely it must be too;

- What it's saying about hell;

- What it's telling us about science and biology;

- How we deal with some of the violence in the Old Testament for which God seems to get the credit; and

- How to deal with some of the (apparently) outdated things it appears to teach, such as women submitting to men and keeping quiet in church. Are these "timeless" truths or time-bound within that era? If the Bible contains a mixture, then why does it? How do we tell the difference?

All of these come under the broader question, "What do we mean by the Bible as the Word of God?"

How Is God Involved in His Word?

You will have noticed that I've been using the term "the Word of God" with a capital "W" and will continue to do so throughout. One reason for that is simply because it's the most common title that Christians give to the Bible. But a more important reason is that it's that very title that leads to many of the questions we're aiming to address, so I want to keep it center stage. Specifically, this happens when by implication Christians grant to the Bible quasi-divine attributes that place it almost on a par with God himself. Non-charismatics may be criticized for turning the Trinity into God the Father, God the Son, and God the Holy Scriptures, but their charismatic brethren can be just as guilty of unwittingly deifying the Bible, too. I think this happens through a combination of seeing a capital "W" (we tend to capitalize words referring to God, don't we?), the slightly ambiguous tag "of God" (the meaning of which people interpret differently: "of" in what sense?), and conservative evangelical tradition in which the Bible is very highly revered, not least when we feel the need to defend it against secular criticism.

The challenge is illustrated by something I came across on a website called biblestudytools.com, under the heading "Bible Verses about the Word of God," where it says: "The Bible is referred to as the Word of God *meaning it can be considered a direct line of communication from the*

Lord ..." (italics added). The sentence then continues with the qualifica-
tion "... interpreted by the authors of the respective books," which adds
to (rather than resolves) the problem of how those two statements are
understood to come together in practice. How can a communication be
both a *"direct line of communication"* and "interpreted by"?

Strictly speaking, of course, the Bible does not talk about itself as the
Word of God, not least because the Bible as we know it today had not yet
come together. Within the Bible itself, that title is reserved solely for Jesus
(John 1)—which perhaps adds to that "quasi-divine attributes" ambiguity
for people. Christians' naming of the Bible as "the Word of God" largely
follows by inference from phrases such as "the word of the Lord" (which
is talking of God speaking generally) and "the law of the Lord" (which is
talking of Torah). I will continue to use the Word of God as a title, but
wherever it appears I mean nothing different than if I'd said "the Bible" or
(as I do occasionally) "Scripture" or "the Scriptures."

God Likes Questions (Even If People Don't Always)

Many Christians have been told by church leaders—or at least, it's been
strongly implied—that they shouldn't ask difficult questions. They should
just trust and believe; not over-intellectualize their faith, not let their
head get in the way of their heart, and such like. If you've experienced
that, and found it disappointing, then this book is for you.

Sadly there is a strain of anti-intellectualism in everyday Christianity,
which is driven by a legitimate fear of intellectualizing faith away; and
especially, heart-centered experiential faith. However, in God's design,
we were made to be inquisitive, thinking people. Jesus said that we should
love the Lord our God with our *minds* as well as our hearts and souls—the
"greatest commandment" embraces all three (Matthew 22:37). I actually
think God likes questions! He certainly isn't fazed by them. Christianity
is never under threat from good people asking good questions with
good attitudes (even though some Christian leaders may feel that they
personally might be!). The famous motto of Anselm, the eleventh-
century Archbishop of Canterbury, was "faith seeking *understanding.*"
Not, however, in the sense of replacing a living faith with intellectual
head-knowledge. He was talking about people who start from a position
of *loving* God but are equally passionate for a deeper *understanding* of
God—who come at understanding from the direction of faith. Who want

to add understanding to that faith. And of course, the Bible has a key role to play in the journey. There's absolutely no need for us to put "faith" vs. "understanding" in competition with each other.

This book will not be one for those who are perfectly happy to start and finish with "the Bible says . . . ." That's great as a starting point, but not if our interest ends there. What we should really want to know is what the Bible *means* by what it says—how we are to best understand what it says, and why it says it. If we're going to properly respect the original writers, that means first wanting to know what it meant to them in their situation, in their day, rather than leaping straight to what it means for us in our situation, in our day. That's important because a basic "rule" of good biblical interpretation is that it cannot mean something now that it did not mean then. Simply to "copy and paste" verses from "then" to "now," as if there was no distance between the two, is to ignore the significance of those verses' original contexts. At best, it's disrespectful, and at worst, it will lead to poor interpretation. Flipped round the other way, the better we understand its original meaning, the richer and more profound will be our application of the text in our circumstances today.

Don't Be Afraid of "Interpretation"

Speaking of *interpretation* . . . for many faithful Bible-believing Christians, that word will immediately ring alarm bells! Most of us like to think we're just reading the Bible (emphasis on the word "just") and we honestly don't think we're interpreting it at all. By nature, evangelical Christians in particular can be a bit suspicious of academics, maybe because we worry that some of them are not really Christians at all—or at least, not Christians like we are. We worry that they're going to interpret it away, dissecting it like a dead rat on a high school lab bench—if it isn't dead already, it will be by the time they've finished. We like to think that our understanding of what we're reading is the same as the original writer intended and the Holy Spirit intended. Especially when what it's saying seems pretty obvious, from what's there on the page. Many Christians have grown up with the idea of the "perspicuity" of Scripture. They may not know the word, but they know the concept, which comes from the Protestant Reformation. Namely, that the Bible can be read and understood perfectly well by ordinary people with the help of the Holy Spirit alone—that it "plainly says what it plainly says," without needing additional help from theologians to interpret it for them.

It's true that lots of the Bible can easily be understood that way. Its message is clear and obvious. It can easily bless people, "speak" powerfully to people, and draw them into a relationship with God—that's especially the case with the Gospels, and lots of the New Testament. It does that all the time and always has. But it's also true that every time we read anything in the Bible we're interpreting, whether we realize it or not. Every time someone "teaches" the Bible in church or in a home group, they're interpreting. Maybe not very deeply, or necessarily very well, but interpreting it none the less. Surprising though it may sound, there's no interpretation-free way of "just" reading. We all bring with us things we already know—or think we know—when we open its pages, things that we've got from somewhere. They form the "spectacles" through which we're reading.

Once upon a time (up to around the beginning of the last century) there was for all practical purposes only one English Bible—the King James Version, or KJV. It's still the single most common English translation. Many, many Christians revere it. I'm not entirely sure why, exactly; perhaps because it sounds old-fashioned to modern ears and so it feels like it "must be" closer to the original (actually, it's not, but we'll talk about that later). Maybe it's because so many verses have become well-known sayings in their KJV form, or because many Christians first learned verses and passages in that translation.

The proliferation of English translations (especially since the middle of the last century) has now made it obvious to every Bible reader that there is such a thing as biblical interpretation and that they can't escape it. Every time a translation renders a verse differently, there's interpretation going on—translation is a form of interpretation, by translators. In today's world, therefore, it becomes increasingly difficult to say *"the* Bible says" when the obvious next question is *"which* Bible says?" Perhaps that's another reason why some Christians want to cling to the KJV as "the" Bible, or at least, use it as the reference point for the "correctness" of every other version—mistaken though that would be. For more on Bible versions, please see the Appendix.

So, we're all Bible interpreters (sorry about that) and the only question is how well or badly we're doing it and where we're getting our ideas from. By the way, there's nothing wrong with having those "spectacles." It's unavoidable. There's nothing any of us can do about it, we just need to be aware of it. And that's not easy, until we see for ourselves that that's what's happening so we can take it into account. As any spectacles wearers will tell you, most of the time we're so used to them that we're not even conscious we're wearing them.

Last thought—if the word "interpretation" risks bringing some of us out in hives, so too can the word "theology," for the same reasons (dead rats and all that). For the purposes of this book, all we mean by "theology" is *thoughts about God expressed in words*—from the Greek *theo* = God and *logos* = word(s). So again—we all "have" a theology and we all "do" theology. The only question is how well or badly we're doing it and where we're getting it from! The aim of this book is to try to help us do it a little bit better and, dare I say, help rehabilitate the Bible for those of us who have found it difficult to defend when faced with the critique of those who want to point out its supposed weaknesses, inconsistencies and flaws.

1

What Is the Bible?

"What is the Bible?" is a question we don't ask very often. We know what it is in one sense—the foundational text for Christianity. We also know that Christians call it the Word of God. What perhaps we don't ask so often are questions about the nature of the Bible and what exactly we mean when we say it's the Word of God.

The word "Bible" doesn't tell us very much on its own—it comes from the Greek word for "book." However, its longer title of "Holy Bible" is more helpful. To speak of something as holy means for it to be "set apart," "separate," and "sacred," having to do with the things of God and for that reason to be respected—if not also revered—as something different and special, on a higher level. In short, in the Christian tradition, it is no ordinary book—it has something of God about it.

But all of that gets us only so far. We can acknowledge all those things and believe all those things about it and yet still not grasp what the Bible intrinsically is and how we should be relating to it. And, for that matter, how God relates to it. How, exactly, were the human writers involved? How exactly was God involved?

Features of the Bible

We talk about the Bible as a book, but it's actually a collection of books—sixty-six of them: thirty-nine in the Old Testament and twenty-seven in the New Testament. So it's more like a library of books, written by lots of different authors. It's also very long—about 800,000 words in English, which is about ten PhD theses. And it's very old, written between about 2,000 and 3,500 years ago, in a totally different world. Much of the Old Testament was happening when Britain was in the Bronze Age. Just think how differently people lived then, and thought then, compared to now. It's almost impossible to imagine. All of which gives us food for thought, when later we start to think about the ways in which what the Bible says is "timeless."

The Bible is also a whole bunch of different kinds of literature. The technical word for that is *genre*, or type. If you go into a bookstore or a library, that's how the books are organized. There are different sections for different categories, such as history, fiction, romance, sci-fi, music, poetry, philosophy, religion and so on. The Bible has all of those, too— well, maybe not sci-fi—but it mixes them all up in one volume, and sometimes even in one book. Which doesn't make it any easier for us, as readers. Especially when we realize that writers in the ancient world didn't follow twenty-first-century rules—or "literary conventions"—in how they wrote. In other words, they didn't write then, the way that we do now; which is really rather thoughtless of them, isn't it? They had categories of literature that we simply don't have, such as apocalyptic—a kind of prophetic literature full of striking, peculiar symbols—which is hard enough to pronounce, let alone relate to.

> It is clear that there are various kinds of literary forms in the Bible. Each of them possesses its own rules of interpretation . . . Each author assumed that his readers would interpret his words according to the rules governing that literary form. If we are not aware of the rules under which the biblical author wrote, misinterpretation almost certainly will take place.
>
> Robert H. Stein, *A Basic Guide to Interpreting the Bible*, 75.

Writers in the ancient world used lots of picture language and stories to convey things and explain things, where we nowadays would expect to find facts and figures and technical information that they really weren't so bothered about. Our way of thinking comes from living in an age of science (a period of unprecedented scientific discoveries that began with the so-called Scientific Revolution of the seventeenth century and continues apace). We expect so much more about "life, the universe and everything" to be explainable now, and for those explanations to be provided in scientific terms.

Perhaps already you can begin to see some of the difficulties, when we're looking for the Bible to conform to the expectations that we bring to it as modern readers, and then either criticize it when it fails to live up to them or alternatively, try to apply everything as if it had been written yesterday. A "flat reading" in which it is assumed that there is as good as no distance whatsoever between "then" and "now" is not the most faithful kind of reading. We should never simply say "the Bible says . . ." (especially when we link it to an authoritative conclusion) without thinking carefully, in an informed way, about what the Bible *means* by what it says—which of course starts with what it *meant* by what it said. Only then can we go on to determine "What the Bible teaches . . . ," then and now.

One of the reasons that writers in the ancient world used picture language and stories is because most people couldn't read or write. The sacred writings that in due course became part of the Bible were not written to be read privately by individuals, but read-out and listened to in a community setting. People didn't have their own personal copies for private devotions. Picture language and stories are great for conveying truths. They're easy to remember and easy to pass on. Many began life passed down by word-of-mouth, before they were ever committed to writing. They also have a "timeless" quality about them. We all love stories and we all relate to stories. We're more inclined to remember them. Stories engage our brains in ways that facts and figures alone rarely do, including, in reflection and imagination. Most of us far prefer to watch box sets and movies than documentaries and lectures.

We also shouldn't forget that it wasn't until the Middle Ages that anyone started dividing the Bible up into chapters and verses. That can be very useful, of course, to help us find a verse or a passage. But it can also make us more inclined to dissect it into bits, like a dead frog in a school biology lab, as if the more we chop it up into smaller and smaller pieces the more we'll learn about how it works. One consequence of the Bible having been divided up in that way is that it can make us inclined to pick out individual verses—especially "nice" ones that we find encouraging—from their original contexts, treating them as self-contained communicative statements. There's nothing wrong with that done well; the problem is when we treat the Bible as if it's primarily a collection of inspirational one-liners with padding in-between.

Reading the Bible with Its Original Audience

"What is the Bible?" may be a question that we don't ask very often, but even less often do we ask the question "What was the Bible to its original audiences?" Obviously that's not always an easy one to answer, given the time and cultural distance involved. But hard though it may be, it's not a question that we can dodge completely; a basic rule of good biblical interpretation is that something in the Bible can never be saying "now" something that it could never have been saying "then." We'll talk more about that later.

When we read the Bible today it's easy for us to assume—to take for granted—that the questions that matter to us in our world must also be the questions that mattered to them in their world. Without realizing that's what we're doing, we approach the text looking for answers to what matters to us, rather than the answers to what mattered to them. In fact, it may never even occur to us to start by asking what questions would have mattered to them.

A classic example of that would be the Creation account in the book of Genesis. When we read Genesis nowadays we're looking for it to tell us *how* the world was made, because that's what interests us in an age of science. Given that interest, it seems "obvious" to us that's what it "must be" about. We're looking for clues to the manufacturing process. Because God is timeless, we assume his Word must be—so we expect what it says about how the world was made to fit with what we know today about how the world was made. Or at least, because of our desire to honor it as "timeless" truth, we try to make it fit—to look for a scientific correspondence between what modern science knows and what the Bible says (as if finding such connections via little clues in the text will somehow ratify the truth of the biblical account). We're wanting it to conform—to offer answers—to what matters to people today. However, in the ancient world people really weren't interested in *how* the world was made; they were interested in why it was made. And who made it. And why the world is the way that it is. And how that affects them and who they are. How they fit into the big picture. What that means for their lives, as readers (or more often, hearers). Who they are, as a people. And who their God is. Not such bad questions, wouldn't you say? But none of them have anything much to do with expecting Genesis to be describing the scientific chronology of a manufacturing process presented in modern terms.

No wonder people nowadays find it hard to make sense of the Creation account, when we're expecting to find answers to questions they weren't asking. The best answer in the world is no use to anyone if it's answering a different question. It's like aliens from Outer Space tuning in to re-runs of Michael Scott in *The Office* (David Brent, in the UK version) and assuming it's a management training video (which in a way it is, but only in a "how not to" sense). Or Tom Cruise in *War of the Worlds*, and assuming it's a documentary on The History Channel (object lesson: "how not to" invade another planet, perhaps?).

So when as Christians we ask "What is the Bible?" we're not asking *whether* it's the Word of God so much as *how* it's the Word of God and what, exactly, we mean by that. We're not questioning *whether* God is uniquely engaged with it in some way; we accept that by faith. What we're enquiring is *how*. And our goal for asking these questions is not simply academic interest; it's so that we can better understand it, better learn from it, and better apply it as God's Word in our lives. Our overriding ambition is relational: to draw us closer to God.

Now one of the first things that's obvious about the Bible is that while it's many other things as well, before anything else it's clearly a book about people and their stories. We may be separated by thousands of years and almost unimaginably different cultural settings, but they were people with life stories just as we are people with life stories. They were people with families and relationships—fathers and sons and mothers and brothers and sisters and cousins—just as we are. People who had life experiences as we have life experiences. Happy times and sad times. Successes and failures. Triumphs and tragedies. Times they did the right things and times they did the wrong things. People who had hopes and fears and joys and sorrows—as we have—and who had to live by faith as we do. Needing to believe in a God they couldn't see, as we do. Wanting to understand him and his nature and his character and his ways of doing things, as we do.

It's very important for us to remember that in most of the biblical period the authors and their audiences were progressively getting to know God as the story unfolded and their understanding of him unfolded. It is only when Jesus enters into the story that God's true identity suddenly becomes clear and visible—the Jesus whom Colossians 1:15–19 says is the exact image of the invisible God: the visible likeness of what God is really and truly like, and always has been like. Jesus' incarnation gave rise to a paradigm shift. It was a change of several orders of magnitude in the revelation of God's nature and character and purposes. Consequently, we shouldn't fall into the all-too-easy trap of reading the text as if Abraham and Moses and David had the same understanding of who God is and what he's like as we do, since they didn't have access to the same information. And in particular, they didn't have Jesus, in the light of whom every previous understanding and assumption of who God is and what he's like needed to be reconsidered. They hadn't had the benefit of 2,000 years of theological reflection after Jesus, as we have—nor did they have the New Testament, the creeds (the core statements of belief of the early church drawn up in the first few centuries after Jesus, from the Latin *credo*, "I believe"), or the insights of the Reformation—all of which are available to us and form part of our "obvious."

The Story of People and the Story of God

But of course, the Bible is not just the story of people, it's also the story of *God*. What we see throughout the Bible is these stories of people intertwined with the story of God. They're stories of people experiencing God in their stories and their families' stories, against the backdrop of a "Big Story" of which the people realized they were part. They're stories of things that happened when God was there with them, and stories of when he didn't seem to be there with them. When we read the Bible, we're observers of how people understood God and found him in their stories, as we do, but we're also observers of how, at times, people misunderstood God and missed him in their stories, as we do. All the individual stories are parts of one big story that is unfolding; a continuous story that has a past and a future. It's a story of people grappling with who God is and what he's like, and how he does things, and what's important to him. It's a story of how people can know him and what his plans and purposes are for them and their world. As we're reading it, the Bible is inviting us into those stories. Inviting us to think about what they tell us about God and what they tell us about ourselves. Also, at times, it's inviting us to second-guess their stories. Where they were understanding him correctly and where they were not. Just as we sometimes do, as we too are learning.

The Danish philosopher Søren Kierkegaard famously said that when we read the Bible, we must constantly be saying to ourselves it's talking *to* me and it's talking *about* me. In other words, we see ourselves in its pages and its stories, as if we're looking in a mirror. The Bible invites us to ask ourselves:

- "Who would I have been in that story?"
- "How would I have responded in that story?"
- "What does the story tell me about who God was for them?" and
- "What can I learn from it about who God will be for me, in what's happening in my life right now?"

One of the most interesting things about the Bible, that people often don't realize, is that most of it isn't commandments and instructions, telling us what to do and what to believe. Around 75 percent is "narrative"; or as we might say, stories or drama. About 15 percent is poetry and song. Only around 10 percent is what's called "propositional" truths—in other words, facts about God and instructions from God: doctrines and statements of belief and so on. The Bible is more "box sets and movies" than it is "documentaries and lectures." Don't hold me to mathematical precision on those percentages, but if around 90 percent of the Bible is stories and drama and poetry and songs, it begs the question: How do they "teach"? Christians have become accustomed to the idea that everything in the Bible is there to teach us something; so how do they do that? What and how are we supposed to learn from them and through them? And of course, as soon as we start to think about answering those questions, we're doing theology! We're doing biblical interpretation!

Now the propositions that are there (the facts about God, the instructions and commands and belief statements and so on) are very important. We need to be clear on that. But all of them come to us within a context. Or rather, within many different contexts. In other words, each is located in a particular place in the biblical story, which it's at least helpful to be aware of and sometimes essential to be aware of, if we are to understand them right. Not all of them are "timeless" and intended to stand-alone, when they're taken out of their context. Even those that are need firstly to be understood within their context before we rush to "copy and paste" them directly into today. A classic example of that is whether some of the Old Testament commandments still apply today. And if they do, how we decide which ones. That's a subject all by itself, that we'll cover in chapter 6.

Even with the propositions, we still need to be doing some theology—we still need to be doing some interpretation. As we said earlier, there is no interpretation-free way of "just" reading. We all read through the lenses of things that we already know (or think we know). We all bring with us pre-formed ideas as to what something means, or "must mean" or "can't mean" or "obviously" means, or that people have told us it means. Those things may of course be right, or they may not be right, but they're all reflecting understandings that we're bringing with us as the lenses through which we're reading. These are called "presuppositions"— an important word to try to remember—things that we take for granted at the outset about what we're reading. We all have them, and we can't change that. The key thing is for us to aim to be aware of it. Whenever we use a phrase like "must be" or "can't be"—or what something "obviously" means—it's our presuppositions talking.

It's helpful for us to be aware that not everyone will be looking at the text through the same lenses that we are. Our "obvious" may well not be their "obvious." Our personal circumstances, life-history, gender, economic situation, Christian background (or lack of it), the place in the world where we are living, and so on, will all have a part to play—however unconsciously—in how we will read the text. A "timeless," impersonal, "objective" reading uninfluenced by any of these background factors is as good as impossible; we just need to see that that's the case.

When we talk about the importance of "context" for what we're reading in the Bible, we mean taking proper account of the setting, or background, in determining what something means or "what it's saying" (rather than, extracting a word, verse, or passage and treating it in isolation). Context is our framework for interpretation. As well as the literary context, it includes the rhetorical context, the historical context, the cultural and social context, the political context, and the economic context. Each of these contextual aspects, which often overlap, contributes materially to understanding the author (and the audience), the events being narrated, and the characters who feature.

Context might be thought of as like a set of Russian Matryoshka Dolls (or "nesting dolls"). Every word or phrase sits in a sentence, in a paragraph, in a passage, in a book; every individual story has a place in the Big Story; each thing that happens is set in a particular place, against the backdrop of what was happening in that place, at that time; every book was written for a particular group of people, by a writer (or writers) with a particular perspective, and so on.

Everything in the Bible was happening in what we would now call an ancient-world setting (obviously they didn't call it that at the time, any more than people called the Middle Ages that at the time), where people thought in ways that are very different from our ways. It was written *by* people with a particular worldview as to "the way things are" and *to* people with a particular worldview as to "the way things are." Notably, this ancient-world perspective would, broadly, have been shared by people throughout the entire biblical period. We'll say more in this in chapter 5.

The ancient world had its particular presuppositions as well. And because of that shared worldview, the biblical writers didn't need to explain things that were seen as patently "obvious" by them and their audiences. We're actually no different, today. We don't usually explain things that are taken to be common knowledge: assumptions that everyone shares— things that everyone already knows—and knows that they know! An example of an unexplained presupposition in the ancient world is how sacrifices were understood to "work." How, exactly, they were efficacious in establishing, maintaining, and where necessary repairing relationship with God (or the gods). The thing about a worldview is that if everyone already knows something, because it's considered "obvious," then no one needs to explain it or bothers to explain it. Unfortunately, that leaves us as today's readers wishing that someone had written something down at the time, for posterity!

As God spoke to and through the biblical writers, he was working with—and working within—that ancient-world worldview and the particular circumstances that people were in at the time. No differently to how he works with and within our worldview as to "the way things are" to us, and what's "obvious" to us, in our particular circumstances. Again, we will expand on this later.

What Exactly Do We Mean by "the Word of God"?

The overarching questions, then, are as follows. How does this book that's both the story of people and the story of God—with our human story and God's story intertwined throughout its pages—become something that qualifies to be called the Word of God? What separates it into a unique category from every other piece of literature that's ever been written and takes it to a different dimension? In what special way is God involved in it so as to affect how we think of it and how we relate to it? How does the divinity of the Bible interact with the humanity of the Bible? In what ways does this dual-authorship work? Does the presence of its humanity alongside its divinity still warrant us calling it the Word of God; and most importantly of all, justify being willing to commit our lives to its authenticity and its dependability?

When we start to look at those questions, the funny thing is that the Bible says very little about itself as the Word of God. This is especially surprising when we consider the time and effort that's gone into Christian organizations' drafting of statements of faith over the years. Many of the ideas about the nature of the Bible that get reflected in those statements of faith—such as, "inerrancy," "infallibility," and "authority"—are drawn from a combination of our tradition and reflections on what the Word of God "must be" for it to carry that title, rather than from express statements found in Scripture itself. That does not invalidate those ideas, of course. Heritage and tradition are important conversation partners (more so than contemporary Christianity often recognizes). But it's important to think through what we mean by these words and from where we are getting the definitions.

One of the very few things that Scripture says about itself, but also one of the most important, is found in 2 Timothy 3:16—that it is "inspired by" God (NASB) or "given by inspiration of God" (KJV). It's highly unlikely the author was intending his own letter to be included in that, of course (he would have meant the Jewish Scriptures), but we may do so now, by logical extension. "Inspiration," in this context, doesn't mean the way we tend to use the word today, when we talk about a brilliant idea, or something that's very creative, like a piece of art or music. In fact, our familiarity with the term being used in that way (focused on the artist) can slightly mislead us as to what the verse is saying. The Greek word here is *theopneustos* and literally means "God breathed," or "God breathed-out." It's describing a characteristic of Scripture. The emphasis is not on the writers being breathed into by God but on the texts being breathed out by God (albeit coming to us, of course through those human writers, which we discuss elsewhere). More recent Bible versions reflect this sense by rendering it as "God-breathed" (NIV) or "breathed out by God" (ESV). Its dynamic imagery is all the more meaningful when we reflect on how the Holy Spirit is spoken of in Scripture as breath, wind, and life-giver (the root word is the same: in Hebrew, *ruah*, and in Greek, *pneuma*). See, for example, how it's used in Job 33:4, John 3:8, John 20:22, and Acts 2:2–4. Saying that God "inspired" the Bible therefore means that he "breathed" the Bible; that the generation of its words reflects his person and presence, making it unique in literature and uniquely authoritative in relation to Christian faith. By extension, this unique, God-breathed status enables Scripture to continue to perform a unique dynamic role, as we engage with God through the texts and bring them into our lives and situations. Hence, God is able to, metaphorically, breathe-out of Scripture to us now, as well.

Now on the surface, the story that we read in the Old Testament is mostly the story of one nation—one family, one group of people—called Israel. But because the God of Israel is also the God of the whole world, the God of every-one and every-thing, the Bible is also the whole world's story. When Matthew and Luke set the story of Jesus in its overarching context in Matthew 1 and Luke 3, Matthew traces the story back to Abraham, the father of Israel, while Luke traces it back to Adam, the father of everyone.

But of course, the Bible is not just a narrative about the past. It's also a narrative about the future—although we shouldn't read it (as some have) as if it's a meticulous, detailed plan with secret coded messages just waiting there for us to crack. If Jesus could say that even he doesn't know the date and the time of the age to come (Matthew 24:36)—only the Father knows that—and that when it does come, it will surprise everyone, because it will come like a thief in the night (1 Thessalonians 5:2), then why do Christians waste their energies trying to calculate dates and times? Trying to find clues that simply aren't there, in a Bible that isn't trying to give them those clues? Or at least, not beyond the simple yet profound pictures of the future that the Bible paints with words, and the sure and certain promises of what God is one day going to do. In the meantime, the Bible encourages us to live as people who believe it's going to happen—and even, as if it's about to happen any time now.

What we see in the Bible, rather than hidden clues and secret messages, are "prophetic pictures" and "prophetic insights" of what that future will be like: the big picture and the key messages. Especially, concerning who we should be and how we should live because of it. We see pictures and insights of what our own future will be like, if we want to be part of it. God's primary interest is not to have us poring over prophetic timelines and prophecy interpretation charts to identify events in the future, but to be drawn into a relationship with him that changes our present. A relationship in which we increasingly become more and more "kingdom people"—eagerly awaiting the fullness of the future kingdom to arrive and doing all that we can in the meantime to hasten its coming.

One reason why so much of what the Bible is wanting to teach comes to us through picture language is because we know that "a picture is worth 1,000 words." And that's particularly so if you're a timeless God and you want to make sure—as best you can—that ancient literature which first had to make sense to people in one set of circumstances will still makes sense to people in another quite different set of circumstances, thousands of years later. Which it will—provided, of course, that we're asking it the right questions and not the wrong questions. Provided we respect it as it is—as it was intended to be—and we don't assume that it "must be" answering the questions that we in our modern world, with our modern ways of thinking, would like it to or expect it to.

The Bible, then, is a Big Story that is both the story of God and the story of people. It goes back to the beginning of time and it looks forward to the end of time. It's narrating a story that has a beginning and an end. It's a story which is very interested in theology (learning about God) and Christology (learning about Jesus), but is really not that interested in biology or cosmology. It's a story that picks and chooses its targets as to what it's wanting to tell us, what it's wanting to teach us, and how it's intending to achieve that. Most importantly, it's a story that is ongoing and embraces the entire cosmos. All of us are therefore included— whether we realize it or not. The story of the Bible is an invitation to see our own lives as part of it. The question, therefore, is what role do we personally want to play? Do we want to bring our story into God's story and under God's story? To have him inhabit our story as he inhabits the biblical story—bringing his dynamic presence into it? Do we want to say, "yes, please" and include ourselves in, or "no, thank you" and exclude ourselves out? When the almighty and supernatural God comes into anything, of course, it's never going to be the same again. And nor will we be. Life takes on a whole new dimension.

Because it sits within this Big Story and is shaped by this Big Story, the gospel is so much more than it's often been reduced down to—as a way of getting individual forgiveness for a list of personal sins and a ticket to heaven. Clearly it includes that, but it's so much more than that. The gospel is the good news that Jesus offers us the opportunity to exchange our old and broken story for a new and transformed one. It's an invitation into the story of God and his plans and purposes for this world. To change stories is to change kingdoms: "For he has rescued us from the kingdom of darkness and transferred us into the kingdom of his dear Son" (Colossians 1:13)—now, "our citizenship is in heaven"

(Philippians 3:20). To change stories is to change the center point of our lives; that which everything else in our lives takes as its point of reference. To change stories is to change whom we serve and how we live. The gospel is an invitation to begin to exchange the bad news of life as it is for the good news of life as God intends it to be, and that one day it will fully become through Jesus. The bad news of life "in Adam," as the apostle Paul would say—what our human life looks like when it's left to our own devices, without God—vs. the good news of life "in Christ," with God. And yet, because we're living in the time between Jesus' first coming and Jesus' return, we're still navigating the challenge of being in two stories at once. A story that still includes bad news even though it's centered in good news. That has tasters and down-payments and first-fruits of the good news "now" but "not yet" all of the good news that is to come. We will talk more about this tension between what we call "the now and the not yet" of the presence of the kingdom in later chapters.

2

The Word of God
or the Words of People?

I n this chapter, we're continuing to look at the nature of the Bible as the Word of God. Once again, we're not asking *whether* it's the Word of God, but *how* it's the Word of God. The reason this is important is because what we have in mind by that phrase, what we think it means, will affect how we engage with the Bible. It will affect how we understand God engaged with the human writers in how the Bible came about. And it will affect how we believe God wants us to engage with it today. How we are to treat it. What principles apply to how we read it, interpret it, and apply it. In short, we're asking what the "of God" add-on means in practice.

We've already seen that there are both divine and human aspects to the Bible. We believe by faith that there is a divine author behind what we're reading—the God who "inspired" it, or "breathed it"—and we're aware, too, that there are human writers through whom it came to us. It has dual-authorship, in some sense. This means that we have some grappling to do, if we're to figure out how these human and divine elements come together, in ways that don't in any way undermine the Bible being God's Word (or that damage the high regard in which we rightly hold it) but at the same time make sense of its human aspects.

Conceptually, this offers a similar challenge to how we understand the earthly Jesus to have been both fully God and fully human at the same time. The early church creed that tried to make sense of this apparent conundrum, after a council of eminent theologians was called together to consider it, is known as the Chalcedonian Creed, from 451 CE. We look to the early creeds to define correct beliefs—that which is considered orthodox ("properly Christian") rather than heretical ("not properly Christian")—and this is the one that addresses the humanity and divinity of Jesus. Here's an extract from the Chalcedonian Creed:

> [Jesus was] perfect in Godhead and also perfect in manhood; truly God and truly man, of a reasonable soul and body; consubstantial with us according to the manhood; in all things like unto us, without sin; begotten before all ages of the Father according to the Godhead, and in these latter days, for us and for our salvation, born of the virgin Mary, the mother of God, according to the manhood; one and the same Christ, Son, Lord, Only-begotten, to be acknowledged in two natures, inconfusedly, unchangeably, indivisibly, inseparably; the distinction of natures being by no means taken away by the union, but rather the property of each nature being preserved, and concurring in one Person and one Subsistence, not parted or divided into two persons . . . .

Some of this is quite difficult language—who uses "consubstantial" these days, in everyday conversation? All it means is, "made of the exact same stuff." (Some of the language they used has challenges in the original Greek as well, that we needn't go into.) But the Chalcedonian Creed is important because the controversy that the council was originally called to deal with was to do with what we might call the balance between Jesus' divinity and Jesus' humanity: how he could be properly and fully *both* God *and* man at the same time, without either aspect being diminished as a consequence. We will be turning our attention to that in chapter 9.

Perhaps you can already see how there is a similar challenge for us in relation to the divine and human elements of the Bible.

Let's highlight some of the key phrases in that Chalcedonian Creed:

- "The distinction of [divine and human] natures being by no means taken away by the union."
  - We can see both divine and human elements present, without one overwhelming the other.
- "In all things like unto us, without sin."
  - Fully reflecting what we are like, in every way apart from sinfulness.
- "To be acknowledged in two natures, inconfusedly, unchangeably, indivisibly, inseparably."

- ■ We recognize and accept that both humanity and divinity are present at the same time (without either separating them or confusing them).

- "Perfect in manhood."

  - ■ Perfect *in human terms*. Although human perfection is different to divine perfection (as humans are finite and God is infinite), natural frailties and limitations are not imperfections in humans. In other words, a perfect human is a perfect *human*, and thus still a limited, finite creature.

Critical to our understanding of the incarnation is that the full and complete humanity of Jesus—being perfectly human, not just perfectly God—was God's clear and deliberate intention from the outset. There was no bias (or weighting) towards his nature as God versus his nature as a human being. Jesus' human nature was fully present and fully visible, precisely because God intended that it should be. Some of these important themes are sourced in Hebrews and Philippians.

> For surely it is not angels he helps, but Abraham's descendants. For this reason he had to be made like them, fully human in every way. . . . Because he himself suffered when he was tempted, he is able to help those who are being tempted.

Hebrews 2:16–18

> For we do not have a high priest who is unable to feel sympathy for our weaknesses, but we have one who has been tempted in every way, just as we are—yet he did not sin.

Hebrews 4:15

> Have this attitude in yourselves which was also in Christ Jesus, who, although He existed in the form of God, did not regard equality with God a thing to be grasped, but emptied himself, taking the form of a bond-servant, and being made in the likeness of men.

Philippians 2:5–7

For us properly to understand Jesus—and for him to be a role-model for us, in living in the power of the Holy Spirit and "doing the stuff that Jesus did" (as John Wimber, the main founder of Vineyard Churches, famously put it)—it's essential that we get our heads around Jesus being fully and completely human. He wasn't able to do what he did "because he was God" but because of the anointing of the Holy Spirit. If that hadn't been the case, he wouldn't be a role model for us, because we're obviously not God. We'd still be able to admire him, but not model ourselves on him; he wouldn't have been our perfect human example.

Grappling with the Both-And: "Fully God" and "Fully Human"

Christians generally—and charismatic Christians in particular—tend to have more of a hard time with Jesus' humanity than they do with his divinity. There seems to be a tendency to overemphasize Jesus' divinity and underemphasize his humanity. Many of us really don't like to think too much about Jesus being fully human. Maybe that's because the main challenge that we feel we have with our friends is convincing them that Jesus was the Son of God rather than "just" human. We worry about dragging him down to our level—even though, if we take Philippians and Hebrews seriously, Jesus' full humanity is *vital* to understanding him and what he's done for us.

Philippians 2:5–7 is saying that Jesus voluntarily laid aside (the Greek word means "emptied himself of") everything that would have been incompatible with being fully human as we are, excepting only sin. In other words, he laid down everything to do with "being God" that would have given him an unfair advantage in "being like us" and in living life as we have to—the important thing being that he did so by divine choice.

This begs the question: might the ways in which Jesus as the Word of God (John 1) is fully God and fully human at the same time help us to grasp how the Bible as the Word of God is fully God and fully human at the same time? Might that correspondence work well as a picture or analogy for understanding the nature(s) of the Bible, following the framework of the Chalcedonian Creed?

- If the "distinction of natures" is "by no means taken away by the union" of the two together, we would expect both divine and human elements to be apparent within the text, without "confusion."

- There would be no bias or weighting toward the Bible's divinity over against its humanity. God would have held back from including anything that would have been inconsistent with the knowledge and the lived experience of its human writers at the time (such as, little clues to scientific facts that people wouldn't become aware of until many thousands of years later). There would be no divinely planted anachronisms or secret clues for us to discover and claim that these somehow validate the Bible as "timeless" truth!

- Although both divine and human elements would be apparent, they would be "inseparable"—we wouldn't go on a search to separate out the "divine bits" from the "human bits," because *all* of it would be the Word of God in the sense that all of its content would have been given to us in exactly the way that God intended. The human as well as divine elements would be an inherent part of his design and plan. The "human bits" would not be mistakes, flaws, or design weaknesses.

- The Bible would be "perfect" in human terms; even though if we judge that against what being perfect means in divine terms, it would obviously be lacking in comparison, due to the inevitable, natural frailties that are part of being human. The full and complete humanity of the Bible—being perfectly human alongside being perfectly divine—was God's clear and deliberate intention for it from the outset. It was not a design error! It was as he intended it should be and how it should come to us: hence, fully reliable and fully trustworthy.

Given the struggle for Christians coming to grips with Jesus' two natures, it's unsurprising that Christians also tend to have more of a hard time with the humanity of the Bible than they do with its divinity, and for much the same reasons. We really don't like to think too much about the sense in which the Bible as the Word of God includes it being the words of people as well. As with Jesus, the battle many Christians feel they have with their friends is convincing them that the Bible isn't "just" a human book. They fear that acknowledging its humanity will undermine its claims to divine authority. It's the humanity in the Bible that gives Christians the most difficulties in defending it as "the Word of God." I think that's mostly down to what both its critics and its defenders "read-into" the phrase—what it "obviously" must mean and the characteristics it therefore "must have." We're back to the assumptions that flow from that appendage "of God."

It's easy to assume that the "of God" bit means that the divinity of the divine author of the Bible always overrode the humanity of the human

authors. The consequence being that people expect it to possess characteristics that it never intended to (such as, being "perfect" in matters of
biology, cosmology, science, and so on). That kind of wrong expectation
will lead us to be expecting the Bible to answer questions that it isn't trying to—about things that it isn't saying. However, once we understand
that its humanity is there by divine design—and quite deliberately hasn't
been overridden or covered-up—then we will be able to see that there's
no flaw that needs defending.

We can see in typical modern statements of faith some tenden-
cies, when they're talking about the Bible, to do what Christians do with
Jesus—to overemphasize the divinity at the expense of the humanity.
Words such as "infallible" and "inerrant" are fine if what we mean by that
is *fully reliable, entirely trustworthy,* and *exactly as God intended*—but
not if what we mean would be undermining the Bible's genuine humanity that God included within it by design. Not if what we mean is being
"perfect" in matters, e.g., of biology and cosmology. Not if what we mean
is being perfect in terms of worldview. Not least because we'd then have
to ask: perfect according to the terms of reference of *which* worldview?
The worldview held by which people group, in which place, in which era?

As with Jesus, once we downplay the Bible's humanity, we're not understanding it right. We'll be looking for the wrong things in it and claiming the wrong things for it. We will be defending things that need not be
defended and in the process losing (rather than gaining) credibility both
for ourselves and for the Bible.

Something else that many modern statements of faith do—and this
is because those who draft them realize that the Bible is not "without
error" in some modern senses of that phrase—is to locate the "without
error" only in what they call the "original manuscripts" (which are sometimes called the "autographs"—or the "originals"—which mean the same
thing). This is meant well, but is ultimately rather embarrassing, since
biblical scholars know full well that no such original manuscripts exist.
The way that the Bible came to us via multiple editors, redactors, and
copyists is far more complex than the simple image of a single writer
composing a primordial "original" version implies. Well-intended though
it may be, trying to argue for Scripture's absence of "error" (and hence,
its authority) on the basis of documents that do not exist is, frankly, not a
great strategy. Especially when it is then necessary to go on to argue that
the copies of the texts that we do have (from which our English Bibles
are produced) are close enough to those non-existent originals to still be

fully authoritative in all material respects. This is very much wanting to have our cake and eat it! What is happening here is that we are trying to shoe-horn an ancient text into a modern way of conceiving the features that we think the Bible "must have" if it is the Word of God. Even if such originals did exist, they would still have had human features embedded in them from the outset. The prevailing knowledge of human physiology did not change between the "original" and the subsequent "copies." Nor did people's understanding of the cosmology of a flat earth and tiered universe change in the time between the original author and a subsequent copyist. It's when we feel compelled to over-state the Bible's divinity (its "must have" features) that we get ourselves tied up in knots in these kinds of ways.

The "Rules" of the "Interpretation Game"

With all that in mind, let's talk a bit more about biblical interpretation. And here it's helpful for us to know some of the "rules of the game." If we go to watch a new sport for the first time, our enjoyment and our ability to grasp what's happening will be far greater if someone's explained the rules to us beforehand. Equally, if we want to play the game ourselves, we need to learn the rules and follow them. It won't work for us to be "self-taught" or just guess from what we see on the field—or worst of all, make up our own rules as to what "obviously" or "must be" going on.

> Think for a moment of a European soccer fan attending his first (American) football and basketball games. In football the offensive and defensive players can use their hands to push their opponents. In basketball and soccer they cannot. In basketball players cannot kick the ball, but they can hold it with their hands. In soccer the reverse is true. In football everyone can hold the ball with his hands but only one person can kick it. In soccer everyone can kick the ball but only one person can hold it. Unless we understand the rules under which the game is played, what is taking place is bound to be confusing. In a similar way, there are different "game" rules involved in the interpretation of the different kinds of biblical literature.
>
> Robert H. Stein, *A Basic Guide to Interpreting the Bible*, 75–76.

In the same way, when we're interpreting the Bible, we have to be "playing by the same rules" as the biblical authors. We've already said that the Bible is the story of people—and their stories—that were being lived out at particular places, in particular times, in particular contexts. Everything we read is therefore "time-bound" in that sense. But we also know that it's the story of a timeless God, intertwined with those people and their time-bound stories. So if we're to make sense of the Bible for our story— the story we're living in—we have to figure out how and in what ways that original biblical story is "timeless" vs. time-bound. Which means, we have to get to grips with its humanity and its divinity. Because if we can't grasp that, we'll never be able to explain to our friends how the Bible is "true"—and how it has authority—for us and our lives. We need to understand how the two elements are present and work together in what it's communicating.

When we approach the Bible as readers today, it's easy for us to think that God wrote it for us—for you and me, in the twenty-first century—because that's where we're reading it and we (rightly) expect God to "speak" to us through it. We believe it to be a "living" and "active" Word, based on, for example, Hebrews 4:12: "The word of God is living and active and sharper than any two-edged sword." All of which makes it easy to forget that before the Bible ever says anything to us today it was saying something to an original audience.

One of the first "rules of the game" for interpreting the Bible is therefore to ask ourselves "What did it mean to them, then?"—the writers and audiences by whom and for whom it was originally written. That doesn't mean the Holy Spirit can't speak to us in other ways through a verse or passage now. We will be looking later at how to get that balance right. But we should always start by wanting to know what a verse or passage would have meant then. It's important that we fully respect the original writers and their original audiences. After all, it meant something to them in their day before it ever means something to us in our day. If it hadn't meant something significant to them, then, it would never have been cherished as something "from God" that needed to be preserved and handed down to future generations. If it hadn't made sense to them at the time it was written . . . if it hadn't communicated something that they saw as very important for them . . . if it hadn't had a profound sense of God about it . . . then it would never have found its way into the Bible so that we could read it, or Martin Luther and John Calvin could read it, or Billy Graham could read it, thousands of years later.

In his book *The Blue Parakeet*, Scot McKnight perceptively observes that in "those days," God spoke in "those ways":

God spoke in Moses' days in Moses' ways, and
God spoke in Job's days in Job's ways, and
God spoke in David's days in David's ways, and
God spoke in Solomon's days in Solomon's ways, and
God spoke in Jeremiah's days in Jeremiah's ways, and
God spoke in Jesus' days in Jesus' ways, and
God spoke in Paul's days in Paul's ways, and
God spoke in Peter's days in Peter's ways, and
God spoke in John's days in John's ways,
and we are called to carry on that pattern in our world today.

Another of the rules of the game is that what we're reading can't possibly mean something now that it couldn't possibly have meant then. Which is different from saying that God can't speak to us now in a way that is not the same as its meaning then—but that's something we'll look at later. God speaking *meaningfully* to me *through* a verse or passage is not the same thing as *the meaning of* a verse or passage. Different "rules" apply to each.

That leads on to recognizing that, for God's communication through the Bible to have made complete sense to the original writers and their audiences, he would have to have used language and ideas and illustrations and concepts that they would have been familiar with, and that they took to be "obvious" or self-evident in their world. God would have had to "locate" himself in their time and context, in order to be able to successfully communicate within and to their time and context. Not least if they were to recognize that what God wanted to communicate was special and needed to be cherished and preserved. In that communication, God would have to have "laid aside" or "emptied himself" (in Philippians 2 terms) of knowledge and concepts that he knew perfectly well but humanity would only become aware of in eras yet to come. For example, he wouldn't talk about things that would only become "obvious" or self-evident in the twentieth century, or the twenty-first century or even, the twenty-fifth century. (Imagine how hard it would be for us to be hearing God now, if he were to communicate knowledge and concepts from the twenty-fifth century.) He wouldn't embed hidden clues in the text for future generations to find, to somehow prove the Bible's "timeless" knowledge. The exception to this, in relation to "hidden clues" (and here, a footnote would have been useful!), is prophetic words, such as Old Testament passages that were foreshadowing Jesus as the Messiah. However, two cautionary notes. Firstly, the manner in which the New

Testament writers interpreted Old Testament prophecies should not be taken as a license for us doing the same today. Secondly, we need to be extremely cautious about finding things that it's highly likely are not there in the first place, especially if they are being claimed to affirm things to do with, e.g., outer space, alien life, medicine and science, specific dates and future events affecting specific modern countries like the US, and so on. The idea of hidden clues and embedded coding along the lines of *The Bible Code* (a 1997 best-seller by Michael Drosnin), or gnostic varieties of hidden secret knowledge, should be handled with the utmost care to say the least. In my lifetime, speculation of that sort, identifying a particular political or military figure as the Antichrist (until he then retired or passed away), or identifying the European Union as the ten-horned beast of Revelation when Greece joined its ranks (later quietly dropped when Spain and Portugal also joined a few years later and the math no longer worked) has been an ongoing embarrassment.

How God Works with and within Our Time-Bound Contexts

In order to successfully communicate to and through the original writer to his audience, in their context, God had to "play by the same rules" as the biblical authors. He had to "speak in Moses' days in Moses' ways." He had to work within the conceptual framework of what people at the time thought was "obvious" about life, the universe, and everything—only deviating from or challenging that "obvious" where he felt it was absolutely necessary. For example, we see an important example of God challenging his people about some of the prevailing "obvious-es" at the beginning of Leviticus 18, verses 1–4:

> Then the LORD said to Moses, "Give the following instructions to the people of Israel. I am the LORD your God. So do not act like the people in Egypt, where you used to live, or like the people of Canaan, where I am taking you. You must not imitate their way of life. You must obey all my regulations and be careful to obey my decrees, for I am the LORD your God.

Then follows a list of commands and guidelines that reflect and define not acting like—not imitating—the Egyptians and the Canaanites. The particular matters that are listed were no doubt totemic examples of those peoples' ways of life. However, God did not override or overturn all of what people at the time thought was obvious about life, the universe, and everything—how science and biology worked, how society should be ordered and organized, and so on. He focused on the most important things for them, then, at that time. Specifically, he didn't try to make their societies conform to how a twenty-first-century western society thinks everything should work. Nor for that matter, how a nineteenth-century or sixteenth-century society thought things should work. He picked his targets.

In summary, God "accommodated" the people he was engaging with in terms of starting from "where they were at," just as he does with us. Of necessity, he spoke into, within, and through their time-bound contexts. He "accommodated" those contexts, in order that they could grasp what he most wanted to convey at the time—which were his most important "theological" concerns (as we might call them). He didn't seek to correct everything in a society that was less than ideal, nor to correct contemporary beliefs about "the way things are" that would, in the future, be shown to be wrong, not least in matters of science, physiology, cosmology, and so on. His goal was to communicate effectively to particular people—in a particular place, time, and culture—that which was most important for them to know, in ways they would be able to relate to.

Let me give an example of what I mean. Let's say I could jump in the DeLorean Time Machine (from the 1985 movie *Back to the Future*) and go to see John Calvin, one of the great heroes of the Reformation, for a cup of tea. But I only had one hour before heading back to my own time. I'd have to make a choice about what I was going to talk to him about. I'd have to be really disciplined. Talking to the most important theologian of his day, my priority would have to be what was most important theologically, at that time, for the people of that time. I'd need to make sure I didn't get sidetracked and waste time talking about things that were really not the most important—even if some of the things happening in that society were less than ideal and arguably I should be aiming to "correct." I'd also have to bear in mind that however important those were, and people would eventually realize they were, I would be achieving absolutely nothing if Calvin wouldn't be able to "hear me" on them at the time, through the cultural filters of his day. There would be plenty of things I could tell him, of course, and put him right on—things we know today about science and cosmology and technology, and even things like equality and human rights. I'd have to be very disciplined. It would be so tempting to want to "correct him" about all sorts of things, especially if I wanted his subsequent writings to be "without error" (so that twenty-first-century readers would not be able to criticize what he wrote on those grounds). For example, neither Calvin nor Luther believed that the earth revolved round the sun (nor for that matter did anyone in the Bible either). They thought the earth was the center of the universe and the sun revolved around us. People at the time thought that was "obvious." Calvin said that people like Copernicus, who were saying the earth revolved around the sun, were "deranged" and "madmen," possessed by the devil. So, wrong though Calvin et al were about that, he and I could have wasted the whole hour arguing about something that I'd never have been able to convince him about. If I were to lead with that in our conversation—even though it would have been "true" and even though "keeping quiet" about it would put me at risk of being accused of allowing him to continue to believe something that "wasn't true"—he almost certainly would have thought I was nuts and wouldn't have listened to anything else I had to say, let alone pass it on as truth to other people. The wisest thing for me to do, therefore, would be to accommodate how people saw things, stay silent on the stuff that wasn't vital to address at the time, and just focus on what was most important at that time for the people of that time. Maybe I might also carefully sow just one or two little seeds, just to get them thinking; just a couple of things that, over time, would become really important, but people wouldn't have made sense of at the time, like equality and human rights (in which I'd need to play the long game).

Can you see how in relating to the biblical writers and their audiences Almighty God might have done precisely the same kind of thing, for precisely the same reasons? How that would have been the necessary and wisest thing for him to do, as well. How he, too, would have decided to "accommodate" some of what people saw as "obvious" about life at the time and chosen to stay silent on some of the stuff that he could have said but they wouldn't be able to hear. Even though, by staying silent on things that people in the ancient world were currently getting "wrong" in areas such as science and geography and cosmology and physiology (not to mention, areas like equality and human rights), it would put the Bible at risk of being accused by future generations of saying things that were "wrong" or "outdated" in modern terms. Such criticism emanates directly from our claims for the Bible's "timelessness."

John Calvin often spoke of God accommodating himself to our human understanding, although the idea did not originate with him (he was building on the insights of some of the church fathers, such as Tertullian, Origen, John Chrysostom, and Clement of Alexandria). In his *Institutes of Christian Religion*, Calvin likened accommodation (or as Augustine called it, condescension) to the way in which a nanny would speak to a child. Michael Tinker, in his article "John Calvin's Concept of Divine Accommodation," expands on how this works:

> In talking to a child we may speak in a way that does not express things "as they are in themselves," but in a way that still conveys truth about those things. It may be that when trying to explain to a child that someone has died we do not explain all the scientific reasoning behind their death, explaining the spread of the cancer and how it destroyed other cells, or whatever the fatal illness may have entailed. We may not even use the word "death" as they probably won't have the capacity to understand the word. Rather we may talk of somebody "leaving." Although this does not explain everything about death it does help the child understand the truth that the person is no longer physically present. Such ways of talking about death do not explain everything about the event, they do not explain the event in all its truth, however they convey sufficient truth, tailored to the recipient's capacity, for that recipient to understand what is happening, however limited that understanding is.

Tinker goes on to note that adults also do this when speaking to each other:

> We speak in ways that are not altogether "true" scientifically, and yet what we say does convey some truth that is useful. Many will, without hesitation, talk of sunrise and sunset. Most people know that this is not true, scientifically. We know that, in reality, the earth revolves around the sun due to the gravitational pull of the sun and at the same time the earth revolves on its own axis, etc. Then why do we still talk of "sunrise" if it is, in fact, untrue? We still speak of it because, despite being "untrue," it still conveys some truths, namely that we see the sun "rise" and "set" each day . . . whilst it remains untrue scientifically.

Communication Theory

What we're talking about here is what's called "communication theory" and it's important because the Bible is an act of communication. And, it's not an act of communication by God in a vacuum. It's an act of communication *by* God *to* people *through* people, so our humanity is unavoidably involved in that.

It's helpful to think a little bit more about how communication works. The first and most obvious point is that communication is not all about the communicator in isolation. They say "it takes two to tango," and so too does communication.

Let's say that I am invited to be a guest speaker at a church in another country. The first thing I have to do is to think about my audience. For any communication to succeed, the communicator has to be wise in "accommodating" where their audience is "at"—where they will be "starting from." So, I will be asking myself whether I am talking mainly to people who would say they were Christians, or people who wouldn't. What's their church background—their "PCE" as John Mumford calls it: their "Prior Christian Experience"? What's their age profile and their cultural profile? What kind of country are they living in, politically, economically, and socially? What's been happening to these people? And what's it like to live in their world, with their particular concerns and hopes and fears? My awareness and willingness to take account of all of these things will have a profound impact on whether I'm going to communicate with them successfully. My overriding objective is to bless them with what God has for them now—what's most important for them now. It is not to show them how much I know and how much I could tell them, by dumping lots of information on them. If they couldn't take it in, it wouldn't be effective. For my communication to succeed it has to "work" for them as the hearers, not just me as the speaker. I have to use language and concepts and communication styles that my audience is already familiar with—that they can easily relate to—because they see them as "obvious" in their world. I need to "situate" what I'm saying within their cultural assumptions or they will "miss it." I must be disciplined and selective. This is not the time or place to teach lots of new and different language and concepts and communication styles and cultural assumptions that my audience isn't familiar with and doesn't see as "obvious" in their world, even if those would be true and even if they would be better. I have to accommodate "where they are at"—and to "start where they are at"—if I'm going to communicate what's most important in what God has for them at that time.

The renowned Old Testament scholar, John Walton, says:

> There can be no question that accommodation is essential in
> God's communicating with humans. Every act of communica-
> tion requires accommodation that will tailor the communica-
> tion to the needs and circumstances of the audience. Without
> this, effective communication could not take place.... [E]very
> successful act of communication is accomplished by various
> degrees of accommodation on the part of the communicator
> for the sake of the audience. Accommodation must bridge the
> gap if communicator and audience do not share the same lan-
> guage, the same command of language, the same culture or the
> same experiences.

The Lost World of Scripture, 39, 43.

OK—so what might that look like in what we find in the Bible? Borrowing
from the Chalcedonian Creed, we "acknowledge" its two natures (divine
and human) and that "the distinction of natures" is "by no means taken
away by the union." In other words, we can see both divinity and humanity
distinctly present within it. We then add this additional dimension
that communication theory offers us. As Walton puts it, to "tailor the
communication to the needs and circumstances of the audience," which
every successful act of communication needs to do. Hence, we find in the
Bible both the substance of what God wanted to communicate to people—
the "what"—and the means by which he chose to do it—the "how." What
we see in the Bible is "both-and"—the substance of the communication
and the means of the communication combined together. The substance
is blessings and promises and teachings; what we might call the theology.
The means of conveying that are stories, parables, legends, songs, and
poems, using the genres and the literary styles of the day, framed by the
worldview of the day.

Understanding the Bible therefore requires us to differentiate somewhat between the cargo and the vehicle that's carrying it. The substance
of the communication—the theological truths that God wanted to be
conveyed—will be "true." That's what God intended to communicate and
why it's completely reliable. But we don't need to have the same expectations of the means as we do of the substance, because that's where the
accommodation to the audience comes in. The truth-conveying vehicle
that God used need not be "true" in that sense, any more than a poem,
a parable, a story, a legend, or a piece of art has to be "true" for it to be a
great way of communicating truth. Any artist or poet or songwriter—or

any author who's ever used metaphor or analogy or story, as C. S. Lewis did with Narnia—knows that full well.

So let's relate all of this back to some of those words and concepts that we commonly encounter in statements of faith, when people are talking about the nature of the Bible. The *substance* of the communication that God intended will be inerrant, infallible, and authoritative. But the *means* that he used to convey it may well be cultural, transitory, and therefore fallible. Inerrancy and authority are located in what God intended to convey. Accommodation for the sake of the audience—in culture and genre and worldview—is located in the vehicles he chose to best convey it. So we just need to avoid confusing the two and claiming for the vehicles properties that are really only appropriate to speak of in relation to the cargo. The creation account in Genesis 1 is a classic example of where we can see all of this at work, making sense of five short statements about what Genesis is (and isn't) trying to tell us:

1. The Bible is not a science textbook.

   - Its intention is not to give us a scientific explanation of how the world works but a *theological* explanation of how the world works.

   - Any information we find in the Bible about the material world is either something that everyone could see for themselves at the time or represents the typical way of thinking of the ancient world.

2. There is no new scientific revelation in the Bible.

   - God resisted the temptation to offer new scientific insights, or little clues for us to find later, about how the world *really* worked.

   - One very good reason for that is because over time scientific understandings of how the world works change. So which particular understanding, at what point in time, would God have chosen? It would be rather arrogant of us to assume he would obviously have chosen our day; especially as our present knowledge will almost certainly be superseded by discoveries in the future.

3. God chose human communicators located in a particular point in time, language, and culture and communicated what he wanted to communicate through them into that particular world.

   ▪ God was first communicating something to *their* world before he was ever communicating something to *our* world, or the Reformers' world, or Billy Graham's world. Many statements in Scripture are indeed "timeless," but they always come to us within the "wrapper" of a time-bound scriptural context, because there's no other way they could have come to us. Indeed, everything that comes to us in Scripture is within a time-bound context. We cannot therefore avoid the need to discern the difference between "truths" and "wrappers" and the extent to which, at times, both may be visible—challenging though that may be.

In terms of how the original audience would have understood Genesis:

4. They weren't in the least interested in *how* the world was made, they were only interested in *why*, and by whom, and why the world is the way it is, and how that affects them and who they are—what that meant for their lives.

   ▪ Genesis has all the right answers, but they are answers to *its own* questions answered in *its own* ways.

And then finally

5. We need to respect the original authors by respecting their literary styles and genres, instead of finding fault with them or trying to make them into the literary styles and genres of our day.

   ▪ This includes respecting their use of "picture-language" and painting "prophetic pictures." Respecting the way that they would integrate what we would call history with what we would call legend. Respecting their right to be selective about which bits of a genealogy they would include and which bits they would leave out. Respecting their need to communicate with their audience in ways that conform to how communication works.

   ▪ If God could "lower himself," as it were, to respect and work with all of that in what he put into the text, then we should be happy to do the same in what we bring out of the text.

All of which means that when we look at Genesis and Revelation—and lots of what comes in-between—we are looking for truths about *theology*, not truths about biology or cosmology. In academic terms, we're studying in the arts and humanities department, not the mathematics and science departments! We're looking at how the biblical authors communicated truths in a world that was a hearing-dominant culture rather than a text-dominant culture; where there was no need for the vast majority of people to be literate—only a few scribes, to create archives and draw up the occasional contract (rather like lawyers and notaries do today). What mattered most was conveying the important theological truths for that time, in the context of its time, in ways that would most easily be remembered and passed on.

Creation in Genesis through the Lens of Communication Theory

If you're not generally familiar with Genesis 1, maybe have an open Bible alongside you as we close the chapter with how some of this works out in practice.

Genesis 1 verse 1. "God created the heavens and the earth." The surrounding nations had their own legends about how the world was created by various gods, often through conflict. Genesis is saying "no"—the world was created by *one* God, the one true God, and he did it by the power of his spoken word: "God said let there be . . . and there was." In Genesis, there is no divine battle with opposing forces necessary for creation.

To reinforce the fact that Genesis 1 is not intended as the account of a manufacturing process, the Hebrew word for "made"—as in, God *made* or God *created*—is never used in the Bible in a manufacturing sense, only in a "bringing it about" sense. For example, in Psalm 51:10: "Create in me a clean heart, O God," where this obviously has nothing to do with manufacturing a physical heart. It's about bringing something into being in a transforming sense.

Genesis 1, verse 3. The reason that light appears here, even though the sun and the moon aren't created until verse 16, is because the ancients didn't realize that light came from the sun. Which is understandable, when you think that even when the sun is covered by cloud, it's still light in the daytime. This is not an "error" in a scientific chronology of manufacture, because that is not the narrative's role or purpose.

Genesis 1, verse 6. "Let there be a firmament dividing the waters under the firmament from the waters above the firmament." As Tremper Longman and John Walton observe, in *The Lost World of the Flood*, "the narrative reflects an ancient cosmology of subterranean waters beneath a flat earth and waters suspended above the firmament" [note the implication, in the blue sky] "that could be released by opening the gates of heaven." The presence of waters "beneath" was consistent with observable natural springs and waters "above" with rain. In the account of the flood, Genesis 7:11 says "the windows of heaven" (KJV)—or "the floodgates of the heavens" (NIV)—were opened, and it rained. This is not just poetic language—it reflects the ancient world cosmology of a flat earth, like a disc, with the firmament sitting on top like a silver-domed cloche over a plate in a fancy restaurant. The "floodgates" or "windows" in the dome of the firmament were like windows set in a pitched roof in an attic room. The source of the flood was God releasing the floodgates, or opening the windows, releasing the waters held back behind the dome.

The presumption of a flat earth is why Psalm 103:12 was such great news, when it said that God has removed our sins from us "as far as the East is from the West." If they'd known the earth was round, it wouldn't have been such great news, because those sins would have ended up coming back to us.

Genesis 1, verse 16. "God made the two great lights, the greater light to govern the day, and the lesser light to govern the night; He made the stars also." Arguably, the reason the sun and the moon are not given names and it's emphasized that it was God who made them is because it's telling people that the sun and the moon and the stars are not gods, as the surrounding nations thought. They're just things, created by "the" God. They're not given names, in this Jewish account, because to give something a name in that culture was to give it significance. Even in that small detail, God was working within the culture of the day as part of his communication of truths—truths that were theological in nature, not cosmological in nature.

Genesis 1, verses 26 and 27. The pinnacle of God's creation, man and woman; made in God's image and likeness. In the ancient world, an image or an idol was believed to carry the "essence" of that which it represented. The other nations therefore made images of their gods, believing them to carry that essence with them. In contrast, Genesis is saying don't make images of your God (cf. Exodus 20:4; 34:17, etc.) because God has created *you* to be his image and likeness, and for *you* to carry *his* essence in this world. Radically different! It's interesting that the New Testament Greek word for "image" is *eikón*—from which we get "icon."

The surrounding nations believed that humans were created to be the slaves of the gods, of low value and expendable, but Genesis is telling its audience that we were created to be of the very highest value. Made in God's "image" and "likeness"—pictured as friends, walking and conversing together in the Garden in the cool of the day. Deeply theological!

Genesis 1, verse 31. Each day that God spoke and created something, he said it was "good." And then on the sixth and final day, after creating humanity, he saw everything that he'd made and said it was "very good." Notice firstly a distinction between "very good" and the Platonic idea of "perfection," which precludes any change or development (since any change would, by definition, make it worse). The creation in Genesis was "very good" in the sense of being entirely as God intended that it should be. "Saving" that once "very good" creation is not about simply returning it back to some pristine original state (still less, one characterized as a "perfect" state). Instead, it's a rescue plan to allow it to reach the destiny for which it was originally created. Despite everything that's gone wrong with it since . . . despite that image of God in us having become dirty and torn and damaged, like an oil painting waiting to be restored . . . despite the damage that sin has done and that we have done . . . and despite our mess-ups . . . God still believes that it is worth saving and we are worth saving. Not just giving up on and starting again. The redemptive message of the biblical story does not begin with "original sin" but with the "original goodness" that came before it.

It's because God sees things that way that through Jesus each of us has the hope of resurrection and our world has hope of resurrection—of being rescued and made new, with all the bad stuff gone from our lives and from the world we live in.

By the way, biblical hope doesn't mean "just hope for the best" or "hit and hope" (as a golfer might say), it means "confident and enthusiastic expectation!"

Genesis 2, verse 2. We often talk about a seven-day creation, but technically it's a six-day creation, because on the seventh day God rested—which is where the Jewish Sabbath came from, the commandment that on one day each week God's people should rest as well. What that meant was not just a lazy day of doing nothing—lying in bed, or going shopping. Rather, it was a day set apart for enjoying God together and enjoying his creation together. It was an "enjoying" day. And that's a great way for us to think about, in our case, Sundays—a day of enjoying God together and enjoying his creation together. Not so much as a command but an invitation and an encouragement, because it's something God would like to be doing with us! Something he would enjoy just as much as us. Just as he did with Adam and Eve, before things started to go horribly wrong.

Some Final Thoughts

I hope that this chapter has been useful in helping us to grasp the Bible's humanity alongside its divinity. It's important for us to navigate the ways in which it is both the Word of God and the words of people without its status being felt to be diminished as a result. We should respect the Bible for what it *is* and not try to defend it as something it was never intended to be—sanitized of the times in which it was written. Without doubt, the Bible is permanently relevant and contains "timeless" truths; however, even that which God intends to be "timeless" within it is coming to us in Scripture in a time-bound context that may well imbibe time-bound features. Distinguishing between context and contents—that which is "timelessly" true and that which is a product of its times—requires interpretation, with discernment. Not least because none of us ever see "truths" in a "pure," objective, timeless way—we always see them in a cultural context, through cultural lenses (whether ancient or modern ones). This is what makes the whole issue so complex and our desire to be "biblical" and embrace Scripture's authority so challenging. It is too easy to polarize and at one extreme reject anything that is not amenable to the contemporary mindset—purely on subjective grounds, of "that was then, this is now"—or, at the other extreme, to insist that everything "the Bible says" must be permanently applicable *as written*, in order to be honoring it as the Word of God. However, the fact that this matter is challenging does not mean we can avoid engaging with it. Yes, there will be a tension, but it's one we need to embrace, not shy away from.

In closing, remember that the Bible's intrinsic humanity is not a weakness, a mistake, or a flaw. It reflects the divine author's conscious communicative approach, working with the human writers, such that the Bible's words would work both for their original audiences and future generations, in accordance with his inerrant and infallible intentions! The Bible's intrinsic humanity does not in any way diminish its standing as the Word of God, nor its authoritative status for our lives and faith. But it does mean that at times we will need to work a bit harder at it as today's readers.

3

The Bible Story as a Box Set

If someone was to ask you "What's the Bible all about?" I wonder how you'd explain it? Normally with a book you can get an idea from the contents page, but try that with a Bible and you won't get very far. Lots of the chapter titles seem to just be people's names. There are also some weird-sounding ones, like Numbers and Revelation. Most people who try reading the Bible cover-to-cover give up by about Leviticus. There seems to be some kind of chronology at work—we can follow a storyline in parts—but then it seems to skip to another part of the story and it's not always clear quite how it got from there to here. If only every chapter began as box sets do, with "Previously on . . . ."

The Old Testament is definitely the hardest part. No wonder that some Christians just skip it completely because—if they're honest— they're not entirely sure why it's there in the first place, so they just begin the story with Jesus. And that's OK to a point, especially for someone just starting out. But the obvious problem is that the first three-quarters of the Bible is what happened before Jesus. He entered into an existing story of God and people that had been in process for thousands of years, and it happened that way for a reason. In the earliest days of the church, of course, the Old Testament *was* the Bible. From the outset, its status as Scripture was a given (the discussions in subsequent centuries focused on which books to include within the New Testament canon) and when that status was challenged—notably, by Marcion, in the second century, of whom more anon—the church fathers expressly rejected the challenge and chose to retain the Old Testament. Although the Old Testament may be testing for us to figure out, it is most certainly an integral part of the Big Story.

Perhaps precisely because of the difficulties people have in figuring out the Big Story of the Bible, many Christians simplify things by going straight from the "fall" in Genesis, when Adam and Eve eat the fruit they were told not to (as "the problem") to Jesus' death on the cross (as "the solution" to the problem). Almost as if nothing of any real significance happened in between. From which point, the telling of the story then leapfrogs to our personal salvation now. And from there, to our destiny in heaven. Not quite a hop, skip, and jump (as the Triple Jump used to be called, in Track and Field), but pretty close to it.

Telling the Big Story of the Bible

So what exactly is the Big Story of the Bible all about? And how can we explain it to people, without using lots of religious words and concepts that they have to Google? How can we put back in all of the ingredients that this foreshortened way of telling the story has missed out?—without hopelessly confusing everyone, or needing a theology degree to grasp it.

Ideally, to do justice to the story, we will find a place for:

- How it all began
- What went wrong
- Why it went wrong
- What God did about it
- Why Jesus came
- How Israel fits
- How the church fits
- How we fit, and
- How it will end.

In this chapter, I want to suggest a way of looking at this Big Story of the Bible that you might find helpful. Acknowledgments up front— I've been very influenced in this by a number of others who have thought about it in similar, dramatized ways, notably: Scot McKnight (*The Blue Parakeet*), Tom Wright (*The New Testament and the People of God*), and especially Brian McLaren (*The Story We Find Ourselves In*), so a big "thank you" to each of them. Their influences will be obvious and I commend their versions to you (and their books).

My own version presents it as a Bible Story Box Set—seasons one to three. Season one is what we call the Old Testament, season two is the New Testament, and season three is the one we're in now, where God invites us to be the cast.

Obviously, we could have had ten or twelve episodes in each season, as many box sets do, but that would take too long and be too hard to remember. So instead, we're going to focus on eight key words within the seasons, that all begin with the letter "C." As they say on Sesame Street, "This chapter is brought to you by the letter C." To remember this version of the Bible Story, all we have to remember is eight words.

The Pilot Episode: Creation

We start with the pilot episode—"C" for **"creation"**—which sets the scene for everything that happens in the story. As the story unfolds, we see themes in creation reappearing in season two and then again in the finale in season three. In creation, we see God "speaking into being" an incredible cosmos full of beauty, complexity, diversity and mystery. The pinnacle of his creation is people, because unlike everything else, we were made in God's image and likeness. And when he's finished, God looks at the whole package and says, it's "very good" (Genesis 1:31). This way of telling the story doesn't start with something called original sin in Genesis 3:6—it starts further back, with original goodness in Genesis 1:31. And despite the problems that surfaced, God has never stopped seeing things that way. Even in its damaged state, and us in our damaged state, God believes that it is worth saving, and we are worth saving. Not just giving up on and starting again.

The "creation" episode is telling us that God made us to be in a relationship with him. Our capacity to know him personally is part of being made in his image. It was part of our human destiny. The "creation" episode pictures that in Adam and Eve walking and talking with God in the Garden of Eden.

Because we were made in God's image, we were made with the capacity for our lives to be defined by love, just as God is defined by love: love for each other, and love for him. But in order for our love for God to be real and to mean something, God had to take a risk when he created us. Love always involves risk. We can't love someone without taking a risk as to whether they will love us in return. To love is to make ourselves vulnerable to being rejected and being hurt. The risk God took in creating us was giving us choice, in what we call "free will." The reason he did that is because there had to be the option, built-into the way he designed his creation, of more than one story to live in. Otherwise, we would be like robots, programmed to love him. If God forced us to love him—or forced us to love each other for that matter—it would be deeply unsatisfying. When Adam and Eve choose to do the one thing—the only thing—that God had asked them not to do, eating the fruit of the tree in the middle of the garden, they were exercising that free will. Keep in mind that this is against a background where God had said: "You're free to eat from *every other tree* in the garden" (Genesis 2:16). There was only one "don't do this" negative commandment.

The point of that tree in the middle of the garden is not so much the tree itself. It wasn't that it had some kind of magical properties—that eating from it would, somehow, impart knowledge of good and evil. It wasn't that God intended them to be kept ignorant. The story is not so much talking about the nature of the tree as the nature of what Adam and Eve chose to do. Which is, the *one tiny little thing* that God had specifically asked them *not* to do. The story is about them saying to God: "We'll decide for ourselves what's right and wrong, thanks very much. We'll decide for ourselves how we're going to live." Even in something as apparently petty as eating or not eating from one particular tree they wouldn't be told. They were opting out of God's version of the story and rejecting God's place in the story. Arguably, the particular tree wasn't that important; the fact that God had asked them not to do it was more important. He could have said: "Don't fish in that river, or don't go up that mountain, or don't eat from that tree on the far side of the garden" or any number of other things instead. The main point is that *God said it*, whatever it was. Rather like with some of the more obscure commandments in the later law that weren't necessarily that important in themselves—their importance lay in being things that God had said to do or not to do. They were markers, to test whether God was going to be allowed to decide what was right for people (what's right in his eyes) or whether people were going to insist on deciding what was right for themselves (what's right in our eyes). This might remind us of the later time, in the era of the judges, where it says: "In those days there was no king in Israel. People did whatever they felt like doing" (Judges 17:6 in *The Message* paraphrase).

So the question that God was posing to Adam and Eve—and the question that he poses to us as well, especially in a postmodern world, where we don't like being told what to do by anyone—is whether they would do what he said just because he'd said it, or only if they personally "agreed" with it.

All that said, we shouldn't assume there was no significance to the tree's name. But if so, its significance was not that Adam and Eve were not supposed to acquire knowledge of good and evil. It wasn't that God wanted to keep it from them. Learning what's right and wrong is part of growing up, and growing up well. The question was simply *when* and *how* they were going to go about that. Was it to be a knowledge of good and evil from God's perspective, or their own? Were they going to be "self-taught" or "God-taught"? His version or their version?

Changing tack a little bit, when we read about "Adam and Eve" we need to know that there's some word-play going on here that would have been "obvious" to the original audience, because the Hebrew word *'adam* is the word for "mankind" or "humanity." So the story is not just talking about one man and woman, it's talking about all of us. It's not just picturing what they were like and what they did and why—it's picturing what *we're* like and what *we* do and why. It's not just their story, it's *our* story too; a story that repeats itself again and again throughout human history. We can see ourselves in Adam and Eve, just as we can see ourselves in many of the other biblical characters, from Genesis onwards.

Season One: Crisis

As we move from the pilot episode further into season one, this "very good" creation soon ends up in **"crisis,"** our second "C" word. As the human stories unfold in Genesis, we see selfishness, independence, and a desire to be in control starting to dominate human life. Adam and Eve, Cain and Abel, Lamech, and the Tower of Babel are all painting a picture, not just of one crisis of one couple eating some fruit that they shouldn't have done, but a whole series of crises. Of relationship breakdowns between people and God and people with each other. Family, work, and society all become damaged. As tribes and nations evolve, they become competitive and aggressive and violent. Life becomes about getting, not giving. About living life to love and serve me rather than loving and serving each other (let alone loving and serving God).

Creation, as God designed it, began with just one story. But now another story has emerged: a parallel story. Humanity has started writing its own independent story and writing God out of the plot.

One of the first consequences of things going wrong is that Adam and Eve pick up a distorted idea of who God is and what he's like. Fear replaces love in how they see him and what they think he's like. Fear replaces love as the primary characteristic of God in their minds. Adam says: "I was afraid of you, so I hid" (Genesis 3:10). This idea, that God is first and foremost to be feared rather than loved, starts to take hold in how people think of him. It's become pervasive ever since—so much so, that some Christians even start the gospel with that, trying to scare people into the kingdom rather than love them into the kingdom.

As the story continues, the image and likeness of God in which humanity was created gets more and more dirty and damaged and distorted. Like parallel lines that slowly but surely start to diverge—and the gap is increasing. So much so, that sometimes you'd think that image and likeness had been lost completely. Humanity embraces what we call "evil." We see stories of personal violence, military violence, and economic violence. It's as if even the natural world has somehow been knocked off kilter—with earthquakes and hurricanes and tsunamis—natural disasters that mimic and mirror the spiritual and relational disasters. And because the wrong choices that we make when we ignore God have consequences—especially, relational consequences—this selfishness, independence and desire to be in control causes the loss of intimate, personal relationship with God. The kind of people that we became separated us from him; we became incompatible.

So how could God restore this creation, that began so very good? Already in the story of Noah and the Ark we see that a straight-remake of Adam and Eve, just starting again with the same raw materials, is not going to be the answer. Just getting rid of all the really bad people like that wouldn't be enough, because the problems of human nature will just replicate, time and time again. Aleksandr Solzhenitsyn was surely right when he said that the line between "good" and "bad" doesn't run between groups of people—the goodies (like us) and the baddies (like "them")—it runs down through every single one of us. And over time that line shifts position, especially when we're under pressure.

Season One: Commitment

As season one continues, we very soon see this "crisis" that people have made being met head-on by a **"commitment"** that God makes—our next "C" word. This refers to a divine *promise*, which he repeats, time and again, to different members of the cast throughout season one. A promise that he will never rescind and that, fortunately for us, our failings can neither cancel nor invalidate. A promise that depends on *him* and his character alone, which guarantees that he will see it through to its conclusion. The technical word for this commitment—a word that we can use instead, if we want—is **"covenant."** God irrevocably committing himself that he will rescue the story.

The rescue mission begins with a family that grows to become a nation. A family that God miraculously brings into being through an elderly couple who are far too old to have children: Abraham, and Sarah. God chooses the most unlikely heroes, as he so often does throughout the story. This is something that he seems to specialize in—just to keep reinforcing the point that this is all going to be *God's* doing, not our doing.

A key verse in the first unveiling of this rescue plan is Genesis 12:2, where God says to Abraham: "I will make you a great nation, and I will bless you. I will make your name great, and you will be a blessing." And that early mission statement is still central to the plan, even now. God says to all of us, "I will bless you, not just so that you're blessed—but so that you will be a blessing." God never makes us great for any other reason. If we're not interested in being a blessing, we shouldn't be surprised if God chooses to bless others instead, who are.

So God chooses this people—this nation that becomes "Israel"— and gives them a calling to "model" to the nations what human life looks like when it's lived God's way, with God in the center, within this broken and damaged world. But as the story continues to unfold, what we find time and again is that being the people of God doesn't come naturally. The crisis of human selfishness and independence is too deep-rooted. It's too embedded in human nature.

Season One: Commandments

As God engages with Israel once they're delivered from the oppression of Egypt, and free for the first time to lead their own lives as their own nation, he defines for them what "living right" looks like, in what we know as "the

Law"—a series of divine expectations—in "C" for **"commandments."** According to the Jewish Talmud, there were 613 of them: 248 positive ones (do this) and 365 negative ones (don't do that). These expectations are wide-ranging, from what some would categorize as "civil" instructions (how to run the country) to "ceremonial" instructions (how to run your religious practices) to "moral" instructions (how to behave personally). We'll come on, in a later chapter, to talk about why these categories are not a particularly helpful way of dividing up the law, and especially not a very Jewish way of looking at it, but for the moment it simply illustrates the wide range of things that this framework of expectations for their corporate and personal lives embraced.

There's a quite a lot of confusion in Christian thinking about "the law" and from that confusion derives Christian concerns about the dangers of legalism. Not least, confusion about what the New Testament has to say about it, especially in Paul's letters. Again, we'll look at that later. But for the moment it's worth just being aware that "law" is not a helpful way of translating "Torah" because of the legalistic overtones that come with its modern usage. The meaning of Torah is "instruction" or "teaching," which the word "law" (as we think of it, especially since the Reformation) fails to convey.

It's important always to remember that it was *God himself* who gave these instructions and teachings to Israel (it was the law *of God*, not the law of Moses). He gave them with the expectation that they could and would keep them. Nowhere in the Old Testament is there any suggestion that Torah was burdensome or impossible to keep. Nor is there any hint that a future Messiah would be the only one who would ever be able to keep it. This does not mean for one moment that the people of Israel always succeeded in keeping it, of course! But it does explain why Torah itself included provisions to deal with that; specifically, in regular sacrifices for sin and the annual Day of Atonement. Failures were foreseen from the outset, so provisions were built-in. Availing one's self of those provisions in Torah was therefore part of keeping Torah! If no one ever availed themselves of those provisions, they would have been failing to keep those parts of it.

God did not give them Torah knowing full well that no one would ever be able to do it. That would simply be cruel. No loving parent would ever ask things of their child that they knew full well were impossible from the outset. Rather, God gave Torah to his people for their blessing, with every expectation that they should and would be able to live by it and cherish it as a gift from God. Unsurprisingly, this is precisely how the biblical writers understood it. When the Psalmist talked about Torah in Psalm 119:97–106, for example, he was surely not deluded:

> Oh, how I love your law!
>   I meditate on it all day long.
> Your commands are always with me
>   and make me wiser than my enemies.
> I have more insight than all my teachers,
>   for I meditate on your statutes.
> I have more understanding than the elders,
>   for I obey your precepts.
> I have kept my feet from every evil path
>   so that I might obey your word.
> I have not departed from your laws,
>   for you yourself have taught me.
> How sweet are your words to my taste,
>   sweeter than honey to my mouth!
> I gain understanding from your precepts;
>   therefore I hate every wrong path.
> Your word is a lamp for my feet,
>   a light on my path.
> I have taken an oath and confirmed it,
>   that I will follow your righteous laws.

That said, of course, the more commandments there were, the more there were to (fail to) live up to. And, those commandments were originally given to a nomadic, desert people. As society grew and evolved, and moved into a more settled environment, including urban areas, the more commandments were needed—or perhaps better to say, the more interpretations were needed. Flipping to a present-day example to illustrate that: does switching on an electric light or stove count as "working" on the Sabbath? Or is the commandment envisaging an underlying principle, rather than a "rule" as such? Not to be taken literally. Either way, how does an individual know what is the correct application? "Please tell me what I should do about light switches and stoves on the Sabbath!" is a reasonable question, for a command that needed interpreting!

This was why, of course, in the time of Jesus, rabbis were forever being asked their opinion about interpretations of Torah. Jesus included. On many occasions. And, it's why there were different "schools" of rabbinic thought. Hence the occasions when Jesus said, "You have heard it said . . . , but I say to you . . . ."

This is one of the problems of "righteousness"—in other words, doing "what's right," so that one is "right with God" and "right with others"—being defined by a set of rules (do this, don't do that). Ultimately there aren't enough rules in the world to cover everything. And, the potential interpretations of the ones you already have will be almost endless. Remembering them would be a practical impossibility for the ordinary person, let alone living up to them. And how is one to know which interpretations of which laws are "right"?

There was clearly nothing wrong with God's gift of Torah as a starting point for defining what it looked like to live as the people of God, once Israel was freed from the oppression and the lifestyle practices of the Egyptians and able to be self-determining. Perhaps the challenges and the questions posed by Torah, as the life of the nation evolved, were intended to lead Israel to a realization that "Surely, Lord, there must be more than this?" More to it, in other words, than a relationship shaped and defined by rules (however good and God-given those rules in themselves might be).

As we move into season two, we see some people—some of the Scribes and Pharisees that Jesus engaged with—appearing to lose sight of the end game. Acting as if the rules were the thing, and getting the rules confused with the relationship. Putting the cart before the horse, as it were. But let's not rush ahead of ourselves . . . !

Throughout season one, we see a series of divine initiatives to "force quit" and "re-boot" human life—through Noah, then Abraham, then Moses, and then the various judges and kings leading Israel. We see them having their ups and down, with some triumphs along the way, but ultimately ending up roughly where they started. As I think God always knew that they would. Whatever ways we organize human society and however hard we try, we'll never succeed on our own in being a people of God. Just telling people to be nice and to follow the rules isn't going to do it. Something fundamental about who we are—something in our metaphorical DNA—had to change, and only God himself could bring that about. Only he could repristinate creation and somehow bring divinity and humanity back together, in a "new model" of what it looks like to be human. A restoration of the "image of God." Retaining, in the new design, our free will, which remains so important in God's relational approach, but at the same time breaking the grip of the hostile cosmic powers ranged against us that keep damaging us and our societies, including in particular the one that we ourselves set in motion and continue to fuel, that we call "sin."

Season One: Conversations

We see these human failings over and over again in the remaining episodes in season one, where there's an extended period of "C" for **"conversations."** The Old Testament prophets are engaging in ongoing dialogue with the people on God's behalf. We see a continuous battle for hearts and minds. Will the people turn back to God and his story, or keep choosing their own story? The exact same questions and the exact same choices that we ourselves face.

All the episodes in season one are telling us—all the "conversations" are telling us—that whatever the form of government, whether it's judges or kings or priests or prophets, whatever gifted individual is leading us and whatever political system is in place, human nature means it's never going to work long-term. Even the very best set of rules will never be more than a Band-Aid. Saving humanity from itself requires "something more."

After the period of the kings (notably, King David and his son, Solomon), Nebuchadnezzar's army captures Jerusalem, destroys the temple, and exiles the Jewish people to Babylon (modern-day Iraq). We see them asking themselves—and asking God—why are these things happening to us? Whose fault is this? Why has God allowed it? Again, the kind of questions that we, too, often ask. The Babylonian exile was deeply traumatic for Israel—an exodus in reverse. Even though a return to the land was permitted after the Persian King Cyrus conquered Babylon, and construction of a new temple began, scholars like Tom Wright argue that exile remained a major theme in the consciousness of first-century Jews at the time of Jesus. Not least because Roman occupation meant they were still, in effect, "exiled" in their own country, under pagan rulers, prompting those same questions to resurface.

As we read the stories about Israel in the Old Testament, we need to realize that the stories aren't there to tell us how bad Israel was and how Israel failed. Israel is not there for us to "beat them up" and talk about how bad they were. Israel is there as an example for us. Their story of one nation is showing us things that are true of *all* nations. Their story of one people is showing us things that are true of *all* people; very much including us. Their stories mirror *our* stories. We see ourselves in their stories, and that's not always pleasant for us. The point is, if it had been any other nation, the story would have turned out the same way. Israel's story is there to generate a realization and desire for God to do "something more" for all nations. For God himself to intervene and do something spectacular, unexpected, and unprecedented, that will be a "game-changer" for human life. The Big Story was always supposed to ultimately reach all nations, starting with and through one nation; the problem is, it got no further than the first nation. The troubles Israel had were a microcosm of the troubles the whole world has.

As season one draws to a close, God reiterates and renews his commitment to rescue his creation and we begin to see hints of how he is going to do that in Jeremiah 31:31–34:

> "The days are coming," declares the LORD,
>   "when I will make a new covenant
> with the people of Israel
>   and with the people of Judah.
> It will not be like the covenant
>   I made with their ancestors
> when I took them by the hand
>   to lead them out of Egypt,
> because they broke my covenant,
>   though I was a husband to them,"
>   declares the LORD.
> "This is the covenant that I will make with the people of Israel
>   after that time," declares the LORD.
> "I will put my law in their minds
>   and write it on their hearts.
> I will be their God,
>   and they will be my people.
> No longer will they teach their neighbor,
>   or say to one another, 'Know the Lord,'
> because they will all know me,
>   from the least of them to the greatest,"
>   declares the LORD.

Bringing this covenant commitment into being is what Jesus is talking about in season two when he shares bread and wine with his disciples at the Last Supper; when he says: "This cup is this new covenant in my blood," the ultimate commitment that God could make, to our broken and damaged story. Making a covenant in the ancient world was sealed with a sacrifice that became the centerpiece of a familial meal. Sharing in the meal marked the sharing in a new familial bond between two parties that were previously estranged. The greater of the covenanting parties was committing to be the provider and protector for this newly extended family.

Season Two: Christ

Which brings us to the center-point of the whole Box Set: the pivotal moment. The fulfillment of Jeremiah's words, in season two and the coming of Jesus—"C" for **"Christ."** Season two is when God himself steps into our story, taking all of its damaging and destructive consequences upon himself. Enabling our story to become one that's re-centered in life instead of death—a story of "new life" replacing "old life." 1 John 3:8: "The reason the Son of God appeared was to destroy the devil's work." In John 10:10, Jesus says: "The thief comes only to steal and kill and destroy. I came that they may have life, and have it abundantly."

Our human story is resurrected with Jesus, enabling us to rejoin the story of God "in Christ," as the apostle Paul would put it. In the person of Jesus the Son, God himself comes into our world and into our humanity to rescue it from within. To experience life as we do—becoming one of us "in every way" apart from the commission of sin. Including, sharing in the traumas and the hurts and the pain that come with being human—the damage that sin does to us and our world. He experienced the consequences of living in a broken and damaged world as we do, finally being falsely accused, wrongly convicted, and murdered. The last and final desperate act of a broken and damaged humanity: the ultimate rejection of the Creator. And yet at the cross, what looked to be a defeat turns out to be the exact opposite. It's the pivotal moment when the damaging and destructive forces that have made themselves at home in this world go into reverse and begin their retreat. Just as when the snow begins to melt in Narnia and the power of the White Witch begins to fade. God's future is arriving in our present. A bridgehead has been established. The kingdom of God is here—the rule and reign of God has begun, even although the "good news" is currently co-existing with "bad news" until Jesus' return.

Rather than speak of Jesus' "miracles," it's better to speak of them as "signs" and "wonders," because the healings and the nature miracles were not the end-game. Nor were they to "prove he was God." They were signposts, pointing to the wonderful way that the world will one day be, cleansed and healed from everything that has infected and harmed it. Every hostile force that's currently present within it destroyed—every enemy of human life and flourishing, whether in the spiritual realm or the natural realm, including death and the things that lead to death. Everything restored to a state of "shalom" (meaning not simply "peace," but "when the world is all as it should be"), the way that it was meant to be.

Jesus became the first of a new kind of people of God, according to a new pattern; a new way of being human. In Romans 5, Paul pictures this aspect of Christ's work of atonement in terms of an "Adam-to-Christ" contrast. "Sin" and "death" came into the world through "one man" (Adam) and his "disobedience"; but now the defeat of sin and death has come into the world through "one man" (Jesus, "the second Adam," or the "new Adam") and his "obedience." Through Jesus, God invites us to exchange the story of the first Adam for the story of a second Adam—a story whose outcome is life, instead of a story whose outcome is death. (See Romans 5 and 1 Corinthians 15). The gospel is an invitation to change stories, with a different outcome.

Pictured in Jesus' virgin conception, God was "breaking the line of succession" of what humanity had become and was continuing to reproduce. (In the ancient world, their understanding of biology was that babies came only from the male sperm.) To be "born again" is to be remade in the image and likeness of God through the image and likeness of Jesus. "To all who received him . . . he gave power to become children of God" (John 1:12).

One of the fourth-century church fathers, Athanasius, famously said this of Christ's work in restoring the image and likeness of God in humanity:

> You know what happens when a portrait that has been painted on a panel becomes obliterated through external stains. The art-ist does not throw away the panel, but the subject of the portrait has to come and sit for it again, and the likeness is re-drawn on the same material. Even so was it with the All-holy Son of God. He, the image of the Father, came and dwelt in our midst, in order that He might renew mankind made after Himself.

On the Incarnation of the Word, 14.1

Season Three: Cast

And then in season three, the resurrected Jesus offers us the opportu-nity to join him in this new version of the story—for us to join the cast. Through the indwelling Holy Spirit, he gives us the power to reject the competing stories that life wants to offer us, in favor of a new and better one, in a "Jesus-centered" relationship not a "rules-centered" relationship. In season three, we're called to live out this story as the "C" for **"cast"** together. The individualistic way of thinking of our modern western world has confused a "personal" relationship with God with an "individualistic" relationship with God. To continue with the "cast" metaphor, Christianity is not all about monologues or soliloquies. It's not about a few leading men and leading ladies—however much modern evangelicalism might love to put its heroes on pedestals. In the words of John Wimber, "Everyone gets to play." We are a kingdom of priests. Just like biblical Israel, we too are called to be a people who will "model" what it looks like to live together and love together and give together and serve together when a community is centered on Jesus. A people who will join him in his mission not just to "proclaim" good news but to *"be"* good news, in the bad news of life as people presently have to live it. To show the world around us who God is and what he's like—how he's changed us and how he can change them—by the power of the Holy Spirit. People who don't just want to be blessed, but who also want to be a blessing. All of which should be just another way of saying "doing church" and "being church."

What's so exciting about season three is that we're in it now. We're not just re-reading the old scripts of seasons one and two, or watching endless repeats. Nor are we just in the audience, watching. We've been empowered by the Holy Spirit to "do the stuff" that Jesus did. To put "markers in the sand" as Jesus did, for the arrival of the kingdom. Not simply marking that the kingdom came in Jesus, but that it never left, and it's advancing. That the future kingdom is coming towards the present.

We're in season three and the episodes are still being recorded. So as trained actors who are steeped in the characters and the themes and the events of seasons one and two, we are being invited not just to re-shoot the old episodes but to continue the drama with new scripts that we ourselves are writing. To take the story forward in fresh ways that are completely faithful to the past characters and wholly consistent with the story so far. Faithful to the Executive Producer—God himself—who's there in person, on the set, working with us.

Finale: Completion

And then finally we reach the finale, which has already been scripted ready to shoot—with a heavenly cast ready to take over from us and enact the final scenes—in "C" for **"completion."** This episode is already "in the can," as they say. How it's all going to end is all scripted, with all of the cues and prompts and rehearsals done and dusted—the story coming to its completion in all of its fullness. And just like at the very start of the story in the pilot episode—and for the same reasons—we see it being described to us in "picture language." Painting a picture with words, this time in Revelation, of what it's going to be like.

> Then I saw "a new heaven and a new earth," for the first heaven and the first earth had passed away, and there was no longer any sea. . . .
>
> And I heard a loud voice from the throne saying, "Look! God's dwelling-place is now among the people, and he will dwell with them. They will be his people, and God himself will be with them and be their God.
>
> He will wipe every tear from their eyes. There will be no more death or mourning or crying or pain, for the old order of things has passed away."
>
> He who was seated on the throne said, "I am making everything new!"'

Revelation 21:1–5

God speaks, and he creates a new cosmos—just as he did at the beginning, when he spoke that first cosmos into being. The reason there's no longer any sea is because in the ancient world the sea was symbolic of chaos and disorder—hostile forces breaking out in natural disasters. But all of that will be gone, along with sickness, sin, and death. We see "God's dwelling-place is now among the people" just as it was in the Garden of Eden. Just as he promised it would be in that renewed covenant (Jeremiah 31), when he said: "I will be their God, and they will be my people." He will "wipe every tear from their eyes"—with "no more death or mourning or crying or pain"—because "the old order," which is characterized by those things, has been destroyed. God is making everything new and once again, he's speaking it into being. Re-creating everything that was so "very good" about that original creation, but with all of the bad stuff that invaded it taken out. So too, all of the people who still want to do bad stuff and live in their own version of the story will be taken out (we see all of this being pictured in the Parable of the Wheat and the Weeds in Matthew 13:24–30).

The good news of the gospel is that, through Jesus, this is what's coming! God's future is coming into our present, in all its fullness. When we pray "Your kingdom come, your will be done, on earth as it is in heaven" in the Lord's Prayer, *that's* what we're praying. When we pray for people and their situations, we're asking: "Lord, would you bring a foretaste of your future into our present? Bring the way things will be into the way things are." Technically, it's the Disciples' Prayer rather than the Lord's Prayer—it's how Jesus taught *us* to pray—but let's not be picky!

So to paraphrase Charles Dickens, season three is the best of times and the worst of times. It's the best of times because Jesus has come. In his death and resurrection, he's defeated all of the powers ranged against human life and flourishing. He's rescued the story. He's ascended to the heavenly realms as the first-born of a new way of being human—the first human to be "born again" as a new person—as we are invited to be, in his image and likeness. A new way of being human; a new way of being *'adam*. And Jesus has not then left us alone. He's poured out the Holy Spirit, bringing new life and new power into human life, so that we may experience the first-fruits of the future, as a down-payment or guarantee of the coming kingdom. But it's the worst of times too, because there are still tears in our eyes to be wiped away. There's still death and mourning and crying and pain around us. We see the kingdom come "now," but "not yet" in all its fullness. It's "both-and." So we still need faith and trust that in God's good time he will complete the story, while we're living in this "now and not yet" era. Good news people still living in a bad news world.

Personalizing the Big Story

So this has been the Bible Story Box Set, seasons one, two, and three. With just eight words that we need to remember, if we want to tell the story that way.

Pilot Episode:	Creation
Season One:	Crisis
	Commitment
	Commandments
	Conversations
Season Two:	Christ
Season Three:	Cast
Finale:	Completion

Obviously, we don't have to tell it that way—there's more we could include and there's some we could leave out. There's some we could explain differently and some we could emphasize more. The important thing is that each of us, as Christians, should have our own "version"—"oven-ready" as it were. A way of telling the Big Story that makes best-sense to us; one that is easy for us to tell and easy for others to relate to and remember. One that we can tell without using lots of religious words, so that it has the best chance of "making sense" to someone with little or no church background.

The way that we tell the story should never be simply theoretical or theological. We, personally, are part of the story. We engage with it in a personal way. Since it's a relational story, how we personally encounter God within it is integral to our telling of it; how his story became my story and continues to shape my story. The traditional way to describe that is "my testimony" (although bear in mind the phrase will sound odd outside of Christian circles). The ways that God and his story impact me and my story are central. We want people to see how the Big Story affects our stories in practice. What God's invitation to come into his story looks like—what new life looks like, when we encounter that story.

The challenge is always to be asking ourselves—are we really living in *God's* story, or have we just imported a few features of his story into ours? Have we just made our own story a bit more religious? Whose story are we really living in? We can't have a foot in both. Colossians 1:13 says that "he has rescued us from the kingdom of darkness and transferred us into the kingdom of his dear Son." Too many Christians commute between kingdoms. The gospel is intended as a one-way ticket. To mix my metaphors, you can't be transferred to another football team and continue to play for both teams.

The Big Story of the Bible is an invitation to bring our story into his story. To challenge us that we need to make a decision—for today to be the day in our life journey when we decide to change stories and bring our story under the story of the Savior of the world. The story we live in involves a choice. God won't force anyone to love him and he won't force anyone to be part of his story, any more than he did at the beginning. The question is, do we want to be just spectators, while season three plays out in this world through his church? Or do we want to join the cast?

— 4 —

The God of the Old Testament and the God of the New Testament

The question we're going to look at in this chapter is one that for many people is a big one, if not also an insoluble one: Is the "angry, violent God" that we read about in the Old Testament the same as "that nice Jesus" in the New Testament? Can they possibly be the same? And if so, how?

In case you've not read much of the Old Testament, let me offer some background as to why people wonder about that in the first place. There are certain passages in the stories of Israel's battles with the Canaanites—after God rescues them from slavery in Egypt in what's called the exodus—that seem to command, or at least to condone, genocide towards the existing inhabitants of the land. Nowadays, if it wasn't in the Bible, we would call that "ethnic cleansing." Actually, even although it is in the Bible, it still sounds like ethnic cleansing. And, God having "told them to do it" is often given as the reason. However, this seems completely incompatible with everything we know about the nature and character of Jesus in the New Testament, from everything he said and did. If John 14:9 is right, that anyone who has seen Jesus has seen the Father, then how do we reconcile this apparent contradiction in how God comes across? Did he somehow "change" in the period between the Canaanite conquest and the incarnation? Or was Jesus angry and wrathful, too, but just kept it to himself most of the time? That may sound slightly facetious, or even offensive. It's not meant to, but I have actually heard that argued—that just because Jesus comes across as nice doesn't mean he didn't feel that same kind of divine anger and wrath deep down.

Let me be more specific about the problem, highlighted in passages in Deuteronomy and Joshua.

> When the LORD your God brings you into the land you are entering to possess and drives out before you many nations . . . then you must destroy them totally . . . and show them no mercy. Do not leave alive anything that breathes. Completely destroy them . . . as the LORD your God has commanded you.
>
> Deuteronomy 7:1-2 and 20:16-17

> They devoted the city to the LORD and destroyed with the sword every living thing in it—men and women, young and old, cattle, sheep and donkeys.
>
> Joshua 6:21

> When Israel had finished killing all the men of Ai in the fields and in the wilderness where they had chased them, and when every one of them had been put to the sword, all the Israelites returned to Ai and killed those who were in it. Twelve thousand men and women fell that day—all the people of Ai. For Joshua did not draw back the hand that held out his javelin until he had destroyed all who lived in Ai.
>
> Joshua 8:24-26

> So Joshua subdued the whole region, including the hill country, the Negev, the western foothills and the mountain slopes, together with all their kings. He left no survivors. He totally destroyed all who breathed, just as the LORD, the God of Israel, had commanded.
>
> Joshua 10:40

It's texts like these that cause people to ask the perfectly reasonable question, what's the moral difference between modern ethnic cleansing in places like Rwanda, Bosnia, and Kosovo and the Canaanite genocide in the Old Testament? If it's morally wrong in the twentieth and twenty-first century CE, why wouldn't it also be morally wrong in the fifteenth- and thirteenth-century BCE? How does these events being in the Bible make them any different? What's the moral difference between Joshua believing Yahweh wanted him to wage a Holy War against the Canaanites and Osama Bin Laden believing Allah wanted him to wage a Holy War against America? And all the more so when we contrast these Old Testament verses with what Jesus said and did in the New Testament.

> You have heard that it was said, "Love your neighbor and hate your enemy." But I tell you, love your enemies and pray for those who persecute you, that you may be children of your Father in heaven.
>
> Matthew 5:43–45

So—a bit of a contrast, and hence a bit of a problem.

Dawkins, and Marcion

Funnily enough, that well-known atheist Richard Dawkins has picked up on this, with a few choice words in his popular book, *The God Delusion*.

> The God of the Old Testament is arguably the most unpleasant character in all fiction: jealous and proud of it; a petty, unjust, unforgiving control-freak; a vindictive, bloodthirsty ethnic cleanser; a misogynistic, homophobic, racist, infanticidal, genocidal, filicidal, pestilential, megalomaniacal, sadomasochistic, capriciously malevolent bully.
>
> *The God Delusion*, 31.

I think we get where he's coming from.

Now it may not surprise you to know that Richard Dawkins isn't the first to have a problem with this "Old Testament God." Someone called Marcion, who was a bishop in the early church in Rome in the second century, had a big problem with him as well. Marcion's problem went further: he wanted to reject not only the Old Testament as Scripture but also everything from the books that now compose the New Testament that made any reference to the Old Testament (in an act of textual genocide, one might say). By the time he'd finished, less than half of it was left. Of the four Gospels, only Luke survived. And even from the books that Marcion liked, he took out all the verses he didn't agree with. So how did Marcion explain the difference between the God of the Old Testament (that he didn't like) and the God of his shrunken version of the New Testament (that he did like)? Very simply, he concluded that the Old and the New Testaments must have been talking about completely different Gods. He decided that there was a "Supreme" God—a God of Love, over and above everything—but that he wasn't the one shown in the Old Testament. The one we see there is an inferior, lesser one. A "Creator" God who made everything, and who features in the Old Testament stories, but who is basically a nasty piece of work, rather like Dawkins described. Seeing what was happening in the world, the Supreme God—the God of Love— decided to reveal himself in Jesus. Even though he had no responsibility for the creation, he decided to get involved, to defeat that nasty, horrible, lesser God and rescue us from him.

The debate about Marcion was one of several doctrinal controversies in the early church that had a number of positive effects. Firstly, it spurred them on to formalize exactly what they did believe. The Old Roman Creed—an early antecedent of the Apostles' Creed, which is still in use today to define core Christian beliefs—was promulgated in Rome around the time of Marcion. To what extent it was in response to Marcion, we don't know; in any event, the Creed made clear that there is only one God, who is the same God in both Testaments, and addressed a number of Marcion's other heresies along the way (for example, his claim that Jesus suddenly appeared on earth as a full-grown adult, rather than, "born by the Holy Ghost of the Virgin Mary"). Secondly, it was Marcion who provoked the church to clarify the canon, affirming both the place of the Old Testament and the books that should comprise the New Testament (on which there was already broad consensus, but not at that point formalized). In case you're wondering whether any other church fathers sided with Marcion, they didn't. In fact, he managed to successfully unite every other Christian writer of the day against him. We still use the word "Marcionite" to describe someone who tries to reject the Old Testament from the Christian Bible.

Ways of Addressing the Problem

So Marcion may have been wrong, but how do we answer our question? It may not surprise you to know that Christians have come up with different ways of dealing with it.

One is the classic way, of just ignoring the problem! They just read the New Testament instead and say "It's all a bit too complicated for me . . . ." Which works fine for some people—so if that's you, just turn to the next chapter.

Another is to say, "Well, those genocidal stories may sound bad, but I'm sure God knows best. His ways are not our ways. He must have had his reasons for it, we just need to trust him." And in a way that's OK. If that's enough for you—again, turn to the next chapter.

Another approach goes beyond "God knows best" and tries to explain it—and justify it—on the grounds of what awful people the Canaanites were. That they were evil and immoral and did bad things, like idolatry and child sacrifice and prostitution. So, basically it's saying that "they deserved it" as some kind of divine punishment, enacted through Israel, because it was important in God's eyes to rid the land of their bad influence. However, there are some problems with that way of looking at things. Firstly, there's no evidence that the Canaanites were any worse than any other nations at the time that did similar things. Secondly, does that really justify the wholesale slaughter of everyone, including women and children? Isn't that still genocide? Don't people who want to commit genocide always justify it on ethnic cleansing grounds, as the Nazis did in the Shoah?

And then there's the Calvinist view, that you'll hear from people like John Piper. In an interview on his Desiring God website—titled *What Made It Okay for God to Kill Women and Children In the Old Testament?*—Piper explains what he thinks "made it okay":

> It's right for God to slaughter women and children anytime he pleases. God gives life and he takes life. Everybody who dies, dies because God wills that they die.

The Calvinist view gives God the "credit" for everything. Whatever happens, it must have been God making it happen—which therefore includes natural disasters, murders, rapes, sexual abuse, and so on. The technical term for that is "meticulous sovereignty," which some might call "micro-management." Calvinists believe that God is in direct control of everything, like a machine operator pulling all the levers and flicking all the switches of how the universe "works." Everything that happens is because "God does it." They feel that if we don't give him that level of credit, however unpalatable it may seem, then it somehow diminishes his status as Almighty God, entitled to do whatever he pleases, without having to explain himself to us. However, this does mean that Calvinists have to use some highly technical arguments to try to overturn the obvious conclusion that this view of God's sovereignty can only mean he is directly responsible for all of the evil in the world. You will need to read those arguments in greater depth, to take a view as to how convincing they are.

And then finally, some say that the slaughter of the Canaanites never actually happened. It was just bravado—just a style of speaking, a literary device—and the Israelites were never intended to carry it out literally. Or, alternatively, that it was a "gloss" added into the story by a later writer who was expressing the anger and frustration that people felt against the Canaanites in his own day; wishing that the Israelites had indeed wiped them out earlier. Certainly it's been observed that people groups supposed to have been wiped out (or commanded to have been wiped out) pop-up again shortly afterwards in the biblical account. But of course, there are problems with those explanations, too! For one thing, it's hardly taking the text seriously to say "Although that's what it *says* happened, it never did happen." That's not a very "conservative" reading of what "the Bible says . . ."! But perhaps a bigger problem even than saying the text doesn't mean what it plainly says is that it doesn't help us with some of the other troublesome stories in the Old Testament, such as those that Phyllis Trible has called the "Texts of Terror" (in her book of that name)—sad stories in which women are victims: Hagar, Tamar, an unnamed concubine and the daughter of Jephthah. Unless, of course, we want to say that those stories never really happened, either. That approach also doesn't help us with what the Psalmist says in Psalm 137:7-9:

> O Lord, remember what the Edomites did
>   on the day the armies of Babylon captured Jerusalem.
> "Destroy it!" they yelled.
>   "Level it to the ground!"
> O Babylon, you will be destroyed.
> Happy is the one who pays you back
>   for what you have done to us.
> Happy is the one who takes your babies
>   and smashes them against the rocks!

So, you may have heard some of these various ideas and you may even like some of them. Many Calvinists, I know, find comfort in an explanation that places God "in control" of everything that happens to that extent, even if there are some uncomfortable aspects that come with it. In its favor, it is at least simple and easy to explain. It maintains the apparent integrity of the text taken at face-value (it doesn't require any sophisticated nuancing), although it does so, arguably, at the cost of the integrity of the God behind the text.

Just to be clear, in raising doubts about the Calvinist view, I would in no way wish to diminish God's sovereignty, power, or authority. I would never suggest that his standing as Almighty God and Creator does not grant him the absolute right to do as he pleases, without being answerable to us for it. None of that is in question. It's not what God has the *right* and *power* and *authority* to do, but what he *chooses* to do and how he does and doesn't go about it.

The Nature of God, and the Nature of the Bible

The reason that different Christians have come up with different ways of dealing with this question of how to reconcile the "God of the Old Testament" with the "God of the New Testament" seems mostly to come down to a combination of (i) how they see God and (ii) how they see the Bible.

In terms of how people see God, what I mean is, the kind of God they think they're relating to today. Whether he's the kind of God who couldn't possibly have done that or commanded that. Or alternatively, whether he's the kind of God who, left to his own devices, could quite possibly smite some of us in the way he smote the Canaanites (if it hadn't been for Jesus stepping in to protect us and taking all that smiting on himself). Some Christians think there's every possibility that from time-to-time God might well choose to smite people nowadays anyway, despite Jesus. Especially those whom they see as particularly "bad" people. Stories abound in the media of Christian public figures controversially attributing tsunamis and other such natural disasters to the judgement of God on the victims, for their supposedly sinful ways. The story of Ananias and Sapphira in Acts 5 offers biblical evidence, they say, that such divine smiting can still occur in a new covenant context.

In terms of how people see the Bible, I mean the extent to which they believe the cultural assumptions of that era were impacting on how people were hearing God "speak." A little? A lot? Or not at all? Are these in fact stories of people hearing God correctly, that we are to take at face-value and find other ways of dealing with, in terms of what we find problematic in them, or might they be stories of people hearing God inadequately? Are we supposed to simply believe what they were hearing, or to challenge what they felt they were hearing? Is this Scripture's divinity showing through, or its humanity showing through? To what extent are we to factor into these particular stories of Scripture what we read elsewhere in Scripture, to help us make sense of them? Most obviously, of course, I'm thinking here about what we know of Jesus. To what extent might these early stories reflect that there was "development" going on, as the people of God were on a journey to a fuller and better understanding of God that would ultimately be revealed fully and perfectly in Jesus? These are interpretive questions that require interpretive decisions.

What is sometimes overlooked by critics such as Dawkins, when he attempts his character assassination, is that there are other Old Testament texts from the exact same period that offer a very different perspective on the nature and character and ways of God. Insights that need to at least be placed alongside the problematic texts and be taken seriously in their own right. For example, Leviticus 19:34: "The foreigner residing among you must be treated as your native-born. Love them as yourself, for you were foreigners in Egypt. I am the LORD your God." That is as plain as your nose. So when we place a text like that alongside the texts we looked at in Deuteronomy and Joshua are we seeing an inconsistency in the Word of God? A contradiction in terms? Or, is it illustrating that Israel's understanding of God was indeed in a process of development? Is it a case of different (and ultimately incompatible) lines of thinking being visible at the same time during that process? To what extent might Israel's fear and anxiety as a small, threatened, and vulnerable people have contributed to how they were understanding and "hearing" God in relation to the treatment of the defeated Canaanites following a crucial military victory? How are we hearing the voice of humanity alongside the voice of divinity in the text?

Asking Questions of the Stories

If we consider what we looked at in chapter 2 in relation to "communication theory," we might ask ourselves to what extent God may have chosen not to intervene in some of the things that—in their day and time—people saw as "obvious" in terms of "how the world worked" and "the way things were" in society, not least in terms of warfare. The extent to which God may have held back from "challenging" things that reflected taken-for-granted cultural features of the world at the time but which have since been recognized (often, it must be said, only many thousands of years later) as inappropriate in a civilized society. To what extent did he work with how people saw things at the time and within the constraints of how they saw things at the time, as well as sometimes challenging how they saw things at the time? It does seem that in the various stories and commandments we see God doing some of each. He by no means "tolerated" everything for the sake of a need to communicate with people in ways they would be able to "hear." At times, for example, he very directly commanded them not to adopt the practices of the surrounding nations—such as in Leviticus 18:1–3:

> The LORD said to Moses, "Speak to the Israelites and say to them: 'I am the LORD your God. You must not do as they do in Egypt, where you used to live, and you must not do as they do in the land of Canaan, where I am bringing you. Do not follow their practices.'"

We could never accuse God of imbibing what people would later call "the spirit of the age," but there certainly do seem to be some societal matters with moral and ethical dimensions in which we do not see God "speaking out"—slavery and the place of women being fairly obvious examples.

So when it comes to the problematic texts in Deuteronomy and Joshua that we began with, how might God be inviting us to engage with those stories? Perhaps he would encourage us to ask ourselves whether this is an example of religious zeal going badly wrong. A warning against being so passionate for God that we want to eliminate people that we see as our God's enemies. Are we seeing an example of how people at the time thought about their gods—of the kind of things that gods "obviously" wanted their servants to do (like, eliminate their enemies who were following the "wrong" gods) and the kinds of things that the gods would "obviously" therefore tell their servants to do on their behalf? We will see in the next chapter that in the ancient world the place of God (or, a particular society's gods) was central in everything that happened. Divine counsel was sought on everything. There was no sacred/secular divide, so God or the gods (or at least, spiritual forces) were understood to be in everything, directing everything, and taking the credit or blame for everything. Rather the opposite problem to the assumptions of our world today, one might say!

Given all of these factors, we are at liberty to look at some of these stories and to say "No, that's not what our God would say or do, because that's not what he's like." The Bible invites us to not just "absorb" the stories but to do "midrash" on the stories, as the rabbis would. The meaning of midrash, as a form of study, includes "seeking" and "enquiring," often in a group setting. Hebrew scholar Wilda Gafney says that midrash "asks questions of the text; sometimes it provides answers, sometimes it leaves the reader to answer . . . ." We're invited to argue with the text, just as Abraham argued with God about the fate of Sodom in Genesis 18:23–33. Notice here that the basis of Abraham's argument centers on what he knows God to be like:

> Abraham approached [the LORD] and said, "Will you sweep away both the righteous and the wicked? Suppose you find fifty righteous people living there in the city—will you still sweep it away and not spare it for their sakes? Surely you wouldn't do such a thing, destroying the righteous along with the wicked. Why, you would be treating the righteous and the wicked exactly the same! Surely you wouldn't do that! Should not the Judge of all the earth do what is right?"

What the stories and statements in the Bible are telling us—and how God wants us to reflect on them, and engage with them—may not always be as we have assumed. Just as an appropriate definition of the Bible as "the Word of God" may not be as we have assumed—the "of God" bit might not be saying what we assumed it was saying. The stories and statements are not there just to be "telling us" things, but also to be "asking us" things—and inviting us to "ask them" things!

Problems with the Bible Having Been "Dictated"

If as many Christians do, we have tended to assume some version of a "dictation" model for how God spoke to and through the biblical authors in writing their accounts—if that's the "mental image" we have of how the Bible came to us—then we will have very little scope for recognizing how profoundly "human" elements came to be there along with profoundly "divine" elements. According to a "dictation" model, all of the Bible would be "the words of God," word-for-word, as written. It would then be difficult to explain how God could have "said" something that was clearly rooted in the worldview and culture of its day—such as, what victors always did with their vanquished enemies and their possessions—that we consider abhorrent in our day. (This lies behind why some Christians feel the need to look for reasons to explain and justify "why God said it"—that's where their model for understanding the nature of the Bible as "the Word of God" leads them.)

Out of interest, Muslim scholars believe that the Qur'an was dictated by God in precisely that fashion, and that the Qur'an they have today is word-for-word the same as "the original." It's also why they prioritize reading it in Arabic. All of this, understandably, influences their hermeneutics. Muslims view the fact that we see the human voice within the Bible as well as the divine voice as a poor attempt to evade the obvious conclusion that it can't therefore be "the Word of God" (as they define it). They find it incredulous that Christians should claim the divine status of the Bible to be located in the inerrancy of "original manuscripts," when, apparently, God did not foresee the need to preserve any of them, to substantiate that. Finally, they fail to understand how we can happily read any number of quite different English versions of the Bible and call them all God's Word. It's not difficult to see where they're coming from.

Obviously, belief in word-for-word dictation is a view, and has at least the superficial advantage of offering what we might feel is a "high view" of God's role in Scripture. But is it really possible to sanitize any human writing—however much God is involved—from all of the cultural, moral, and ethical assumptions of its times? To step completely outside the framework of how people saw "the way things are" in their day? And in the case of the conflicts with the Canaanites, for the writers not to be influenced by the fear and anxiety they felt towards those people—fearing for themselves and their wives and children that, if not eliminated, their opponents would simply regroup and come back at them even more powerfully? That kind of fear, gripping a small minority group surrounded by far more powerful enemies, can be a very potent force. Hearing God objectively within that kind of context is deeply challenging, not least if you are still trying to get to understand him and his ways. We know that in the ancient world, people always went to war in the name of and on behalf of their (tribal or territorial) god and "the best god won." Victory was, of course, always credited to the will of one's god and so too were the things that victors typically did. Their god was doing what they were doing, so to speak, since they were his instrument, and vice versa.

Although it's a commonplace assumption in everyday Christianity—albeit, more implicit than explicit—few if any scholars subscribe to a word-for-word dictation model for how Scripture came to us. In the various ways in which the Bible reflects the humanity of its writers, it doesn't seem to correspond to anything remotely like that. When we read prophecies from different prophets, for example, their own personalities and vocabularies very much come into play. That is even more the case when we move beyond prophets into the rest of the Bible and the different literary styles that are evident, in, e.g., the New Testament writings. All of which makes "dictation" tricky. Even where the prophets appear to be quoting God directly, if they are speaking as ambassadors, commissioned to convey a message, this would not necessitate it being a previously memorized, divinely-authored script. It is not necessarily indicating how, exactly, they metaphorically or audibly "heard" God in relation to what he wanted conveyed. We can but speculate, of course, on the extent to which how we hear God today does or doesn't correspond to how biblical writers heard God then

Why We Have No "Gospel according to Jesus"

In the New Testament, it's remarkable that in a book called the Word of God we have nothing written for us by Jesus; even though he perfectly well could have done (either directly or through the common means of dictating to a scribe). Have you ever wondered about that? Why did Jesus deliberately choose to have his story conveyed only through the remembrances of others? If God had wanted to give us something that could hardly correspond more precisely to anyone's definition of "the Word of God," he could have done so through the authorship of a book called "The Gospel of Jesus," instead of the ones authored by Matthew, Mark, Luke, and John. If Paul could employ a scribe to take dictation for him, when he was writing to his churches, surely so too could Jesus. That would indeed have been an original manuscript or autograph worth having! In the Gospels, we have variations in what appear otherwise to be the same stories, and in how Jesus' words are quoted in some of those stories. These variations are of no significance in the context of an eye-witness's recollection—indeed they add authenticity, since no two eye-witness accounts are ever identical—but it hardly fits with the level of precision that one would expect if God himself had dictated it. Such variations could so easily have been eliminated in that "Gospel of Jesus" we might have wished for.

The idea of some form of divine dictation going on also doesn't fit stylistically with places where, for example, at the beginning of his Gospel, Luke says:

> Many people have set out to write accounts about the events
> that have been fulfilled among us. They used the eyewitness
> reports circulating among us from the early disciples. Having

carefully investigated everything from the beginning, I also
have decided to write an accurate account for you, most hon-
ourable Theophilus, so you can be certain of the truth of everything you were taught.

Luke 1:1–4

That really doesn't sound like God talking, does it? Or what about the
apostle Paul in 1 Corinthians 7:12: "Here I want to add some suggestions
of my own. These are not direct commands from the Lord, but they seem
right to me" (TLB). Is that or isn't that "the Word of God"? Was Paul
wrong here? Was he just being modest? Or, do we take what he said at
face value and conclude that we might need to slightly re-think what we
mean by that phrase, the Word of God. In particular, to re-think how
God decided to interact with people in giving the Bible to us.

Let's be clear on this: I'm suggesting that the Bible is the way that it
is, with its human elements visible—sometimes painfully and embarrass-
ingly visible—as the result of divine choice, not divine weakness. If it was
designed by God to be "the way it is," then it's "the Word of God" the way
it is. Which means we will need to stop insisting that the Bible "has to be"
something we've assumed that it "must be"—possessing features that we
feel it "must have" or "can't have"—in order to fit our definition of what
being "the Word of God" must mean or can't mean! And in particular, to
over-state the features of divinity that it must have.

This is the right moment to bring back Jesus to front and center
stage in this discussion. If the coming of Jesus is the pivotal and critical
event of world history . . . if Jesus is at the very heart and center of the
story of God and his creation . . . if it is Jesus who "makes sense" of the
story . . . if all authority in heaven and earth has been given to Jesus
(Matthew 28:18) . . . and if he and the Father are one (John 10:30) . . .
then we should be looking to Jesus as the obvious answer to this question
of the relationship of the God of the Old Testament to the God of the
New Testament. Jesus would be the only correct "lens" (or "spectacles")
through which we approach it. Stated bluntly, therefore, wherever we
see any divergence between the nature and character and behavior of
Jesus in the New Testament and the apparent nature and character and
behavior of God in the Old Testament, we must say it is only Jesus who
reflects that same, one God perfectly. So whenever we see something in
the Old Testament that appears on its face to be inconsistent with Jesus,
it requires a bit more thought. Not because those problematic passages

are not equally the Word of God . . . not because they're "in error". . . not because, as Marcion argued, they're portraying "a different God". . . or as Dawkins argues, that they're exposing a "bad" God . . . but because there's something more going on within God's ways and purposes in how he's designed and delivered this Word of God to us.

We've already looked in chapter 2 at how communication "works" and the need for the communicator to "accommodate" the person with whom they need to communicate. In biblical terms, this meant that God himself had to operate within frameworks of understanding that "worked" for the world in which the biblical writers were living. What was communicated had to have "made sense" to people at the time before it ever became something with application to us in our world.

We have a young man in our congregation who fled his home country for the UK because his life was under threat for his Christian beliefs. He barely speaks a word of English and no-one in the church speaks a word of his language. This makes communication very challenging! He speaks his own language perfectly well, of course, but we're finding it really hard to understand him—to "hear" what he's saying. It's literally "foreign" to us. One of the consequences of this communication gap between us is that when we're engaging with him, we focus only on the things that are most important. Another is that we tend to simplify things a lot more. And we resort to more use of pictures! I suggest that the same kinds of circumstances and priorities prevailed in God's communications with people in different eras of biblical history as well. God speaks "his language" perfectly well; but we as his people sometimes find it hard to understand him—to "hear" what he's saying. It's "foreign" to us. So, because of this communication gap, God focuses on the things that are most important at that particular time. He simplifies things a lot more. And he, too, resorts to more pictures!

Cover-to-Cover, the Bible Is a Relational Story

Although the church fathers decided that both Old and New Testaments should be in the Bible, they called them "the Old" and "the New" for a reason. The word "Testament" here means an agreement defining the relationship between two parties, in this case, humanity and God. "Covenant" is an alternative word that means the same. "Old" and "New" are not entirely helpful terms—I would prefer "earlier" and "later" because they better reflect the continuity. In any event, the Old is talking about the part of the Bible that frames and describes an earlier way of relating to God (the very earliest ways in which God's people understood him, pre-Jesus). The New is talking about the part of the Bible that frames and describes a later way of relating to God (the ways in which God's people later came to understand him in the light of Jesus).

It would be disparaging to speak of the Old Testament period being "darkness" and the New Testament period being "light," but there is a useful metaphor in there somewhere in relation to the light by which we see God (as with all metaphors, so long as we don't over-work it and push it too far). In Matthew 4:16, Matthew quotes a prophecy of Isaiah that Jesus' coming fulfilled: "The people living in darkness have seen a great light; on those living in the land of the shadow of death a light has dawned." In John 8:12, Jesus said: "I am the light of the world. Whoever follows me will never walk in darkness, but will have the light of life." The revelation of who God is and what he's like from the past has suddenly been taken to a whole new level of visibility and clarity by the revelation of who God is and what he's like in Jesus. In biblical language, it is indeed like light penetrating darkness. If we think about the difference between what it's like trying to read a book in a darkened room compared to what it's like when someone turns on the light, we can see why Matthew and John are saying: "That's what it was like for us" when Jesus came and "lit up" our understanding of God. It's like when dawn breaks. No wonder we talk about something "having dawned on us." The Book of Hebrews explains this difference between the earlier understanding of God and the later understanding in these terms: "In the past God spoke to our ancestors through the prophets at many times and in various ways, but in these last days he has spoken to us by his Son . . . The Son is the radiance of God's glory and the exact representation of his being" (Hebrews 1:1-3). There's a qualitative difference in the divine communication, and there's a progression going on. Not, we hasten to add, within God himself—he's the same God that he's always been—but rather, in how he is understood. C. S. Cowles says that the coming of Jesus "represents a whole new order of divine disclosure." A different order of magnitude from the prophets' past understanding of who God is, compared to the fresh revelation of who God is that we see in Jesus.

The journey of revelation narrated in the Bible was a long one, with a fair number of communication challenges for God to overcome along the way. Remember where the story began, early on, in Genesis 3, with Adam saying "I heard you walking in the garden, and I was afraid of you, so I hid." Compare that to the reality of the God who in the Bible says "do not fear" 365 times (according to Rick Warren), once for every day of the year. Remember how when Moses and Joshua were first learning about who God is and what he was like—around the time that we encounter those genocidal texts—and God speaks to Moses through the burning bush in Exodus 3. During that conversation, Moses has to say to him "Excuse me—but which god are you . . . ? What's your name? Which god do I say is sending me?" Compare that to the innumerable names of God, illustrating the attributes of God, that we encounter later in Scripture. Compare that to the Jesus who was given the name Immanuel: "God with us."

So as modern Christians—or even as modern atheists—we shouldn't read into the story an assumption that the characters at the time had the same understanding of who God is and what he's like that's available to us now, thousands of years later. Especially, the understanding that we've had since the coming of Jesus and the availability of the New Testament (and with the benefit of our own personal copies of it). It's not fair to judge those who featured early in the biblical story, who didn't have the benefit of our understanding, as if they did have or should have had, just because their stories are included in the same Word of God. We worship a timeless God, but the biblical characters had a time-bound relationship with him, rooted in the times in which they lived.

The likely reason Jesus said John the Baptist was the greatest of the Old Testament prophets (Luke 7:28) was because John had experienced Jesus and the inauguration of the kingdom of God (Luke 7:22). His understanding was therefore way beyond what any previous prophet's had been. When Philip, one of Jesus' disciples, said to him in John 14, "Lord, show us the Father and that will be enough for us," Jesus answered, "Don't you know me, Philip, even after I have been among you such a long time? Anyone who has seen me has seen the Father. How can you say, 'Show us the Father'? Don't you believe that I am in the Father, and that the Father is in me?" They're inseparable and always have been—they are one in heart and mind and purpose. God has always been like what Jesus is like. In John 5:19, Jesus says "I do only what I see the Father doing—whatever the Father does, the Son also does." And plainly, we do not see Jesus committing genocide. On the contrary, we see Jesus loving his enemies and telling his followers to do the same.

The fact that as human beings we will one day stand before God as Judge to give an account of how we have chosen to live this life does not mean that we are standing before a God who was whispering genocide into the ear of Joshua. To enquire about the right and best way of reading the genocidal texts is not to diminish God's role and rule as Judge of the cosmos or to deny that there are consequences to opposing God's agenda. But if we have a Jesus-centered faith, we must necessarily have a Jesus-centered view of the world and adopt a Jesus-centered framework for interpreting the Bible. It's not that before Jesus no one had ever encountered God, or no one had ever heard God speak to them or reveal something of what he's like to them, it's just that the quality of the picture people were seeing wasn't the same.

God Pictured in Jesus

I wonder what kind of TV you had in your house when you were growing up? Do you remember how bad the picture quality used to be, until fairly recently? Maybe if you're as old as me you might remember having to move a portable aerial around the room, to try to get a better signal? If we go back further in time, until the late 1960s television pictures were all in monochrome, before the advent of "glorious Technicolor." Compare all that to the latest Ultra High Definition 4K models. It's hard to believe the difference in the sharpness and clarity of what we see now compared to what we used to see in the past. We didn't even realize how bad the pictures were at the time—we had no concept then of how good they could be and one day would be. And it's the same with the pictures we see in the Old Testament of what God is like. They're picturing the same God, but the sharpness and clarity of the image is completely different. I remember when our grandson Laurie was five years old and he was at our house watching television. He said to his grandmother, "Nanna, why is your television so blurry?" When I heard the story later, I was so ashamed! Up until then, I'd thought the picture was pretty good. And we might say the same about the "blurry" picture of God that people were seeing in the Old Testament before Jesus.

Hebrews 1:3 tells us that Jesus is "the *exact representation* of God's being." The Greek word that's used there originally meant an instrument used for engraving. Later it was used for the impression made on coins; which is why some translations of Hebrews 1:3 say that Jesus is "the perfect imprint" of what God is like; "the exact likeness" of God's being; "an exact copy of God's nature" and "the flawless expression of the nature of God."

If Jesus is, indeed, the flawless expression of the nature of God and if God is indeed unchanging in nature and character—the same yesterday, today, and forever—then any previous understandings of who God is and the kind of things he says and does will always be in need of adjusting, to the extent that they fail to correspond to the nature and character of God that we see in Jesus. The Jesus who is the flawless expression of the nature of God is the "lens" and "spectacles" through which we need to see everything that came before—and, for that matter, anything that comes up now. Anyone who claims to be speaking for God in our day can be judged—and should be judged—on the basis of whether that looks like and sounds like the Jesus we know in Scripture.

Before the Bible is ever an instruction manual or a list of things God wants us to believe, first and foremost it's a story. I don't mean it's a "fairy story" or "fiction," I mean it's mostly narrative: The stories of peoples' lives and their experiences of God, of which we are observers and eaves-droppers. Stories in which people get things right and get things wrong. In which they do things that are right and things that are wrong. In which they get God right and get him wrong. And the Jesus who is the center-point and fulcrum of the scriptural story provides the rule or measure (which is the literal meaning of the word "canon") to help us know which is which as we go along. In chapter 1, we spoke about "seeing ourselves" in the Bible's stories, as they invite us to ask ourselves questions such as "Who would I have been in that story?"—here, we are asking how would Jesus have featured in the story? As the famous Christian wristlet asks us, WWJD ("What would Jesus do?") in that story? What would he have said and done; how would he have featured, had he been there; how would he have interpreted events and spoken for God in that situation?

And if sometimes this means that, as ordinary Christians, we need some help in figuring some bits of it out, then so be it. If it means that sometimes we need to live with some level of ambiguity as to what is happening in those stories—and how they may be reflecting the divinity and humanity in them requires some nuanced thought—then again, so be it. While we're doing that, let's do what John Wimber said and center our time and attention on "the main and the plain" in Scripture, without allowing the more difficult bits to distract us or put us off.

Welcome the Challenges in the Bible

Over many, many years the people who wrote and compiled the Bible had every opportunity to sanitize it and to take out the bits they didn't like, as Marcion wanted to do. They could have taken out all of the bits that might put people off, or that people might misunderstand. But they didn't do that—they left it all in. They didn't sanitize anything. They decided to allow the Word of God to speak for itself—"warts and all." And that's because it's not just the story of God alone, it's the story of *people* and God. And as soon as people are allowed into the story, there will be people messing up the story and people messing up in the story. The Bible is not just a story of God speaking, it's a story of people hearing. People who get things wrong at times, as well as right at times (just like we do). The Bible does not only feature perfect people who get things right. Far from it. Most if not all of the great characters had plainly visible flaws—like Abraham, Moses, and David. That's what you get, when you allow people into the story! So it's hardly any surprise that we should see people like us and our stories mirrored in the Bible—and thank God that we do! It means there's hope for us, when we see ourselves in its pages. Even when that's a bit embarrassing. W. C. Fields apparently said "Never work with children or animals" in making movies, because they are so unpredictable and will steal the scene. God himself might well have said that about working with people.

So—does God command genocide? No. People do. What kind of things does God command? When Jesus was asked which was the most important commandment, he said it was this one (in fact, he "cheated" a bit by answering it with two—because, in God's perspective, you really can't separate one from the other; it's both-and).

> "Love the Lord your God with all your heart and with all your soul and with all your mind" [Deuteronomy 6:5]. This is the first and greatest commandment. And the second is like it: "Love your neighbor as yourself" [Leviticus 19:18]. All the Law and the Prophets hangs on these two commandments.
>
> Matthew 22:36–40

All the Law and the Prophets—all of the story of Scripture that came before Jesus—hangs on—and has always hung on—these two commandments. Everything God "commands," everything God "says," every attitude that God asks his people to adopt, and every action he asks his people to enact, ever since the beginning of the biblical story, can and should be filtered through these two.

We are invited to question the text. We are invited to enquire *what* a text is there to teach us and *how* it is intending to go about teaching it to us. Once we stop seeing everything through an assumed lens that it's "God saying this"—following the assumptions and implications of a quasi-dictation model—then what a text is wanting to teach us may not necessarily be as we have assumed. We are invited to ask how the human-ity of the Bible has interacted with the divinity of the Bible in what we're reading. Rather than assume the Word of God to be "worldview-free" (because of the "of God" tag) instead we need to recognize that all com-munication must of necessity be set within a worldview, since that is an unavoidable aspect of "context."

The question then becomes: How do we relate (if not also translate) what God said then, within their context, to what God is saying now, in our context? How are we to filter it, in relation to the cultural elements— a lot, a little, or not at all—while remaining completely faithful to the divine author? What are the texts and stories telling us about hearing God within a worldview and within a context? For example, we might want to ask those kinds of questions about what Peter writes, in 1 Peter 2:18: "Slaves, in reverent fear of God submit yourselves to your masters, not only to those who are good and considerate but also to those who are harsh" (some translations say "those who are cruel"). Is that not astonish-ing advice, from our worldview's perspective? But once we move away from a starting assumption that because it's "the Word of God" this must mean that it's "God saying it" in a dictated sense, so we're never allowed to ask questions of it, our approach is transformed. The scriptural text is not like a fearsome sergeant major on a parade ground who responds with "Because I say so" to any recruit with the temerity to ask a question.

God has intentionally given us the canon of Scripture with the times in which it was written reflected in its pages. The Bible is culturally situ-ated, not culturally sanitized. If God had removed stories and teachings in which the cultural conditions, worldview, and social context of the times were embedded, we wouldn't have had a lot left. Equally, since sani-tized stories and teachings would have made far less (if any) sense to the people at the time, they may well then never have been preserved for us.

The upshot of these features, however, is that we clearly have some translation work to do, in which some aspects will be easier than others— depending in particular on the degree of distance between "how people saw things then" and "how we see things now." We also have to remember that each of the biblical authors, especially in the Old Testament, was situated in a particular place in the story in which (to say the least) they didn't have the benefit of knowing the final outcome as we do now. We have the whole story laid out before us—they were experiencing only a snapshot, as it was being written, in real-time.

The crucial place of Jesus in helping us to grasp and interpret the divine role in the story, as it's emerging, can hardly be overstated. Everything God commands and everything God says will always correspond to Jesus—it will always "look like" Jesus and "sound like" Jesus. He is our perfect "lens" for knowing who God is and what he's like and always has been like. Jesus is our "picture of God" in ultra-high definition.

How the Biblical Writers Saw Their World

(And Why That Matters to Us)

O ne of the difficulties that we're often unaware of when we're watching a period drama on television or in a movie is that, although
the costumes and the locations may be authentic to that period, and perhaps the odd phrase here and there—"verily, verily, I say unto thee"—the
mindset of the characters in terms of how they are "seeing the world" still
follows today's ways of thinking. Unless we're aware that different eras
had very different ways of thinking, that will completely pass us by. We
won't even notice it. Many, or even most, period dramas have what we
call "anachronisms" embedded in them, because it tends to make them
more watchable for today's audience. But what then happens is that the
production ends up as a contemporary drama—with a modern moral
framework and social conventions—in which the actors are just "wearing
period clothes."

An "anachronism" is something from one time period that has
been inappropriately placed in another time period. Examples in a
drama would include a Roman centurion seen wearing a wristwatch, or
using a catchphrase or expression that is blatantly from the present day.
However, we don't see an embedded anachronism in terms of attitudes
and ways of thinking about life anywhere near as easily as we see a
wristwatch! An anachronism can also be the other way around—when
someone today is reflecting attitudes and ideas that are thought to be

"outdated." You've probably noticed that a lot of traditional Christian thinking is criticized for that, exemplified in areas such as sexuality and sexual ethics, and the church's traditional approach to the appropriate roles of men and women. Here we are seeing glimpses of a clash of worldviews, specifically how what some would call the "biblical" worldview seems to be out of synch with the contemporary worldview. We will explore all of this in more detail in this chapter.

To begin with, you will appreciate from everything we've been saying in the chapters so far that, in communicating to and through the biblical writers in bringing the Bible to us, God worked with, in, and through their cultural norms and ways of thinking about "the ways things are." Meaning, how they saw what was "obviously" the case (and not the case) in terms of how life "worked": what things were obviously right and wrong; how society should obviously be governed; how people obviously fit into society; where and how God (or the gods) obviously fit into society, and so on. Given that God worked with people in this way and appears to have refrained from challenging many of the "obvious-es" of those eras, we clearly have a bit of work to do in bringing the text from "then" into our lives and experiences "now."

What Is a *Biblical* Worldview?

In particular, we need to figure out what a "biblical worldview" is, both in the sense of the "worldview" that God holds (so to speak), as the author behind the Bible, and in the sense of the worldview that the biblical characters and authors held—how they would have "seen the world" in their time. We need to ask ourselves to what extent those are the same thing. This is extremely important, because one would expect that "God's worldview" (if we can call it that) is one that he would always have held throughout all times and that (since God cannot lie) would be "timelessly" reflected in the text. When therefore we speak of a "biblical" worldview we need to know which of these two different ways of defining it we're talking about and how they correlate—to what extent we are seeing each reflected in the text.

You'll have noticed already how many times I've been using the words "obvious" and "obviously." Whenever we use those terms, in that kind of context, it's our worldview speaking. Examples of things we might

see as "obvious" today—things that "common sense" tells us—would include the following:

- Democracy is "obviously" the best form of government;

- Slavery is "obviously" immoral and wrong; and

- Women are "obviously" of equal worth as people in their own right
  and should have equal opportunity with men.

It perhaps won't surprise you at this point when I say that in the ancient
world, in each of these examples, they thought the exact opposite was
"obviously" the case. Their assumptions were not our assumptions. What
is generally accepted as "common sense" to us was not what was "common sense" to them.

    This comes into particularly sharp relief, of course, when worldviews
clash. The ordination of women and women serving as bishops in the
Anglican communion is one example that continues to divide people.
Some conservative churches are happy for women to "share" thoughts
but not "teach." Some ask women to speak from the floor rather than the
pulpit to (somehow) reinforce this (supposedly significant) distinction.
However, even conservative churches seem happy to allow women to
teach children (despite the risks to the children that must surely pose)
and, of course, to do dangerous work as overseas missionaries (explain
that one if you can). As will be apparent from my parenthetical comments
here, I'm struggling to stop my own worldview showing through! Most
recently, a clash of worldviews has come center stage in attitudes towards
same-sex relationships.

    In these matters, we see a further aspect that gets caught up in the
mix; namely, "tradition." The nature of tradition is that it's "rearwards
looking." It speaks of how we have previously done something or previously thought about something—"how we've always" done it, or thought
about it. Often that is not literally the case, but it might just as well be,
so embedded can the ideas be and so passionately can they be held. So
although tradition very much has its place and needs to be respected
(we should by no means dismiss something just because we say it's "old
fashioned"—that in itself would be a worldview speaking) it's also easy to
see how what we've always said, or always done, or always taught in our
tradition can get caught up and commingled with what the Bible says.
Especially when we move seamlessly from "the Bible says" to "the Bible
clearly teaches" (as if the latter is automatically the same as the former).

This then gets further complicated by what we mean by a "biblical" worldview—which of its two senses—and whether we are appropriately discerning which we are seeing, in particular instances.

Let me offer a simple and hopefully not too controversial example from the New Testament, when the apostle Paul writes to the church in Corinth and says this:

> Judge for yourselves. Is it right for a woman to pray to God in public without covering her head? Isn't it obvious that it's disgraceful for a man to have long hair? And isn't long hair a woman's pride and joy? For it has been given to her as a covering.
>
> 1 Corinthians 11:13–15

"Isn't it obvious?" says Paul, in this NLT translation. Remember that "obvious" is a worldview speaking. In the more "literal" (word-for-word) translation in the NASB, it says "Does not even nature itself teach you that...?" In other words, Paul is saying that this is all about what's "natural" vs. "unnatural."

This might strike us as very surprising—whoever has seen a painting or movie featuring Jesus in which he doesn't have long hair? Have the painters and the screenplay writers never read 1 Corinthians 11:14? Even more surprising, Acts 18:18 tells us that for a period of time Paul himself grew his hair long, after taking a vow—presumably, a Nazirite vow (see Numbers 6:5).

Not to unduly pre-empt what's coming later, but a postmodern would likely say at this point "What's 'long' for you is not necessarily 'long' for me.... Who decides what 'long' is?" But I digress....

Distinguishing "Timeless" from "Time-Bound"

I imagine some Christians, in their desire to take the Bible appropriately seriously and honor its "timeless" truths, really do feel that men shouldn't have long hair and that women really should. And the same with women and head-coverings. But in my experience, that's relatively rare. Most of us take it for granted that what Paul would have had in mind when he spoke of what's "natural" vs. "unnatural" are things that are "timelessly" the case. In other words, that he had in mind the same list of things that we too would think are natural and unnatural. We struggle to conceive that his list would include things that were thought to be the case in his world but aren't thought to be the case in our world.

Which brings us back to the way in which we're defining "biblical" worldview—based on how the Bible characters and authors saw the world in their time-bound context, or based on how God sees the world in his timeless context? Again, we have to ask ourselves how the two correlate, in order for us to be faithful in honoring and applying Scripture today. We need a methodology. No-one is saying there is no potential for overlap and that the one cannot legitimately be the same as other at times (of course not). But we do need to be aware of the potential for taking biblical terms (like "natural" and "unnatural") and reading today's meanings into them—and more specifically, our own sense of their meanings, since opinions may reasonably differ as to what does and doesn't count as "natural" and "unnatural." Good interpretation always starts with what the text meant then and recognizes that it will not mean now something that it didn't mean then; still less should we read our contemporary meanings into their words. This illustrates the care we need to take, if we're to use "biblical" as an adjective and in pronouncing on what "the Bible clearly teaches."

Now we may think that hair length and head coverings are fairly obvious examples of things that are very much bound up only in the worldview of the biblical era, rather than being "timeless" truths. But in dismissing them (so lightly), we're doing an act of biblical interpretation, whether we realize it or not. The grounds on which we're dismissing them are based on personal judgment, as to what's "obvious" to us. And we may be right in that. But to be reading the Bible well, we're going to need to articulate some better methodology than just deciding each case on what we personally see as its individual merits. For example, consider something else that Paul says is also "obvious" by nature—something that "nature itself" teaches us is wrong—and that is, homosexual behavior. Many who would say that Paul is "obviously wrong" in what he sees as "natural" and "obvious" about male and female hair length (that it's a time-bound perspective that needn't carry-over into the present day) would also say that Paul is equally obviously "right" in what he sees as "natural" and "obvious" about same-sex relationships. The question is, do we have a methodology that we're following, so that we're being consistent in making those decisions? On what grounds is the one "obviously" different to the other (it may well be, but why)? Are we perhaps more influenced than we realize by arguments drawn from "tradition"—what we've "always said" or "always believed"—rather than "what the Bible clearly teaches"? Again, that does not make it wrong (we should never simply dismiss tradition), but as soon as we say that something is what "the Bible clearly teaches," we're interpreting.

Much will depend of course on how we understand (how we decide) that which is "timeless" in Scripture vs. that which is "time-bound" in Scripture. Where in the text are we seeing the perspective that the biblical characters held—how they would have "seen the world" in their time— versus the perspective that God has and always has had throughout all times? How easily can those be distinguished? Are they at times inter- twined, and if so, how do we discern between those two elements in things that are said and events that occur? Clearly, what we are wanting to hear is the voice of the divine author through the voice of the human writers.

Let's shift gear a little bit. We have identified a "biblical worldview" in the sense of the perspective as to "the way things are" that the biblical writers had. But there's a further element, which is the worldview shared generally by people in the ancient world. There would have been a very considerable overlap, of course. It would be wrong to imagine that the Bible characters and writers had a totally different perspective to their contemporaries—a totally different set of ideas about what was "obvious" and "natural" about human society and the way the world worked.

Plainly, there are times in Scripture where we see a stark contrast in what God said he wanted from his people in how they lived compared to the surrounding nations. God appears to have zeroed in on certain things to make Israel particularly distinctive. A great deal of the law is all about that. At the same time, though, God appears to have been self- restrained in what, at particular times, he chose to highlight and what he chose to remain silent on—presumably to ensure that what he saw as vitally important at that time did not get lost in the mix. Six hundred commandments are hard enough to remember and prioritize, let alone six thousand, as they could so easily have ended up with! The New Testament expresses similar concerns for God's people to be morally distinctive from the Greco-Roman society in which most of the early churches were situated. Paul writes to his churches and says, in effect, "Don't live like they do and do the things they do," with concrete examples of particular things that he felt should be highlighted—behaviors that should be distinctive of the people of God compared to those around them. Remember that Paul's churches were mostly made up of gentile former pagans, with little or no background in good Jewish ethical lifestyle practices.

So, although it would be wrong, for many reasons, to speak of an ancient-world worldview in the singular, the prevailing worldviews during the biblical era shared a common set of "obvious-es" about the way things worked in society, relationships, biology, cosmology, the spiritual world (the place of God or the gods), and so on. There were, of course, different cultural influences at work in different places and periods, whether that was from Egyptian and Canaanite cultures at the time of Moses, Joshua and the early Israelites, or from Hellenistic (Greek) and Greco-Roman cultural influences (alongside Jewish ones) in first-century Israel and its Mediterranean surroundings in the first few centuries of the early church. Nevertheless, the core features of how people of the time saw the world—their lists of "obvious-es"—were broadly the same.

Our purpose here is not to identify and debate these differences, but to focus on what they had in common, and in particular, to see the radical differences between ancient-world worldviews in biblical times and the worldview of the modern era onwards. And the reason for that, of course, is because we need to allow these differences to inform our understanding of what we're reading in the Bible. If we as its readers have a very different set of "obvious-es" and what's "common sense" compared to its writers, then "Houston, we have a problem." The potential for a dislocation—between what it was saying then and why, versus what we might now assume it was saying and why—will be considerable. Stated more positively, if we can grasp those worldview differences and apply them, it will really enhance our understanding of what we're reading.

A final point to frame what we're going to be saying in this chapter is that we will be considering worldviews within a specifically Western context. We will not be looking at differences between the Western worldview and those prevailing in Asia, or in, say, Islamic countries. For anyone who wants to dig a little deeper and engage more with worldviews—including the aspects that we will not be covering—I recommend a short and very readable book called *Why the Rest Hates the West*, by Meic Pearse, a church historian, theologian, and former church planter.

A Very Short History of Worldviews

With this framework in mind, we shall now be focusing on the ancient-world worldviews reflected in the Bible and comparing and contrasting them with the worldviews of the modern era and the postmodern era, beginning with some time-frames. The first thing to acknowledge is that worldviews do not change overnight. There is a transition process that may take many decades or more, so we need to be circumspect about assigning dates. This is particularly so in relation to past eras, when communication (and hence, the spread of cultural influences) was much slower.

The period during which ancient-world worldviews prevailed goes back essentially to the dawn of time. It embraces the entire biblical period and continued through the Middle Ages, during which time people would have had broadly similar takes on "the way things are and should be" in society, etc.

Modernity began to take over from the mid-sixteenth century, continuing apace through the seventeenth and eighteenth centuries. The key influences that characterized it and shaped it were the Scientific Revolution, the Industrial Revolution, and the Enlightenment (or, the Age of Reason). To which we should also add, the Protestant Reformation. Modernity saw dramatic changes in how society was organized (such as, migration from a rural agrarian society to an urban industrial one). The economic system and way of thinking about commerce that we call "capitalism" is part of modernity; so too, colonialization and modern slavery.

Characteristics of modernity that are particularly relevant for our purposes, in regard to "how people think about things"—including how they now began to think about Christianity and the Bible—include, at various levels:

- Autonomous individualism: personal freedom from traditional shackles of authority, family and community;

- Increasing emphasis on personal rights over duties and responsibilities;

- Separation of church and state (with senior clerics no longer embedded in the heart of government);

- The primacy of scientific method and scientific ways of thinking;

- Everything, in principle, being knowable by rational, empirical methods of study;

- Rejection of the hegemony traditionally asserted by religion in providing the answers to "life, the universe and everything" (now told to stay out of everything except its own "spiritual" matters);

- Disdain for mystery (lack of certainty being a weakness);

- Truth is universal: the same for all people everywhere, regardless of culture and circumstances;

- Truths are established (proven) by the presentation of rational evidence;

- All knowledge on a subject is built on one foundational truth;

and, not least, the impact of all of the above in how Christians think of the Bible as the Word of God, how it should be studied, and the nature of Christian faith, church, the gospel, how to do mission, and many other things.

Based on these Modern ways of thinking (the "epistemology" of Modernity), continuing progress towards a better, more enlightened world was assumed to be inevitable—once freed from the "dark ages" of ancient world and mediaeval ignorance, superstition, and the crutch of religion. Scientific discoveries challenged the authority previously asserted by the Bible—including on subjects such as the origins of the cosmos and human life. Modernity introduced an intellectual skepticism towards the supernatural claims of the biblical accounts; the superstitious ancient world and mediaeval eras were derided as backward. Religion's previously unchallenged role in the public space was dethroned, as faith became personal and interiorized (something that we now largely take for granted).

These various influences overlapped and fed off one another. Within today's Christianity, for example, the epistemology of modernity under-lies Reformed evangelical thought on numerous subjects and is at the root of many of its clashes with—and rejection of—the epistemology of postmodernity. The proliferation of denominations and independent churches is a by-product of the Reformation. Evangelical suspicion towards a "social gospel" is buying-in to modernity's view of what the church should and shouldn't be getting involved with. And few if any Christians today would challenge "following the science" (e.g., in relation to the Covid-19 pandemic) rather than consulting the clerics and theo-logians, as would have been a first port of call in the pre-modern world.

Overall, the period of modernity spans the early-mid-sixteenth cen-tury through the mid-twentieth century, with its ways of thinking still holding significant sway there-after.

Postmodernity began to overtake Modernity from the 1960s onwards, continuing into the present day. Some say that postmodernity is not really a worldview of its own at all, it's simply a form of "hyper-modernity"—modernity on steroids. They say it's just a transitional state before something else emerges. (Certainly, there are elements in postmodernity that it shares with modernity, such as the individualistic way of thinking.) However, we'll treat it as a separate worldview anyway, because of its significance, and say more about it shortly.

Since worldviews do not change overnight and the current one is still emerging, we presently see modern and postmodern thinking co-existing and overlapping, both within society in general and the church. The distinction is typically between older people instinctively thinking in modern ways and younger people instinctively thinking in postmodern ways, with correspondingly different sets of "obvious-es" as the lenses through which they see life (although age by itself is not the sole determinant). In a Christian context, this will impact how each group sees their faith and how they read the Bible. It draws attention to the question as to whether any particular worldview can be thought of as specifically or distinctly "Christian."

OK, so a quick reminder of what we mean by a "worldview." A worldview is the way a people-group "see" how the world works and how society works. The prevailing worldview—"paradigm" is another way of putting it—is "the way the majority think about things, without even realizing they're thinking." It's the sum of all of the taken-for-granted attitudes, values, and cultural markers that define for us "the way things are"—in which words like "obviously" and what's "only common sense" are prominent! This includes what's appropriate and inappropriate in terms of behavior, how we should and shouldn't treat others, and what's fair and what's not fair. It's the (usually) unspoken assumptions that we have about how things are and how things should be. The values embedded in a person's worldview (often unconsciously) are the points of reference that they refer to, to say what's right and what's wrong. This will become clearer when we look at specific examples from each era.

In the Christian world, we may have come across the concept of worldview in preachers talking about "the spirit of the age"—normally in a negative sense, with postmodernity in their sights—seeking to distinguish between that and "what the Bible says." (The German word for it is *Zeitgeist*, but you really don't need to know that unless you want to sound clever at a dinner party. But then you might not get offered dessert. Tricky.) Anyway, the problem with a simple contrasting of "what the Bible says" versus the "spirit of the age"—as good versus bad—is that it fails to take account of worldviews in *how we're reading* what the Bible says. The question implies that the lenses of postmodernity are "the problem," synonymous with the "spirit of the age," such that reading what the

Bible says through postmodern lenses would by definition not be on the list of options. The likelihood, in reality, is that many Christians, older readers in particular, are simply reading the Bible through *modern* lenses, without even realizing that's what they're doing, and unwittingly treating that interpretive perspective as coterminous with "what the Bible says." As the famous phrase has it, a fish doesn't know what water is because nothing else has ever occurred to it. It's just the way things are. Anointing a distinctly modern reading as being "what the Bible says" not only fails to take account of how the Bible would have been read through the lenses of pre-modern worldviews, but condemns any and all ways that it might be read through postmodern lenses, if that would lead to a different interpretive outcome.

The reality is that from a Christian perspective all worldviews have good features and bad features. All worldviews should be subject to critique (which is easier said than done, of course, not least because each of us inhabits a worldview, which embeds certain assumptions in our thinking).

Before we look at some of the core features of the ancient-world worldview, three important points need to be made.

The first is that modern lenses, modern ways of doing theology, modern ways of thinking (modernity's epistemology), and doctrinal formulations produced in modernity have shaped conservative Reformed evangelicalism as we know it. This is not a bad thing per se, since, as we've said, all worldviews have good features and bad features from a Christian perspective—for example, a materialist worldview (whether ancient, modern, or postmodern) is always problematic. Every worldview has elements that fit well with Christianity and elements that do not. It simply means that we need to take an interest in understanding what those are, and in particular not to fall into a too-easy trap of presuming that, because it has been the dominant western worldview for the past several hundred years, modernity's ways are "the right" way—a pure, objective way, and still less, the "biblical" way—while the others are inherently flawed to the extent they fail to correspond to it. Modernity is not the gold standard for judging the others.

The second, that should give us pause for thought, is that since ancient-world worldviews prevailed for the vast bulk of human history—including not only the entire period of the Bible but the first 1500 years of Christian faith as well—it is only in the last few hundred years (since modernity set in) that people have thought in the ways that you and I do now.

And the third is that we should be open to ways in which (notwithstanding its authorship within ancient-world cultures) Scripture includes what we might call a "redemptive trajectory"—embryonic ways in which it begins to prophetically highlight (contra the worldview of the time) things that subsequent eras will perceive to be more visibly reflective of the heart of God. For example, if we read Galatians 3:28 ("There is neither Jew nor gentile, neither slave nor free, nor is there male and female, for you are all one in Christ Jesus") through a redemptive-trajectory lens, we can see implications embedded in that text, today, that may well have passed its original audience by, due to their cultural framework. Our cultural framework, meanwhile, finds it easy to welcome that prophetic statement becoming reality. A further example would be how the teaching on marriage in Ephesians 5 takes standard patriarchal marriage and "infects it" with the gospel, thereby modifying it, even if its original shape can still be seen. We should undoubtedly be open to seeing those redemptive trajectories in Scripture—those "seeds sown."

Ancient World "Obvious" Versus Modern World "Obvious"

So let's compare and contrast ancient-world worldviews—their list of what's "obvious"—with that of the modern world. (We'll defer postmodernity for the moment, since it's a strange mixture, as both an extension of modernity, sharing many of its features, but also critiquing many of the assumptions that underlie it, not least because postmodernity sees modernity as having proven to be morally inadequate and failing to deliver on its lofty original ideals.)

- In the ancient world, society is founded on our religion (on God, or the gods, as the case may be). In the modern world, religion is a private, personal matter.

- In the ancient world, politics and religion (as we now call them) are inseparable. In the modern world, there is no place for religion in politics (notwithstanding that in some countries, such as the US, the extent to which it should still have a place may continue to be debated).

- In the ancient world, life is to be understood by reference to our religion. In the modern world, life is to be understood by reference to science.

- In the ancient world, society is ordered on a divinely-ordained class hierarchy. The common people are accountable to the rulers to whom God has made them subservient. In the modern world, society is ordered on democracy and the leaders are accountable to the common people. Everyone is (or should be) equal.

- In the ancient world, kings and lords have absolute authority and power, which has been given to them by God or the gods, whom they represent. In the modern world, kings and lords are either just ceremonial figure-heads (and hence, powerless) or they're oppressive dictators in "backward" "third-world" regimes.

- In the ancient world, rulers consult the prophets and the theologians. In the modern world, rulers consult the scientists (a government's best defense against criticism is "We are following the science").

- In the ancient world, one's duty and allegiance was to persons—ultimately to the ruling monarch, but cascading down to the humblest subject through a hierarchal structure involving personal "patronage" and "fealty" at every level. As Meic Pearse observes in *Why the Rest Hates the West*, this means that "strong social discipline was imperative. The person who was disobedient to father or master or other figure of authority was, in a very real sense, challenging the entire basis of traditional society. To break the chain at one point was to threaten it at every point." Which helps to explain the savagery and disproportionately (as we would see it) of ancient world judicial physical punishments. In the modern world, by contrast, one's duty and allegiance is to impersonal institutions and to the nation state. Patronage and fealty are no longer seen as "obviously" appropriate to personal ties, but as bribery and corruption.

- In the ancient world, respecting tradition was vital; to change something was risky. In the modern world, innovation is essential; "innovate or die"—change or be "left behind."

- In the ancient world, the existence of a supernatural realm was taken for granted. So too, that God or the gods (or other supernatural forces) were directly responsible for events in (what we would call) the natural world. In the modern world, the exact opposite is taken for granted and ancient world thinking is written-off as "superstition." Everything has, or one day will have, a natural explanation.

- In the ancient world, tradition was revered because the "Golden Age" was thought to be in the past. In the modern world, tradition is sneered at, because the "Golden Age" awaits us in the future. Because of this rearwards-looking perspective, the old were greatly honored (hence, the role of "elders" in the community) because of their greater life experience and knowledge of the past (e.g., what went wrong last time we did some-thing "innovative" and courted disaster, such as planting crops in a different place thirty years ago: the harvest failed and we all nearly died!). Nowadays, the old tend to be seen as "past it" and obstructions to progress.

- In the ancient world, life was centered in the group or community's interests. Decisions, even major decisions for an individual's life, such as who they marry and where they live, would be made by the group or community based on what was best in the eyes of the group or community. In the modern world, life is centered—and decision-making is centered—almost exclusively in the individual's personal choice (and perhaps their immediate, nuclear family).

- In the ancient world, the family (and society generally) was organized on strict patriarchy—the "rule of the man." Women and children were property. A woman was under the authority of her father until marriage, whereupon she came under the authority of her husband. A woman had her rightful place and acceptable roles, based on what was "suitable" for her and "proper." These "obvious-es" were based on the woman's "obvious" inferiority. In the modern world, women have the same status, rights, and freedoms as men and none of the foregoing is the case. (It's notable, however, that it took until late-modernity for such a view to be fully recognized and, even now, in some conservative church circles, a legacy of pre-modern thinking continues, in so-called complementarianism, i.e., that by nature and/or by divine design women have different roles, "complementary to" the male roles, in relation to family and church leadership.)

- In the ancient world, "businesses" were family units, in which all ages in the family would participate. Smallholdings were precious, since having land and the ability to raise crops or animals often equaled survival, and vice versa. (Hence the "shock factor" in the request of the younger son in the Parable of the Prodigal Son. Cashing in an inheritance would have meant selling land. And the even greater shock, that the father was willing to acquiesce to it.) Even larger land-owners with hired hands were essentially family businesses. In the modern world, rather than "staying in" to work, we "go out to work" and the work and family realms are separate. Most people nowadays work for "businesses" not individuals.

- In the ancient world, the individual's obligation and duty to society—to the group and community—was paramount. It took precedence. The individual was first and foremost a contributor. It was taken for granted that "I must obey society's rules." In the modern world, and especially the postmodern world, the personal rights of the individual take precedence. Being "true to myself" is paramount—I do what is "right for me" and "feels right for me." The individual is first and foremost a consumer. I pick-and-mix my own rules.

In terms of morality, the different ways of thinking of the premodern world vs. the modern/postmodern world are illustrated well by attitudes today in strict Muslim countries. In the West, we may perceive them as "backward" and "repressive" (un-enlightened), in matters such as the wearing of the burka, niqab, or hijab (or one of its variations). Whereas, they consider us to be completely immoral in the way that, e.g., sex, nudity, and the female body are allowed to be flaunted and marketed on billboards, movies, and television. Since they see the West as a manifestation of the Christian religion (pre-Enlightenment thinking does not see any natural separation between our modern categories of "religion" and "politics") they understandably look with disdain on people whose religion would uncritically allow and embrace such things. What we see as appropriate personal freedoms, they see as inappropriate, ungodly license. We see similar disparity in how each society thinks about criminal justice and what's considered appropriate judicial punishment. In short, our "obvious-es" are quite different. Our obvious morality and ethics are quite different to their obvious morality and ethics.

Worldview and "the Bible Says . . ."

It will by this point have become fairly clear how, once we are aware of these very different perspectives—these very different ways of viewing the world "then" vs. "now"—it significantly impacts how we understand what is going on in both the background and foreground of many of the Bible stories. It also encourages us to think carefully before we use the word "biblical" as an adjective. It gives us pause for thought before simply lifting a verse from its ancient world context and quoting it as "the Bible says"—as if that, in-and-of itself, makes it authoritative in a present-day situation. It reminds us to keep asking not just what does the Bible *say*, but the far more important question of what does the Bible *mean* in what it says. It reminds us to ask what it would have meant then, for them, and why (even before we think about what it might mean now, for us, and why). We cannot simply "copy and paste" directly from then to now without thinking carefully first; that is not what being "biblical" means, however sincerely we're doing it.

Being aware of these stark differences shows, for example, that far from "elders" being a biblically mandated pattern for how church governance should always work, in the first instance it simply reflects how ancient world governance worked. When it comes to how the place of women was understood, we can see that Paul was not mandating exclusively male leadership as a God-given "timeless" truth, but (at most) affirming what was "obvious" and "natural" in his world for propriety's sake, apparently triggered (and perhaps, only triggered) by the particular circumstances of a troublesome lack of "decorum" in the church at Corinth. In *The Blue Parakeet*, Scot McKnight recounts a conversation with the renowned evangelical scholar and Pauline specialist, Professor F. F. Bruce, in which McKnight was asking the great man for his thoughts on the "timelessness" of what Paul said about women's roles, to which Bruce replied: "I think Paul would roll over in his grave if he knew we were turning his letters into *torah*." It's interesting that the New Testament—Jesus especially—appears to go well beyond what might have been expected for the place and role of women when viewed through the "spectacles" of an ancient world setting. In his closing greetings in Romans 16:7, Paul names Junia as one who is "outstanding among the apostles." Without exception, the church fathers identified Junia as a woman. (Later, mediaeval copyists—who could not imagine a woman being an apostle—changed the name to what they thought was a masculine form, Junias—a name that did not actually exist in antiquity! That's where the KJV gets its "kinsman" from.) More recent "conservative" translations, that should know better, such as the ESV, have no such excuse. It is hard to see how Junia could be credited by Paul as "outstanding among the apostles" (the pre-eminent ministry role in the early church) if she was never permitted to speak or teach. This suggests a localized issue underlying his statements in 1 Corinthians 14:34–36.

It has always struck me as ironic that many conservative evangelical churches that are convinced that 1 Corinthians 14's forbidding of women speaking in churches "definitely does" apply in the twenty-first century are equally convinced that what Paul says in the exact same chapter about practicing spiritual gifts "definitely doesn't." It is all the more ironic when this is the precise context in which the "women keeping quiet" statement appears. If the gifts no longer exist, then perhaps the supposed prohibition on women using those non-existent gifts no longer applies? In any event, it would appear that such churches have drawn their conclusions from selective, pre-existing ideas they bring with them to the passage, rather than through a consistent approach to honoring what "the Bible says."

When it comes to decision-making, Paul's statement in 1 Corinthians 2:16 that "We have the mind of Christ" can be seen to mean not that each of us has the mind of Christ individually, but rather that we collectively can have the mind of Christ corporately (as a group or community). When Acts 15:28 references decisions being taken in accordance with what "seemed good to the Holy Spirit and to us" it really does mean "us" rather than "me." It highlights the difference between group-based ancient world "hearing God" and individualistic contemporary "hearing God." Not just in terms of *how* decisions are made, but also what things are obviously right to factor into those decisions (such as, the interests of the group or community vs. those of the individual).

For us to be aware of prevailing worldviews, as to what was seen as "obvious," will give us fresh insight on how people in Bible times understood the Bible. And not simply in the biblical period itself, but also for the 1,500 years after that, during which substantially similar ancient world thinking prevailed. This would include the era of the church fathers, including the highly influential Augustine, and later the Reformers. Their commentaries, opinions, and interpretations need to be seen in the light of their worldview.

From Modernity into Postmodernity

A couple of final reflections on modernity before we move on. The modern era is characterized as being an age of science. The progress that has been made (and continues relentlessly to be made) is quite remarkable. The progress and success we have seen in matters such as medicine, the natural world, and space exploration lead naturally to the worldview of modernity conceiving everything as ultimately knowable and explainable (not least because we already know so much compared to bygone eras). What we now know about human physiology, for example, makes a great deal of the "knowledge" of the ancient world somewhat laughable in hindsight. However, one consequence is that modernity has trouble with "mystery," because if everything is or should be knowable, then mystery is a negative factor. Mystery is a weakness to be overcome. This is problematic in terms of the element of Christian faith that depends on there being space for mystery. It also impacts on how modern thinkers feel they need to go about arguing for the existence of God and the truth of the Bible. Words like "proof" and "evidence" are commonly deployed. As we've said earlier, the modern era is also the age of the machine. This can be problematic when we say that "God is in control," in that it can be picturing God "controlling" the cosmos in the way that an operator controls a machine—flicking all the switches, pulling all the levers, and pressing all the buttons. Christian faith does, of course, rightly depend on a sense in which God is indeed "in control" of the cosmos. The only question is whether (before the age of science and the age of the machine) we would have pictured "how" he is in control in those kind of terms and whether to be doing so in that distinctly "modern" way nowadays is helpful. I would say not, but some may find it comforting.

So . . . on to postmodernity! Many Christians have been told that postmodernity is "the enemy." And it's not difficult to see why some feel that. Here's a typical example from the bibleleaguetrust.org website:

> The current liberal values, absence of moral absolutes, political correctness, false belief systems are all part of this. Such is the rejection of biblical norms in modern Western society, that the "spirit of the age" is a strong current against Christianity. It is also defensive. Dare speak against it and we are rounded on as "extremists," "intolerant," and almost guilty of "hate-crime." Today's much-vaunted tolerance turns remarkably in-tolerant when we speak up for God's word and His righteousness.

The same article traces the problem back to the massive social and cultural revolution that began with the 1950s and 1960s. The article continues, taking aim at the influence of music:

> During the 1950s, Rock n' Roll came from the USA with Bill Haley and the Comets, and Elvis Presley. The young Cliff

Richard at first modelled himself on Presley. As new bands came, and Rock advanced, its music and lyrics gloried in rebellion against authority, in immorality, outrageous dress, drugs, drunkenness and even witchcraft.

The "Pop" music of the 60s followed, as seen in the later history of the Beatles. It was not just a new kind of music. Music is never neutral. It was a *driven* thing, with a message and purpose. David Samuel summed it up: "Popular music was no longer simply a medium of light relief, but a battering ram for moral and social change."

This coincided with the "cult of the teenager." It goes on:

Before the 1950s and 60s, growing children tended not to have a separate identity. Older sons and daughters looked like smaller versions of their parents in dress, tastes, and lifestyle. It was a straightforward navigation into adulthood. However, Rock and Pop defined a new age group: the "teenager," from 13 to 19 years old. It gave them their own music, and with it their distinctive clothes, haircut, lifestyle, culture, language, and worldview. The post-war baby boom saw many disgruntled and rebellious young people becoming a distinctive section of society.

The BBC (the British public service broadcaster affectionately known as "Auntie" or "the Beeb") is criticized in the article for pioneering "programmes that pushed the standards of taste and decency to limits never before allowed. Swearing, blasphemy, obscenity and violence characterized its output. Satirical programmes mocked politicians and the revered institutions of our country." The Labour Party home secretary at the time, Roy Jenkins, is blamed for helping to "create 'The Permissive Society.' That included abolishing capital punishment for murder, abolishing theatre censorship, legalizing homosexuality, relaxing the divorce law, and legalizing abortion."

One important question is whether this postmodern breakdown in the Christian framework that was perceived to underlie the modern worldview is on balance a good or bad thing, especially for the church— whether "postmodernity" really is "the enemy" that it's made out to be, with the obvious implication that the modernity that preceded it was, by contrast, our friend. Some readers may be shocked that I would even ask such questions, so let's examine them.

Although it would be a stretch to describe the United Kingdom as a Christian country before this point, it was certainly "Christianized." Most of its moral framework reflected Christian roots, however sporadically or imperfectly, at least sufficiently for most Christians to take comfort from that. However, even a cursory reading of the above quotations indicates a degree of cultural disdain interwoven with more clearly Christian concerns. For example, the emergence of something called a "teenager" would seem to be morally neutral (depending I suppose on one's personal experience of teenagers). So too, teenage hair styles and vocabulary. Similarly, musical styles, which reflect cultural preferences rather than moral absolutes. It's funny how God's favorite musical styles (in, for instance, worship music) often seem to coincide with the kinds that we personally like best. And is the abolition of capital punishment really symptomatic of an increasingly pagan society's downward moral spiral?

It would be a mistake for us today to be fervently praying for a *de facto* return to the 1950s—or looking back, misty-eyed, to a past Golden Age of Christianity that never actually existed. In the case of Great Britain, the supposed benefits of being a "Christian country" (to the extent we can call it that) in prior generations were at least balanced out, if not overwhelmed, by the very unhelpful notion that to be born British was synonymous with being a Christian. It's easy for a greater visibility of attitudes and behaviors that are perceived to be "Christian" to be confused with being a Christian country. It's true that religious education in schools was primarily, if not exclusively, focused on Christianity (or at least, Christianity was presented as the correct religion, even if others were studied alongside it). The educational system "taught" Christianity for us, alongside Sunday Schools, which were themselves far more widely attended. All of which meant that people grew up knowing far more about Christianity and the Bible than today, at least information-wise. The question is whether that "education"—the way it was presented and taught—helped or harmed people finding a real, personal relationship with God through Jesus. Did the system "teach" it well? Did people really understand the gospel as a result, or just emerge more Christianized as a result? Or even, put-off as a result? Certainly, I know my parents came out of that system believing that religion should be a personal, private matter, and not to be spoken about in polite company. Their moral framework, which was broadly derived from Christianity, saw no necessity for a personal relationship with Jesus. It made them nicer and better people, perhaps, but it was a very different definition of "Christian" than today. They didn't consciously leave relationship with Jesus out of it, they just never understood that being a Christian included it. Numbers attending churches were sufficiently satisfactory for denominations and clergy to consider things were "fine." The question is whether all of this was lulling the church into a false sense of security—taking comfort in cultural features that should not have been providing that comfort.

The fact that a classical music concert was chosen to celebrate the Queen's 25th Jubilee in 1977, whilst for her 50th Jubilee in 2002 Brian May from the rock band Queen was chosen to open the concert by playing the National Anthem, on the roof of Buckingham Palace, is not *prima facie* evidence of the "spirit of the age" having infected society (as the bibleleaguetrust.org website suggests). It simply reflects cultural preferences; just as some of the great nineteenth- and early twentieth-century evangelists and composers conscripted popular music hall tunes and styles of the day for their songs and hymns (to criticism from their Christian contemporaries at the time).

Modernity, Our Christian Friend? Postmodernity, Our Enemy?

Sincere Christians who berate cultural aspects of postmodernity (and berate the church for being "too close" to the culture) seem to be blind to the flaws in the modernity upon which they look back fondly because of (what they perceive and recall to be) its surface-level Christian features. In postmodernity, by contrast, the prevailing culture no longer serves as a crutch for the church. The strengths and weaknesses of each worldview for the gospel are a matter of legitimate debate.

What we're saying is that there is not and never has been any such thing as a "Christian" worldview or a "Christian" culture to look back on and wish for a return to. There is no current or preceding worldview that qualifies to be called that. There isn't even one that comes close to it. Yes, of course there will be things within every worldview that are antithetical to the gospel and to "righteousness," but they haven't just arrived *en masse* since 1960. All worldviews and cultures have mixtures of good and bad, which we are called upon to discern.

To what extent are we as Christians commissioned to "call out" the bad? To draw "lines in the sand"? To "take a stand"? That's a tricky one. Clearly, depending on what it is we're talking about, there are arguments for doing that. All I would say is that we should pick our targets sparingly and wisely. My two main concerns are these: Number one, in my experience Christians (and the church at large) are far better known for what we are *against* than what we are *for*. This is surely a great shame. Number two, however much we may wish to see transformation in people and society, we must start where people are at. If we cannot genuinely receive, welcome, and accept people to "come as you are" (in another John Wimber phrase) then they will never see or hear anything that will transform them. This has nothing to do with compromising one's moral standards, but it has everything to do with welcoming people as Jesus welcomed them (without the clock ticking on when—and how—they "need to change") and whose job it is to be pointing that out to them (us, or the Holy Spirit). Scripture says "mercy triumphs over judgment" (James 2:13)—which suggests to me that we're called to focus on doing the mercy and leave the judgment to God. He is surely better at that, even though many Christians seem to have a strong desire to do it for him. Yes, he's a God of justice as well as a God of love, and yes, Jesus was filled with truth as well as grace (John 1:14), but the church has often done a very poor job of getting the balance right, at least in how we are perceived. And let's never forget that championing justice is not the same as championing judgment. What we are for, rather than what we're against, should be the hallmark of our gospel. God is only against anything in the first place because it harms his creation, harms people, or opposes his kingdom. We must beware a line of thinking that has as its ambition for society at large to be exhibiting "more holy" behavior. God's ambitions surely start with righteousness in the sense of right relationships in every sphere: people being made right with God, right with one another, and right with themselves. Everything else should and will then flow from that. Transformed people, with transformed lives, transform their world. As stewards of God's creation, we should extend those right relationships to include a right relationship with the environment.

If people are going to give up "the pleasures of sin" (as Hebrews 11:25 puts it) we need to be presenting "the pleasures of righteousness" as the alternative, in ways that sound like good news. The gospel clearly is good news, but the way that Christians explain it hasn't always come across that way. Especially if we think the best way of presenting it is to scare people into heaven (fear is the opposite of faith, not the source of faith). If sin wasn't "pleasurable," in that sense, no-one would be doing it or getting hooked on it. Our calling is to explain why the good news is more pleasurable. Titus 3:4 describes the coming of Jesus as "when the kindness of God our Savior and his love for humanity appeared." Romans

2:4 says it's the kindness (or goodness) of God that leads us to repentance. There's surely a clue here, as to how to approach telling the gospel story.

Postmodernity as Opportunity

The reality is that there are many aspects of postmodernity that are positive for the gospel, even those that at first glance don't appear that way. For example, people no longer think of religion as a private matter that's not to be spoken about in polite company, as my parents' generation did. People today may not have the Christian framework, or know the Bible stories and themes (so there's nothing there deep-down to be "revived" and brought back to life by a good old-fashioned Bible preach, in the classic sense), but they most certainly are aware of a spiritual dimension to life that they're missing. Postmoderns are incredibly open to "spirituality" (as they would call it). Even better, they have fewer preconceived (negative) ideas about Christianity and the church as hurdles for us to get over, compared to those that people used to have. In particular, we don't have to overcome any sense in which to be British is to be Christian or simply "going to church" makes one a Christian. The gospel offer of a personal, restored relationship with God through Jesus is fresh and new to them. (Obviously it helps if the church context in which we're presenting that corresponds well with the postmodern values we've been talking about.)

Even postmodernity's denial that there is such a thing as "absolute truth" is less of a problem than it might sound. Clearly, from God's perspective there is indeed such a thing as absolute truth, but surely we can modestly concede that in this life we humans will never grasp that truth absolutely? As we said earlier, it is only the mindset of modernity that tells us we "must" have an absolute grasp of absolute truth for our gospel to be credible. Just because we can't say everything doesn't mean we can't say anything. Just because there is some mystery doesn't mean there is no clarity. Just because not everything in life (or everything in the Bible) makes sense right now doesn't mean nothing makes sense right now. Christianity in postmodernity can embrace a welcome element of humility which Christianity in modernity sometimes lacked.

Postmodernity has been defined (by the twentieth-century philosopher Jean-François Lyotard, in his book *The Postmodern Condition*) as "incredulity towards metanarratives." That sounds complicated, so let's define those terms. "Incredulity" simply means postmodern people "don't buy it." A "metanarrative" is an overarching story that seeks to explain (if not also dictate) the way things are or the way they ought to be. A metanarrative is a set of rules, or rights and wrongs, by which it is said we should order our lives and our society. Postmodernity is deeply suspicious of any such metanarrative—another term would be a "controlling story"—and the reason it's suspicious is because the metanarratives that postmoderns grew up being told they should believe in have all been seen to have failed. The legacy of two world wars and colonialism and racism and sexism and capitalism and disdain for ecology (and so we could go on) are shameful examples to the postmodern mind of why any and all metanarratives should be rejected. And here is where the big clash comes with modernity: *modernity is all about metanarratives*! "Christian" modernity is all about the vital truth of its own, non-negotiable metanarrative. The gospel is perceived and presented as getting people to believe in and then bring their lives under a Christian metanarrative. Ironically, of course, for postmodernity to propose "the rejection of metanarratives" is in itself to be proposing a metanarrative—a controlling story of the way things ought to be—but it's probably best not to go there!

It's important to stress that postmodernism is not only, or even primarily, opposed to a *Christian* metanarrative (this isn't "all about us"). It's opposed to *any* metanarrative—whether that's the perceived hegemony (controlling status) of the metanarratives of capitalism, Marxism, socialism, or any other -ism. We should also realize that postmodernity criticizes metanarratives not just from a philosophical or "beliefs" angle but because they have been so widely used as instruments of oppression and exploitation. We need to understand the "why" here, because postmodernity is not wrong in that. It's not wrong in relation to what's been said and done in religion's name either, Christianity included. Some contrition and humility—rather than just a reactive defensiveness—will help us greatly. Not least because many postmoderns rightly perceive that the modern Christian metanarrative has had too many features of Western culture wittingly or unwittingly woven into it.

The positives that we can find in postmodernity leave massive space for us to fill with the gospel so long as we are presenting in ways that the postmodern ear can "hear" and relate to—so long as we're able to "speak a language" that they know. Not simply in terms of the words we use but also the concepts and metaphors and examples. There is no point telling people Jesus is the answer to questions that (at this point, at least) they're not asking. They will not recognize Jesus as the solution to problems that they don't feel—it won't work for us to be telling them that they "ought" to feel them. We will never communicate the good news if it doesn't appear to correspond to people's sense of bad news. Fortunately, this ought not to be a problem, because the biblical good news offers a palette of rich colors from which we can paint creative pictures that postmodern people can fall in love with. But we may need to work a lot harder at it than we're used to, especially for a biblically illiterate audience. Simply "dropping Bible bombs on people" (as Mike Pilavachi puts it) and expecting that to work will not do.

Other features of postmodernity are important to understand as well. For example, the belief that there's no such thing as "facts"; that truth is relative, such that "what's true for you" need not be "true for me." Again, this is not as problematic as it first seems, since it leaves massive space for personal testimonies of "what I have found to be true in my life and experience" and can therefore potentially also become true in someone else's life and experience. While postmodernity is uncomfortable with a "Big Story" or "metanarrative" (if that is presented in a clumsy way that includes lots of "trigger words") it is very comfortable with "mini stories," or "local narratives." Hence, a church that presents—and lives out—an attractive narrative of Jesus and his kingdom, which people can see, touch, and relate to as a local narrative or mini-story of the gospel, can thrive even against a background of disdain and distrust for the historic church at large. A "mini story" or "local narrative" easily gets round that. What others have found to be true of church (in a negative sense) need not be true for me!

We also need to understand that "fairness" and "tolerance" are key values for postmoderns. Not wanting to tell anyone what they can and can't do involves some tension when what they might want to do is harmful, of course. Hence, the postmodern standard tends to be "so long as it doesn't hurt anyone else." Clearly, values of fairness and tolerance are not bad in themselves; they only become problematic when they're exaggerated. As the expression has it, "freedom for the pike means death to the minnow" (attributed to R. H. Tawney, the twentieth-century Christian socialist and historian). It is a grave mistake to think that postmoderns do not believe in right and wrong, they just have a more personalized version of it (rather like one might have a personalized version of an exercise plan). Fairness and tolerance rank extremely highly. Postmoderns particularly care about people, and especially those for whom life is "not fair," who have been unsympathetically treated by—i.e., who are victims of—the metanarratives promoted in modernity. People of color, single parents, LGBTQ+ persons, those experiencing economic deprivation or exploitation, refugees, and people in developing nations, would all be seen to be in that category. Postmodern people crave authenticity and they want to believe in something that will change the world for good, not just that will change people's beliefs. They don't want a religion to tell them the things they must believe, they want to see what a religion that believes those things looks like in practice. Is it just another way of presenting a failed metanarrative of the past? If postmoderns thought that metanarratives "worked" for the good of the world, they wouldn't have a problem with them. But since history is suggesting they have always failed, it should be no surprise that postmoderns approach any current metanarrative (any claim to "universal truth," presented as such) with the assumption that it "must be" flawed, so it's only a matter of time before those flaws that are presently hidden beneath the surface are exposed (whether that's flaws in an institution, an ideology, or a charismatic leader).

Postmodernity's loss of confidence in institutions includes the church—and perhaps we should not be surprised at that, given the scale and frequency of abuse (sexual, financial, spiritual, and mental/emotional) that has taken place, about which we should be truly ashamed (whether we personally have directly contributed to it or not). This shameful history leads postmoderns to a rejection of the authority of institutions and those who represent institutions. Genuine contrition, authentic humility, and putting very visible mechanisms in place to avert abuse of any kind is essential, since trust will be at a premium and should not be assumed. Team-centered "servant" leadership, rather than CEO-centered "power" leadership, will also be infinitely more attractive. So too, leadership teams that enthusiastically and co-equally embrace diversity in, e.g., gender and ethnicity.

Keep in mind that a worldview is how people think about "the way things are" and "the way things should be" without realizing they're thinking at all. Another way it is often pictured is that "a fish doesn't know what water is, because nothing else has ever occurred to it" (clearly that's not true of flying fish and one or two others, but all metaphors have their limitations). Hence, simply pointing out to postmoderns that they are "wrong" to think in this, that, or the other way—as if by implication they should simply go back to modern ways of thinking—will not work. People think in certain ways without even realizing they're thinking. We would just be arguing against something that feels completely "obvious" to them. The more we can work with and through things that postmoderns perceive to be "obvious," that also find easy compatibility with the gospel and the kingdom, the more they will be interested. For example, doing things that are meaningful to help those who are less fortunate, through compassion ministries that genuinely prioritize serving and blessing our communities, not just as a Trojan horse for the gospel. The battle is not about ideology or winning an argument. Forget the ideology—they want to see what our ideology looks like in practice, in lived experience. If it's authentic and attractive, they will be the ones asking us about it. Start with what postmodern people can easily grasp and identify with.

No Worldview Is Inherently "Christian"

The challenge for Christians who grew up in modernity is to be able to see the flaws in modernity as easily as they see the flaws in postmodernity. It is so easy to think that modernity was basically a right and good framework for Christianity and the gospel (our "friend") while postmodernity is the opposite (our "enemy"). This is absolutely the wrong starting point.

Evangelicalism has always had a love-hate relationship with popular culture. Perhaps a better way of saying that is that it's always struggling to hold two opposing priorities in tension. On the one hand, evangelicals have always realized that it's essential to communicate within the culture. On the other hand, they also realize that it's essential not to absorb the culture. Seeing the difference between communication-within and capitulation-to is step one, but many Christians struggle with that.

In summary:

- No worldview is more "Christian" than any other, or more problematic than any other. They all have good and bad features that we need to be aware of.

- In particular, modernity is no more a friend of the gospel than postmodernity. Just as we need to understand ancient world worldviews to understand the Bible well, so too we need to understand postmodernity and modernity to understand our mission field well.

- The fact that Christianity and the Bible are no longer generally familiar to postmoderns (through school, family, or church) means we may have to work a bit harder. There's no latent understanding to "revive." "As you know" becomes a redundant phrase in sermons, since . . . they *don't* know! We can't just "name drop" Bible characters and Bible stories and expect our audience to nod, knowingly. However, that also offers the wonderful advantages of (a) a clean sheet of paper, with no embedded religiosity to overcome, and (b) the postmodern openness to—and hunger for—a spiritual dimension in their lives, just waiting for the gospel to fill.

- Postmodernity has features that can be extremely helpful to the gospel. Rather than think of it as something that simply has to be opposed on all fronts, with our job being "to correct" postmodern people and get them to think differently, instead we should reflect on why postmoderns think in those ways—why they have certain feelings towards the rampant consumerism in modernity, for example, and the ways in which the "values" and assumptions of modernity have failed them. Once we do that, we will discover greater respect for them and hence greater empathy for explaining and demonstrating the gospel in ways that make sense to them.

— 6 —

Does the Old Testament Apply Today?

I f you're someone who's read the Old Testament and struggled to figure out why most of it is there, you would not be alone in that. The Psalms can be nice—we get quite a lot of good hymns and worship songs from them—and its poems and songs do seem to present an understanding of God and his ways that seems (largely) compatible with what we've picked up from the New Testament, particularly in the Gospels. And yet . . . quite a lot of the rest of it seems pretty incomprehensible, especially the commandments in Exodus, Leviticus, and Deuteronomy. In fairness, the famous Ten Commandments are pretty straightforward, but according to Jewish tradition, there are 603 more of them on top of those ten, and many are quite obscure (if not occasionally weird).

Something that confuses many Christians is the extent to which God intends that the Old Testament—and especially, the commandments, or "laws"—continue to apply. How do we go about deciding which are still relevant for Christians? Which ones "fall away" and which ones remain as "timeless" in some way? I suspect that many (perhaps even most) Christians approach this on a case-by-case basis, with no guiding rationale as to why this one does apply and this one doesn't. That approach is called "being subjective"—which is another way of saying inconsistent. In other words, how we decide depends on the subject. To what extent is the Old Testament speaking "truth" and authoritative for us, today?

For example, here are some famous verses in Psalm 145:8–9 (you may know them through a contemporary Vineyard worship song, written by Graham Ord):

> The Lord is gracious and compassionate,
> slow to anger and rich in love.
> The Lord is good to all;
> he has compassion on all he has made.

What do you think? It's from the Old Testament, but is it still telling us something that's timelessly true of God's nature and character? Definitely, you may say! Obviously! Vineyard wouldn't have published a song about it, if it wasn't.

But what about, say, 2 Kings 2:23–24?

> Elisha went up to Bethel. As he was walking along the road, some boys came out of the town and jeered at him. "Get out of here, baldy!" they said. "Get out of here, baldy!" He turned round, looked at them, and called down a curse on them in the name of the LORD. Then two bears came out of the woods and mauled forty-two of the boys.

I'm fairly well up to speed with worship songs, but I don't recall any that feature this story. Although I do recall a song many years ago that said, "Pierce my ear, O Lord . . ." (drawn from Exodus 21:6), but I always thought that was pretty weird. . . . Anyway, is 2 Kings 2:23–24 telling us something that is timelessly true of God? That could, quite possibly, happen now? Obviously . . . not? Or, is that "a maybe"?

Banning Shellfish, Pork, and More Weighty Concerns

People often point to the dietary laws in the Old Testament as examples of things that "obviously" no longer apply to Christians today—the prohibitions against eating shellfish or pork, for example, in Deuteronomy 14:8 and Leviticus 11:10. In fairness, it's possible to find a rationale for those laws not applying to us, in Peter's vision in Acts 10 and 11, in which a heavenly voice says to him: "Do not call anything impure that God has made clean." However, from a strict read of what the text actually says, shellfish are not mentioned (only "four-footed animals of the earth, wild beasts, reptiles and birds"). And from an interpretation standpoint (take a look at the very clear context here), what God is speaking to Peter about, using the creatures as a "picture" or metaphor, is his wrong attitude towards "unclean" gentiles being admitted into the kingdom of God.

You may have heard it said that the reason God said don't eat pork or shellfish originally was because they are both prone to disease in a hot, desert climate without refrigeration. That may be so, but was the underlying reason really to do with the health risks? After all, can we really say that refrigeration technology materially improved between Mount Sinai and first-century Jerusalem? If so, maybe that gives us one plank for our platform of how to develop a consistent rationale for which commandments carry-forward and which don't, but it's only going to get us so far.

What about a couple of commandments that are even more puzzling: Leviticus 19:19—"Do not plant your field with two kinds of seed. Do not wear clothing woven of two kinds of material." It's quite hard to see health risks as a particular concern underlying these ones, unless we're worried about static electricity. According to Good Housekeeping's website, "Static is caused by drying or wearing (usually synthetic) fabrics that gather electric charge. An electrostatic charge builds up in your clothes due to different fabrics rubbing against each other." Frankly, I doubt that was much of a problem in the time between Moses and the twentieth century when bri-nylon shirts and acrylic sweaters were invented. Does this commandment now come back into fashion, so to speak?

Obviously, I'm being slightly facetious. But there are some very serious points underlying these questions. For example, Old Testament laws beyond the famous Ten Commandments are by no means restricted to apparently arbitrary (even, inconsequential-sounding) things like dietary restrictions, seed-planting, and fabric choices. There are some extremely serious ones as well. The "two kinds of seed" and "two kinds of material" verse, Leviticus 19:19, sits right in the middle of Leviticus chapters 18 and 20, where we find these two commandments:

> Thou shalt not lie with mankind, as with womankind: it is abomination.
>
> Leviticus 18:22

> If a man also lie with mankind, as he lieth with a woman, both of them have committed an abomination: they shall surely be put to death; their blood shall be upon them.
>
> Leviticus 20:13

I'm referencing the King James Version here because that's often the version that's quoted. The use of "abomination" has a certain ring to it and suggests a considerable gravity. Many Christians would say that these verses offer *prima facie* evidence of God's longstanding disapproval of same-sex behavior.

The point of referring to them here is not to enter into a debate about what view the church should take (or individual Christians should take) towards same-sex marriage or civil partnerships. It's simply to illustrate the challenge—using a very relevant current example, rather than ones that seem to be rather archaic—of finding a consistent methodology for deciding the present-day relevance of verses from the Old Testament that does not simply rely on personal judgments as to which "obviously do" still apply and which "obviously don't."

"They shall surely be put to death"?

You'll have spotted that there are two parts to Leviticus 20:13. The first part pretty much mirrors Leviticus 18:22—forbidding a man to have sexual relations with a man as he would with a woman (I think we know what we mean there). The second part states the judicial penalty for such a transgression: both men shall be put to death. I've read quite widely on this subject, but I don't think I've yet come across a biblical commentator who, whilst disapproving of same-sex relationships, also suggests that the death penalty is appropriate punishment. Nor have I seen any evangelical organization in the US or UK lobbying for the death penalty for homosexual behavior to be (re)introduced into criminal law. (No doubt someone will read this and immediately point me to some organizations that have.) What I do know, according to some quick internet research, is that twelve countries (mostly in the Middle East and Africa) have the death penalty on their statute books for homosexual behavior and at least six of them implement it, including Iran, Northern Nigeria, and Saudi Arabia. Clearly, a number of countries continue to think not only that homosexual behavior should be a "crime" but also that capital punishment is appropriate to that crime. A further sixty-one countries criminalize it without imposing the death penalty, half of which are part of the British Commonwealth. While many Christians may disapprove of homosexual behavior, even strongly disapprove, most would probably feel that to execute people for it is over-the-top as a punishment.

(If you cheated and skipped chapter 5, on "How the biblical writers saw their world (and why that matters to us)" now might be a good time to repent of that decision and go back to it, since "worldview" has a lot to do with why those countries feel as they do.)

However, there is a small problem of consistency here if we are affirming the first part of Leviticus 20:13 (that it obviously still applies) while at the same time denying the second part (that it obviously no longer applies). Some will say, the interpretive principle at work here is that the underlying ethical point of the command is "timeless," but the legal penalty for that offense (situated in ancient Israel) is time-bound. Judicial penalties can therefore change, because they're part of a legal system that changes—and over which Christians have no control—but the sin that's spoken of there is still sin. That sounds logical, but is it quite as simple as that? If Leviticus 20:13 is the command of God in the Word of God, surely we're not at liberty to drop the second part? Isn't that tinkering with God's Word, or selecting only the bits we agree with? If God believed in Leviticus 20:13 when it was first written, presumably he still does now. Otherwise, why would he say it in the first place? Do we have discretion to "update" commandments in those ways?

A further question concerns lesbian relationships. It would be easy to say, "Same thing applies, obviously." And yet, if we're being consistent in following what "the Bible says," we note in both of those Leviticus verses that only male-to-male relationships are expressly spoken about. Hence, it's an act of interpretation to identify an underlying principle in those verses that applies to women also. We may say "Well that's what it means"—or even, "If you could ask the writer, that's what he would say"—all of which may well be the case, but again, those are acts of interpretation, that require a basis. There are no Old Testament verses that expressly talk about female same-sex relationships. (There are several potential reasons for that, but unfortunately the most likely one is the low value and relevance attributed to women in the culture of that era.) In the New Testament, we have just one allusion, in Romans 1:26: "their women exchanged natural sexual relations for unnatural ones." A number of commentators think this is talking about something else—women engaging in "unnatural" heterosexual behavior (such as, sexual activity other than for procreation). The point is that the text itself doesn't tell us which natural ones have been exchanged for which unnatural ones.

Let me add another twist in the tale: The verse immediately preceding the "two kinds of seed" and "two kinds of material" one is Leviticus

19:18, which is the verse that Jesus quotes when he answers the question "Which is the most important commandment?"—"Love your neighbor as yourself." Clearly, that one still applies! Jesus links this to Deuteronomy 6:5, "Love the LORD your God with all your heart and with all your soul and with all your strength." Clearly, that one still applies too.

Clear? Or Not So Clear?

Drawing all this together, then—with a view to trying to form some provisional conclusions—in these three consecutive chapters in Leviticus, 18 through 20:

1. We have a clear example in Leviticus 19:18 of a verse that "definitely does" still apply—"love your neighbor."

2. We have a clear example in Leviticus 19:19 of a verse that "definitely doesn't" still apply—"two kinds of seed and cloth."

3. And we have a clear example in Leviticus 18:22 and 20:13 of two verses that either "definitely do" or "definitely don't" still apply—the "same-sex" ones—depending on the view we take, or the theologians whose opinions we treat as authoritative.

Puzzled yet? We're still looking for a coherent methodology—a way of approaching all these kinds of verses and being consistent in how we treat them for today.

Just let me quickly deal with one thought that might have occurred to you in passing—which is, that the "same-sex" verses are in a different category because they are describing "abominations." The Hebrew word that the King James Version famously translates as an abomination (the NIV translates it "detestable") appears 117 times. In 111 of those 117 times it's talking about other things that are also "an abomination" to the Lord—including rabbits, abusing the poor, not respecting the Sabbath, arrogance, and lying. Oh, and our old friend the shellfish as well. It's true that in Leviticus 20:13 the death penalty is prescribed for the abomination in question, but that was true for many other things as well, such as blasphemy, offering sacrifices to other gods, adultery, a teenage son disobeying or swearing at his parents, and getting one's prophecies wrong (charismatics beware, if that one still applies!). Neither the strength of the language—calling it "an abomination"—nor the severity of the penalty are in themselves telling us something distinctive about how this particular transgression is viewed. Note: one's opinion on whether bri-nylon shirts are also an abomination doesn't come into this.

So, in sum, the process by which Christians decide whether certain Old Testament laws remain applicable to them while others do not is typically somewhat haphazard. Generally, they do so through a personal, subjective decision as to whether or not it seems relevant—or where it sits in our personal moral and cultural compass.

How, then, would biblical scholars guide us?

Approaches in Evangelical Scholarship

Conservative evangelical scholarship generally approaches this by reference to two overarching interpretive principles, reflected, for example, by co-authors Gordon Fee and Douglas Stuart in their classic book, *How to Read the Bible for All its Worth*, which has been a best-seller ever since it was first published in 1982 (and rightly so). Fee and Stuart start with the blanket principle that none of the Old Testament laws apply to gentile Jesus-followers today, because they sit within the context of—they are part and parcel of—a covenant that does not apply. Namely, God's historic covenant with the Jewish people. A covenant is an ancient cultural form of "binding agreement." It's a very important concept for understanding the biblical story, from cover to cover. The word "testament" is another way of saying "covenant." The "Old Testament" is the story of the divinely initiated covenant with the Jewish people in place prior to the coming of Jesus. The "New Testament" is the story of the divinely-initiated renewal of that covenant through Jesus into which gentiles have now been invited, on new terms. Along with conservative evangelical scholars generally, Fee and Stuart say that since the covenant within which those Old Testament laws were given never applied to gentiles, our starting point has to be that none of the laws we find in it apply to gentile Jesus-followers either. Period—or "full stop," as we say in the UK.

Then comes the "however"—the second interpretive principle. That starting point is modified to the extent (but only to the extent) that an Old Testament law is somehow restated or reinforced in the New Testament, either by something Jesus said or something else that the New Testament says. That restatement or reinforcing would then bring it within God's expectations for participants in the new covenant.

How might this help us figure out our "Leviticus 18 through 20" conundrum? To start with the obvious, we were clearly on to something in thinking that the fact that Jesus cited Leviticus 19:18 ("love your neighbor") might put that one in a special category. Equally, though, having Googled it to death, I can find no reference anywhere in the New Testament to God having an issue with flower beds that have more than one type of plant in them, or, wearing a polyester and nylon shirt (the style police might have an issue with it, but that's another matter). Hence, clearly those ones no longer apply. So far, so good. But what about Leviticus 18:22 and 20:13? Neither is directly quoted in the New Testament in the way that many other Old Testament texts are. However, many conservative scholars say that 1 Corinthians 6:9 and 1 Timothy 1:10 are obviously "references back" to these Levitical texts. They see those two verses as "echoing" the Levitical texts in such a way that, effectively, they are "as good as" restated or reinforced. Other scholars, however, say that the textual evidence to support that linkage is questionable. So, whose interpretation are we to go with?

It must be said that whether or not these allusions constitute a restating or reinforcing of Leviticus 18:22 and 20:13 is only part of the underlying question that most people are interested in—the interpreter still has to decide what 1 Corinthians 6:9 and 1 Timothy 1:10 are talking about in their own contexts and in their own right (and so too, a third passage, Romans 1:26–27). There is also the question of whether Genesis 1:27—"male and female he created them"—is offering an exclusive, binding pattern for sexual relations, as many conservatives would say. Again, to debate these texts in not within our purview here.

Whenever there is potential uncertainty of this sort, and we simply have to make our own minds up, there is a danger that something called "confirmation bias" can come into play. In other words, we come to the text with strong views already formed from elsewhere and unsurprisingly we then see in those verses what we expected to find. Confirmation bias can happen either way in the "same-sex" debate, of course, and when we read many other verses as well. Another danger to be avoided is appealing to what are called "arguments from silence" (if you want to sound posh, go with the Latin: *argumentum ex silentio*)—which means, drawing conclusions from what the Bible *doesn't* say, rather than what it does say. That is not usually good biblical interpretation! There are, however, *some* senses in which the Bible's silence can be telling us something. For instance, when we have reasons to think the silence is unexpected in the text. Consider Lamentations, a biblical book in which multiple voices express anguish to God about Israel's ruin and yet the one voice we do not hear is the only voice everyone is listening to hear—God's voice. That is a silence which we can legitimately ponder.

Let's move on to another approach to dealing with whether things we find in the Old Testament still apply today. Some say that what we need to do is to distinguish between so-called moral (ethical) laws, civil laws, and ceremonial (ritual) laws—putting them into one of these three different categories. This is quite an old-fashioned approach, but you'll still hear it said, so it's worth a mention. It defines "moral" laws as those that reflect timeless underlying truths about God's intentions for human behavior. "Love your neighbor as yourself" would be an example of a moral law. "Civil" laws are those that deal with the governance of Israel as a nation, including rights and wrongs to do with the land, economics, and criminal justice. An example of a civil law might be Deuteronomy 15:1: "At the end of every seven years you must cancel debts." "Ceremonial" laws, meanwhile, are those that deal with sacrifices, festivals, and priestly activities. An example of that might be Deuteronomy 16:13, which tells the Israelites to "Celebrate the Feast of Tabernacles for seven days after you have gathered the produce of your threshing floor and your wine-press." In this three-categories approach, the so-called "moral" laws are seen as universal and timeless, while the others applied only to ancient Israel and hence fall away.

Superficially, this approach seems to make some sense. We're used to the idea of asking what the underlying "spirit" (not just the "letter") of a verse has in mind, aren't we?—even when we're looking at the New Testament. Unfortunately, however, a number of problems come with it. Firstly, the Old Testament itself does not divide up its laws in that kind of a way and neither do Jewish scholars. Secondly, it's by no means "obvious" into which of these categories many laws are supposed to fit—even assuming that each law has only one category. And thirdly, it imposes modern categories of thought as to "why" a particular law was there in the first place—it artificially divides-up Torah in a way that would have been unrecognizable to ancient Israel. The whole of Torah defined the covenantal relationship between Israel and God—and what "righteousness" looked like (being right with God in Torah's terms)—so it was all "moral" in that sense. It was all relational, and each law played a part in the overall tapestry. No faithful Jew would have thought of dividing Torah into the "important 'moral' ones" that really mattered and the "merely" civil or ceremonial ones that really didn't matter. (After all, what category of commandment was "Don't eat from the tree in the middle of the garden"—the first broken commandment, from which the rot set in?) When we look at our example passage, Leviticus 19, "Love your neighbor as yourself" in verse 18 is followed directly by "Do not wear clothing woven of two kinds of material" in verse 19. The passage offers no indication that any kind of category shift has taken place between those two verses, moving from a "moral" one in verse 18 to a "civil" or "ceremonial" one in verse 19. The New Testament offers us nothing that looks like a list of the moral ones that carry forward as timeless.

In conclusion, neither approach we've looked at so far—on the one hand searching for the laws that are somehow restated or reinforced in the New Testament or, on the other hand, sifting through for those that seem to be "moral" rather than "civil" or "ceremonial" in nature—seems to be entirely satisfactory. All of which is very tricky for people like us who just want to be "believing" the Bible, taking it so far as possible at "face-value," and placing ourselves under its authority.

Most evangelical statements of faith make reference in some way to the supreme authority of the Bible. However, this issue illustrates that there's a difference between the authority of *Scripture* and the authority of someone's *interpretation* of Scripture. We've said before that (sadly) there is no interpretation-free way of "just" reading and believing. To say that we're simply following what "the Bible says" is not an option. The authority of the Bible does not stand-alone. Its authority comes to us *through interpretation*—and specifically, the interpretations to which we choose to grant authority (whether that's our own interpretations or those of other people). The authority of Scripture means, in *practice*, the authority of those whose opinions we take on board! In his book, *Models for Interpretation of Scripture*, the renowned Old Testament scholar and Anglican clergyman John Goldingay says:

> Scripture is quite normally used in North Atlantic countries simply to affirm and undergird positions. A test whether this is so is to ask when was the last time one changed one's mind (or better, one's behavior) because of something one read in Scripture. In general, we all use Scripture to confirm rather than to confront, merely to "replicate ourselves."

Similarly, N. T. Wright, an equally-renowned New Testament scholar and Anglican bishop, in a 1991 article "How Can the Bible be Authoritative?"

says that "Evangelicals often use the phrase 'authority of Scripture' when they mean the authority of evangelical, or Protestant, theology, since the assumption is made that we (evangelicals, or Protestants) are the ones who know and believe what the Bible is saying." The danger he foresees is that we "move from theology to ideology" and if we are not careful, the phrase "authority of Scripture" can come to mean simply "the authority of evangelical tradition."

Toward Another Biblical Approach

All that said, Fee and Stuart point us in the direction of what might be an alternative approach to this question of whether (and if so which) Old Testament commandments "carry over" into the present. They look to the underlying reason that *aspects* of the Old Testament *ethical* law (their terms, their italics) are restated in the New Testament as applicable to Christians, and conclude that it's because they

> derive their continued applicability from the fact that they serve to support the two basic laws of the New Covenant, on which depend all the Law and the prophets (Matt. 22:40): "Love the LORD your God with all your heart, soul and mind" (Deut. 6:5) and "Love your neighbor as yourself" (Lev. 19:18). Jesus thus excerpts some Old Testament laws, giving them new applicability (read Matt. 5:21–48), and redefining them to include more than their original scope.
>
> *How to Read the Bible for All Its Worth*, 138.

This approach certainly seems to have an overarching rationale that we might look to. In the Matthew 22 passage, Jesus goes on to say why he's answering the question in the way that he does: "All the Law and the Prophets *hang on* these two commandments" (NIV). The NIRV renders it "Everything that is written in the Law and the Prophets is *based on* these two commandments."

Rather than ask ourselves, therefore, in the first instance, whether a particular Old Testament commandment is by nature in the category of "moral" (or, "ethical")—and if so, grant it continued applicability for that reason—instead we ask ourselves to what extent its continued practice promotes and enhances "loving God" and "loving our neighbor." In other words, the combination of these two commandments—which Jesus links in such a way as to suggest they're so closely connected that in practice they're inseparable—offers a "filter" to guide us as to which aspects of which Old Testament commandments have continuing application for us today. Where an Old Testament commandment is clearly and unambiguously restated in the New Testament, of course, applying that filter becomes moot: it self-evidently passes the test, since that's why it was restated in the first place. However, where the continued applicability of a commandment is asserted only on the basis of possible "hints" or "allusions" in the background to the text (or "in the mind" of the New Testament author), it offers us an approach that is centered directly in something that Jesus said. In the parallel passage, in Mark 12, Jesus adds: "There is no commandment greater than these," suggesting that every other commandment should be seen in the light of its subsidiarity to those two. The apostle Paul says something similar in Romans 13:8–10, in which he focuses on the second of the two elements:

> Let no debt remain outstanding, except the continuing debt to love one another, for whoever loves others has fulfilled the law. The commandments, "You shall not commit adultery," "You shall not murder," "You shall not steal," "You shall not covet," and whatever other command there may be, are summed up in this one command: "Love your neighbor as yourself." Love does no harm to a neighbor. Therefore, love is the fulfillment of the law.

In summary, it would not seem unreasonable to propose that for both Jesus and Paul, the present-day application of an Old Testament law for Christians is centered in how well practicing it will promote and enhance the twin concerns of "loving God" and "loving people" or, conversely, will undermine and detract from them. The Great Commandment, as we call it, would therefore regulate the applicability and practice by Christians today of all other Old Testament commandments.

Finally, in view of the degree of interest that exists in relation to what the Bible has to say about same-sex relationships, particularly within the context of civil partnerships and marriage as those are now affirmed by the state and increasingly by public opinion in western countries, here is some suggested further reading:

- Presenting the traditional view: Robert A. J. Gagnon, *The Bible and Homosexual Practice: Texts and Hermeneutics*; Ian Paul, *Same-Sex Unions: The Key Biblical Texts*.

- Presenting the alternative view: John Boswell, *Christianity, Social Tolerance, and Homosexuality*; Robin Scroggs, *The New Testament and Homosexuality*.

- Reflecting elements of both: William Loader, *Sexuality in the New Testament: Understanding the Key Texts*; James V. Brownson, *Bible, Gender, Sexuality: Reframing the Church's Debate on Same-Sex Relationships*.

— 7 —

The Bible and Judaism

I f you've been following "the story so far" you will recall from previous chapters that the Bible—New Testament and Old Testament
together—is one continuous story of salvation. The early church fathers
recognized that the Old Testament was a key part of that story, despite
Marcion's best efforts to eradicate it!

When Jesus was born into this world, as a real human being, he
came into an existing story of humanity and God that was centered on a
particular people-group chosen by God that we know as "Israel." When
Moses asked, "Excuse me, but which god are you?" he proudly identified himself as "the God of Abraham, Isaac, and Jacob" (Jacob later being
given the name "Israel"). Our God's abiding name is the God of Israel.
Israel, meanwhile, is spoke of as God's son, e.g., in Hosea 11:1, "Out of
Egypt I called my son"—a prophecy that Matthew 2:15 links also to Jesus
as God's Son. Prior to the time of Jesus, this relationship had already been
in place for thousands of years.

Jesus' ministry during his earthly life was almost entirely centered
on the Jewish people. Jesus' death and resurrection take place at the
Jewish festival of Passover, when the central and defining event of Old
Testament history—God's liberation of his people Israel from oppression
and slavery, to lead them into a promised land where his presence would
dwell among them—is remembered and celebrated. That we are supposed to notice parallels in the juxtaposition of these two events is plain.

If I was including footnotes, I would use one at this point to observe
how interesting it is that Jesus chose Passover over, say, the Day of
Atonement. Something to ponder, perhaps, not least because the modern

gospel so often starts (and at times, finishes) with "sin." However, we mustn't get distracted. Oh, how I miss footnotes!

Jesus' coming was not an Emergency "Plan B" because the original "Plan A" had not succeeded, although there's a tendency for Christians to think of it in those terms: namely, that Israel failed, so Jesus had to come and sort out the mess. For the typical Bible reader, Israel's failings seem to be particularly apparent in the Gospels, where Jesus frequently clashes with groups called Scribes, teachers of the law, and the infamous Pharisees. Pharisees are a particular case in point because the words "Pharisee," "Pharisaic," and "Pharisaism" have become bywords in popular speech for being self-righteous or hypocritical. One dictionary defines Pharisaism as "Rigid observance of external forms of religion without genuine piety; hypocrisy in religion; a censorious, self-righteous spirit in matters of morals or manners." Ouch! These words are used in church sermons and home group Bible studies every single week as an acceptable shorthand to refer to precisely that kind of attitude and behavior.

So who were all these people and how did they relate to "Judaism"? The first thing we need to know is that (surprising though it may seem) there was no such thing as an "orthodox" Judaism at the time of Jesus. Judaism was never defined doctrinally—i.e., what you needed to believe to be a "proper Jew"—in the way that Christianity is today, what you need to believe to be a "proper Christian." No one spoke for Judaism in the way that, say, the Pope speaks for Catholicism. There was no magisterium. The reason that, in the Gospels, we see various groups (or, "sects") referred to, such as Scribes, Levites, Priests, Zealots, and Pharisees, is because different groups had their own—often passionately-held—ideas as to exactly what Judaism was and should be. (Josephus also names another important group, the Essenes.) Scholars are now aware that there was not one Judaism (singular) at the time, as once was assumed, but various Judaisms (plural) that co-existed, and not always that peacefully! It is precisely as one of these diverse streams or expressions of Judaism that we should classify the earliest form of what we now call "Christianity."

The first "Christians" were Jews who simply saw themselves as practicing authentic Judaism. Indeed, the terms "Christian" and "Christianity" are somewhat anachronistic as well. Neither Jesus nor Paul used them. Jesus-followers, as we should better call them, were just one stream of Judaism amongst the others. What we later come to know as Judaism is largely the product of "the winners"—or perhaps we should say, "the survivors"—after 70 CE, when the Roman legions quashed a

Jewish rebellion and sacked Jerusalem. With the temple destroyed and the sacrificial system no more, the role of the priests and their claims to community leadership effectively ended. Their place was filled by the Pharisees, whose particular emphases (such as a focus on the inner person through prayer and the study of Torah) were particularly well-suited to filling the void. The Pharisees became the natural successors to the religion of ancient Israel and specifically one stream within Pharisaism (that of Rabbi Johanan ben Zakkai).

Jesus and the Pharisees

So, going back to what was happening several decades earlier, in Jesus' day, each of these groups had different ideas as to how "proper" Judaism should be practiced and which things were most important. In particular, everyone was asking why the holy land, the promised land that the God of Israel had given his beloved people, was being trampled over and ruled by pagan armies. Was this divine punishment? If so, when was it going to end? What did they need to do, for it to end? What would bring the Messiah to rescue them? What kind of Messiah would he be? Should they sit and wait patiently for the Lord, or was he expecting them to take things into their own hands (as the Zealots argued). It sounds not dissimilar to Christian denominations, with divergent views about what constitutes "authentic" Christianity today, doesn't it?

Here's where the Pharisees come in. We could talk about the other sects, but the Pharisees are the most well-known and they're the ones that get the worst press among Christians! The Pharisees were surprisingly not that numerous, considering their influence, and they were mostly based in Jerusalem rather than rural areas. They had a very clear view that Israel's woes were all to do with the unrighteousness of the ordinary people, who were not following Torah as they should. What was happening to everyone was God's punishment because of the ordinary people, they said. What was needed was for them to repent and start living righteously (respecting the Sabbath, following the food laws, participating in the temple sacrifices, paying the temple tax, and so on) according, of course, to the Pharisees' particular "spin" on what holiness and righteousness looked like. The Pharisees were "the ones who cared" about "slipping standards" in society, and the slippery slope of ungodly behavior. They were the "Moral Majority" of their day—visible, vocal, and activist! In effect, what they were doing was to extend the holiness laws that applied to the temple and the priesthood to the *am ha'aretz* (the ordinary "people of the land").

Why, then, did Jesus so frequently clash with them? It seems that the reasons for the arguments come down to two things.

Firstly, remember the absence of a uniformly recognized standard against which to define Jewish "orthodoxy" (i.e., "right beliefs") at that time. Different groups were always arguing about interpretation—even, different groups within those groups. Pharisaism had two "competing" rabbinic schools (the House of Hillel and House of Shammai); it was said that if one of them said something "was so" the other could be guaranteed to say it "wasn't so" (although it is noteworthy that despite their arguments they respected each other). Questions kept coming up because one of the things about Torah was that it forever needed interpreting. Not least because it originated when Israel was a nomadic, desert people, but they were now permanent dwellers in both rural and urban environments. The devout were keen to know what leading rabbis thought in answer to various important questions. This is illustrated in times when Jesus says "You have heard it said . . . , but I say to you . . . ." When the rich young ruler asks Jesus, "What must I do to inherit eternal life?" he's asking how this particular rabbi interprets what it looks like to be living as one of the "authentic" people of God. To inherit eternal life (at least for those sects that believed in it) was the destiny of all those who were part of "true" faithful Israel. Hence, the man was asking "How can I be sure that I'm among them?" What was Jesus' opinion? (He wasn't asking, "How do I become a Christian?")

The second reason for Jesus' clashes with the Pharisees is that he clearly saw their fixation on the unrighteousness of the ordinary people as harsh, and unkind—deeply unsympathetic to the circumstances that these poor people found themselves in. The vast majority of the population lived below the poverty line, in a hand-to-mouth existence. The standard of Torah observance that the middle-class Pharisees expected of the working-class ordinary people, aka "the poor," was often beyond them. Economic pressures were overwhelming. If as a day-laborer you had no work (which Jesus chooses as the context for a parable in Matthew 20:1–16) and a pagan Roman employer offered you a day's employment on the Sabbath, were you to say "no" because it was Sabbath, or take the job and feed your family? (Anyone who has worked closely with the disadvantaged knows that when someone finds themselves in that position—such as, being handed a food parcel at a food bank, rather than being able to go to the supermarket—one of the very first things you lose, along with your dignity and sense of self-worth, is the luxury of choice.) The Pharisees' answer was clear: Don't pick and choose the bits of the Bible you accept. (I'm sure none of us have ever heard Christians say that . . . .) But Jesus approached things with a completely different paradigm: "The Sabbath was made for people, not people for the Sabbath." And so, too, Torah. God's laws were not designed for God's benefit, to keep him happy, but for *people's* benefit. Jesus' empathetic conversations with prostitutes and women such as the woman at the well and the one caught "in the very act" of adultery (where was the man, by the way—doesn't it "take two to tango"?) were almost certainly driven by Jesus being very aware of the particular pressures on women within that society. To have no man as protector and provider (perhaps because he had died prematurely, or divorced you, or you had no sons to assume the absent husband's role of protector and provider) was almost certainly to be destitute. In Jesus' order of priorities, he appears to have cared less about the "sinfulness" that the Pharisees were zeroing-in on (not least because of their over-the-top and unsympathetic attitude) and more about how these women were struggling in life and what had led to them being in that awful position in the first place. What we tend to read as lifestyle choices in our prosperous world were more likely survival strategies in that poverty-stricken world. The Pharisees whom Jesus criticized were giving every impression of caring more about the *law* of the Lord than the *people* of the Lord, and in so doing were failing to reflect the heart and priorities of God. Let that always be a lesson to us.

Another example of this—again featuring a woman with no man to provide for her—is seen in the story of the widow's mite. This story is not an object lesson in sacrificial giving, as it's commonly presented—especially by preachers enthusiastic about financing their ministries. The context is as follows. Jesus is teaching in the temple area. In the very last verse of Luke 20, he is criticizing the "teachers of the law" for amongst other things "devouring widows' houses" (or in the NLT, "shamelessly cheating widows out of their property"). The widow's mite story then continues from the very next verse, which happens to be starting a new chapter, Luke 21:1 (this is an example of how chapter breaks can be unhelpful to the flow of a continuing narrative).

> As Jesus looked up, he saw the rich putting their gifts into the temple treasury. He also saw a poor widow put in two very small copper coins. "Truly I tell you," he said, "this poor widow has put in more than all the others. All these people gave their gifts out of their wealth; but she out of her poverty put in all she had to live on."

Luke 21:1–4

According to Torah, widows and orphans in the community were supposed to be looked after (e.g., Deuteronomy 26:12), not least by the temple hierarchy itself. But here in this story, the financial expectations placed on this poor widow (and no doubt Jesus was also thinking of others like her, given that "widows" is plural at the end of Luke 20) were such that these religious leaders were happy to be taking away even the little she had left, leaving her destitute, just so long she was still "behaving righteously" by paying her tithe or temple tax. The clear implications are (1) that the temple authorities (either directly or though their "teaching" on giving) had already taken this poor woman's house—she had lost her home in order to be able to still make her offerings—and (2) that this scenario was commonplace. As one commentator observes, "Asking widows to tithe from their poverty is like using religion to pick the pockets of the poor. The temple should have been giving to her; not the other way around." This story is of religious leaders who prioritized caring about God's law over caring about God's people, with consequences that Jesus saw were breaking the heart of God for the poor.

The arguments among the different groups and the different rabbis (or "teachers") were to do with emphasis and prioritization—where the law "fitted" in everyday life. How it was to be properly fulfilled. How did the "spirit" or the underlying intent "fit" with the "letter"? Whose interpretations were authoritative? Jesus was frequently challenged over "by whose authority" he was speaking and acting—which rabbi, or rabbinic school? Bear in mind that Judaism had always started from right *praxis* (i.e., doing what's right—the technical term is *orthopraxy*) rather than from right beliefs, or *orthodoxy*. Christians are often unaware of that, or treat it negatively, since modern evangelical Christianity in particular has a strong focus on right beliefs and a correspondingly strong worry about anything that smacks of "works." This is the case to a point where it sometimes comes across as if all you need are right beliefs. This difference of thinking—starting with *orthopraxy* rather than *orthodoxy*—is a theological distinction rather than a strength or weakness, and it's certainly not about "works-righteousness" (we'll come on to that in a moment).

With the benefit of this background, we can better understand the Gospels' apparently strong critique of "the Jews" and Jesus' clashes with the Pharisees. These were arguments going on "within the family" concerning what it meant to "live Jewishly" in ways that were pleasing to God—invariably centered on interpretations of Torah—and heightened by the backdrop of those religiously, politically, and economically troubled times, under occupation by the Roman legions.

Some scholars have suggested that while it would probably be going too far to say that Jesus himself was a Pharisee (there is no biblical evidence to suggest this) it's interesting that Jesus appears to debate more intensely and more often with Pharisees than any other group. Oskar Skarsaune has suggested that this in itself may be an indication of closeness, since we debate most vehemently with those closest to us (*In the Shadow of the Temple*, 141). It's certainly true that in the early church we come across Jesus-followers who are Pharisees (Acts 15:5).

But what about all those harsh things that Jesus says? Doesn't he call them "hypocrites" in Matthew 23:27, because they're "like whitewashed tombs which on the outside appear beautiful, but inside they are full of dead men's bones and all uncleanness"? Saying things like that certainly sounds harsh to modern ears. However, Luke Timothy Johnson says that the way that the New Testament talks "is just about the way all opponents talked about each other back then." ("The New Testament's Anti-Jewish Slander and the Convention of Ancient Polemic"). "Knowing that all parties to a debate spoke in a certain way, then," he says, "forces us to relativize our party's version, even with regard to the most hurtful example." In other words, harsh though some of it may sound to us, that was just the way people framed their arguments in that place and time, in their debating style. It's interesting that Luke credits Paul with a "whitewashed wall" figure of speech in Acts 23:3.

Particularly notable in John's Gospel is the very frequent use of the phrase "the Jews." It appears over sixty times compared to just a handful in Matthew, Mark, and Luke. It would be easy from this phrase to think that John is condemning Jewish people *en masse*, but he means the Jewish leaders who are against Jesus. He is not being racist and anti-Semitic in modern terms. What he's talking about is "people who oppose Jesus." Remember that these were debates happening *within* the Jewish community, between fellow Jews who are fellow rabbis. They were not the critique of someone from outside Judaism (Jesus) condemning either Judaism or Jews in general from an external "Christian" perspective.

Problems Caused by Misunderstanding
the Bible and Judaism

A number of problems flow from these mis-readings. Throughout the Christian world, popular preaching takes for granted that for all practical purposes two pretty much fully formed religions called "Judaism" and "Christianity" co-existed from early Acts onwards, meeting respectively in synagogues and churches (or at least, Christian home groups) and competing in the religious marketplace, as modern religions do now. The New Testament is read as if it's telling the story of the successful rise of a new and living faith begun by Jesus ("Christianity") and the concurrent downfall of an old, ineffectual and dying religion ("Judaism") that Jesus and Paul were consigning to the scrapheap because it was "done." It's assumed that we're seeing these two religions constantly compared and contrasted throughout its pages, with Judaism coming off pretty badly. At risk of somewhat over-simplifying to make the point, the assumptions proceed along the following lines:

- Jesus was the first Christian. His arguments with the Jews arose because he was exposing the flawed beliefs and hypocrisies of Judaism and replacing it with Christianity, for which they killed him.

- Jesus was condemning a corrupt religious system in which people thought they could get to heaven by their own good works and meticulous rule-keeping, rather than a living faith centered in the heart.

- The apostle Paul was converted to Christianity from Judaism on the Damascus road (Acts 9). Upon becoming a Christian, Paul repented of his past life as a Pharisee and thereafter taught salvation by faith alone instead of Judaism's works-righteousness, ritualism, and externalism.

- In Galatians, in particular, Paul warns us against Jewish attempts to steal Christians' freedom in Christ and burden them with the legalism from which Jesus came to save us. This is the battle between Christianity and Judaism in a nutshell.

- Humanity is by nature legalistic and tries to please God and get to heaven through its own efforts. Judaism is presented in the Bible as a prime example of that error, and a recurring warning to us.

- The gospel is about salvation by faith and not by works. Judaism, however, is about the opposite.

- The outpouring of the Spirit in Acts, which established the church, was the confirmation of God's endorsement of Christianity over Judaism, as the mantle of being the "people of God" passed from them to us.

Have you encountered any of these assumptions in the Sunday sermon or the midweek Bible study? For many of us, they seem to be pretty obvious when we read the Bible. The problem is, with every single one of them, it's actually "confirmation bias" which is telling us that. Confirmation bias simply means that, when we already think we know something to be the case before we start reading, it's no surprise to us when we come across things that appear to confirm it. We find what we expect to find, from what we already know.

The Old and New Perspectives on Paul

Let us now turn our attention to the apostle Paul. In the world of conservative Reformed evangelicalism, in particular, Paul is front and center stage as the New Testament's supreme theologian, not least because he is credited with a clear articulation of the heart of the gospel in a doctrine that's called "justification by faith"—meaning, that we are saved by grace through faith rather than by works. Ever since the Reformation, the perspective of the Reformers has dominated evangelical thought. "Christianity" and "Judaism" have been seen as sitting at opposite poles in an argument as to how a person is saved: faith vs. works and grace vs. law. Judaism's "legalism" has been assumed to be the "dark cloud" against which the light of Christ was able shine all the more brightly. Paul's "conversion" in Acts is taken to reflect his sudden realization of all this.

So, where did we get this from? Grappling with the corruptions of mediaeval Catholicism and the burden of his own conscience before God, Martin Luther in the sixteenth century suddenly saw himself mirrored in Paul's writings in Romans and Galatians. He saw himself and Paul sharing common ground in their respective struggles—in each case, confronting a corrupt religion of works-righteousness that was placing the traditions of men over the truths of Scripture. He saw them both arguing for the same core truths about the nature of salvation. From that time on, Reformed evangelicalism has read and interpreted Paul and the Judaism of his day through the "lens" of Luther and the Catholicism of his day.

However, Pauline scholars now recognize, thanks to the discovery of considerable new literature from the Second Temple period, that where Luther went wrong was to assume that a supposedly corrupt Judaism of Paul's day held the same view of how one was "saved" (by meritorious good works and religious tradition) as the corrupt Catholicism of his own day. This recent awareness, which has emerged increasingly since the middle of the last century, is called the "New Perspective" on Paul. It is actually more correct to call it a new perspective on the world of first-century Judaism (or, better still, the world of "Second Temple Judaism"). Having carefully reviewed the newly available literature and listened afresh to Jewish scholars, who had been saying such things for years, but had previously been ignored, the New Perspective has concluded that the Judaism of Paul's day never believed one was saved by good works, only ever by faith. The "works of the law"—i.e., following Torah—had nothing to do with *how* to be saved but only how to live as someone who wanted to please God *because* you were saved. In that sense, the thinking is no different from Christianity.

The way I would characterize what Paul was contrasting is:

- Knowing God through a relationship by faith *worked out through Torah* (which up to that point had uniquely defined what it meant to be the people of God since the first Passover and the exodus);

and

- Knowing God through a relationship by faith *worked out through Christ* (now that God had graciously extended the definition of the people of God to include gentiles, outside of Torah, in a new Passover and new exodus).

Paul was not speaking negatively against God's gift of Torah. He was simply saying that the God of Israel had clearly "bypassed" Torah in inviting gentiles into relationship with him through Christ (in Galatians 3:2–5, Paul directly credits the evidence for this in the actions of the Holy Spirit). Why, then, Paul is saying to his gentile churches, are you listening to people who want you to incorporate bits of "Jewishness" (bits of Torah) into that relationship, when God himself didn't ask it of you in the first place? You don't need to put in what God has clearly chosen to leave out.

How Luther was reading Paul helps explain why he was openly critical of the book of James, given that James says things like "faith, if it has no works, is dead" (James 2:17) and, "a man is justified by works and not by faith alone" (James 2:24). We can only really understand Luther's disquiet about James if we visualize ourselves in the situation he and his fellows were facing, within a church that was hyper-focused on the value of works and the traditions of men, to the exclusion of a grace-centered, living faith. Against that background, no wonder Luther concluded as he did, that James had to have been written by "some Jew who had probably heard about Christian people but never encountered any." Once we step out of that emotive situation it becomes clear that, of course, the Christian life includes a concern for "what we do" and "how we live," just as much as "what we believe." James is simply saying that it's "both-and" rather than "either-or." If ever a passage makes that clear it's what Jesus says in Matthew 25:31–46 (note carefully who are the "sheep" and who are the "goats" here).

One of the leading early New Perspective scholars, Ed Sanders, famously said that "the works of the law" were nothing to do with "getting in" to the people of God, but rather with "staying in." Works were not a way of saying "please include me," they were a way of saying "thank you for having included me." They weren't a human-effort-centered way of people qualifying for the kingdom, they were a love-centered response to God's grace in having extended the kingdom to unqualified people. It's easy to forget that "the righteous shall live by faith" (or, better, "by faithfulness")—which we read three times in the New Testament—is quoting the Old Testament (Habakkuk 2:4). That's where the New Testaments writers got the idea from in the first place. It didn't become true in the New Testament, it was *always* true.

The New Perspective came to a similar realization concerning Paul's so-called conversion. Rather than being "converted to Christianity" from Judaism on the Damascus road and "becoming a Christian" instead of a Pharisee, the evidence in Paul's own writings suggests that he had no problem with being a Pharisee before that. All that had happened was that he became a Pharisee *who followed Jesus*.

> ... I myself might have confidence even in the flesh. If anyone
> else has a mind to put confidence in the flesh, I far more: cir-
> cumcised the eighth day, of the nation of Israel, of the tribe of
> Benjamin, a Hebrew of Hebrews; as to the Law, a Pharisee; as to
> zeal, a persecutor of the church; as to the righteousness which
> is in the Law, found blameless. But whatever things were gain
> to me, those things I have counted as loss for the sake of Christ.

Philippians 3:4–7

("Flesh" here meaning, ethnic identity—"being Jewish")

This is not the *curriculum vitae* of a man for whom Judaism "never
worked"—or who was wracked by a version of Martin Luther's famous
anguish, "How do I find a gracious God?" This is a man who had simply
discovered a relationship with God through Christ that he saw as far sur-
passing the one he had known through Torah. A relationship centered in
Jesus the Word of God, rather than Torah the words of God. In Philippians 3:8, Paul doesn't say that Judaism is "worthless," as it's commonly
mis-read to be saying. What he says is that "everything else is worthless
when compared with the infinite value of knowing Christ." He doesn't say
that "it is" rubbish, he says that for Christ's sake he "counts it all" as rubbish. If the Judaism that Paul knew was *actually* rubbish then for him to
say that knowing Christ surpassed it in comparison would be pretty faint
praise! Jesus himself said that teachers of the law who became disciples in
the kingdom had "treasures old" in their storerooms, as well as "treasures
new"—"new gems of truth as well as old," in the NLT (Matthew 13:52).

Scholars today no longer see Paul's so-called "conversion" as the
classic biblical example of someone becoming a Christian, as it's so often
portrayed in pulpits and Bible studies. Not for one moment did Paul ever
feel that he left Judaism. He never thought of himself as changing his
religion (still less, finding faith for the first time, such as when a pagan
becomes a Christian). What happened on that Damascus road was two
things:

1. Paul had a spectacular and supernatural encounter with the risen
   Jesus. He wasn't coming to faith, he already had a faith—in the exact
   same God that he loved and served already, the God of Israel. At
   that moment, Jesus simply came crashing into that relationship,
   revealing himself as divine Son and Messiah in a powerful way.

2. As a consequence of this encounter with Jesus, Paul the faithful Pharisee received *a new calling*—to take the good news of this Jewish Messiah to the nations beyond Israel, a good news that was available to them, too, in a new and unexpected way.

Paul saw that this good news, inviting the gentiles into relationship with the God of Israel, had clearly "bypassed" the Jewish Torah. There was no doubt this was so, because it was attested by the work of the Holy Spirit (Galatians 3:2–5). Once his "theology" had "caught up" and he'd figured out how this wonderful new gift of God in Christ fitted with the wonderful gift of God in Torah that he already knew, Paul committed himself to this new calling.

The Back-Story to Galatians

When we look more closely at the context of Galatians, what appears to be happening is not the typical Christian assumption that a group of religious Jews was trying to sell "Judaism" to Paul's new believers instead of "Christianity." It wasn't about two already fully formed religions competing for members, as we might see happening in the pluralistic religious marketplace of today's world. Rather, it seems that a group of faithful Jewish Jesus-followers had simply drawn different conclusions to Paul on the question of how this wonderful new gift of God in Christ properly related to the wonderful gift of God that Jewish people already had in Torah: a reaction by "conservatives" who saw Paul as too "progressive," or "liberal," in the appropriate basis for gentile inclusion. This group of Jewish Jesus-followers felt it was important for both Jewish and gentile followers of Jesus the Messiah to be practicing the best of both worlds, "both-and," as it were, in a way that Paul apparently did not. Stated crudely, this was not about a group of legalistic Jews insisting that these new gentile converts, who had come to the God of Israel through Jesus, must also share the "misery" of their own religious experience of Judaism.

The answer to the question of the relevance of Torah for gentile Jesus-followers may seem "obvious" to us now, but it would have been far from obvious then, at that very early stage. We need to remember (a) that Christianity was birthed in Judaism (both terms are, of course, wholly anachronistic at this point), extending initially through Jewish synagogues and Jewish communities, so the existing features of Jewish faith were its natural "point of reference" from the outset, and (b) how much faithful

Jews loved Torah. It was embedded in their hearts. It was what they had known, central to their identity as the people of God, for a thousand-plus years. So, even though these faithful Jewish Jesus-followers recognized that God was now doing a new thing—reflective of the prophesied end-times outpouring of the Spirit on the gentiles, drawing them in to the people of God through the coming of Jesus, the Jewish Messiah—why would they not logically assume that Torah would continue to play a central and significant part in this nascent "Christian" relationship with Israel's God? After all, the "new covenant" promised in Jeremiah 31:33 was one that God would "make with the people of Israel"—in which he would "put [his] law in their minds and write it on their hearts"—not one in which Israel and its law would now become wholly irrelevant (as Christians today tend to read that new covenant).

In effect, Paul in Galatians is saying to his gentile converts: "This particular conundrum is really not your problem. Yes, it's a huge problem for my Jewish brethren, that they're still trying to figure out" (exemplified in the debate in the so-called Council of Jerusalem, in Acts 15) "but don't let these other Jesus-followers try to make you gentiles 'bolt on' bits of 'Jewishness' to your faith—telling you that you have to include some of Torah—when the God of Israel himself clearly did a swerve around Torah" (perhaps not the exact phrase Paul would have used) "in pouring out the Holy Spirit upon you. If God himself has so clearly bypassed Torah, then you don't need to go there. This is a question for us Jews to grapple with, it's not one for you."

It was the Galatians' "charismatic" experience of the Holy Spirit absent Torah that for Paul was the conclusive evidence of Torah no longer needing to be the only gateway through which gentiles could access relationship with the God of Israel. The outpouring of the Holy Spirit on the gentiles was a clear sign (long-expected in Jewish tradition, and notably prophesied in Joel 2:28–29) that God had sovereignly acted in Christ to bring about the beginning of the end times in which the other nations would be included. According to the book of Acts, the apostle Peter saw what was happening in those terms, too, in framing his explanation of the day of Pentecost in Acts 2, and especially (in relation to the gentiles) in Acts 10:44–45: "While Peter was still speaking these words, the Holy Spirit fell upon all those who were listening to the message. *All the circumcised believers who came with Peter were amazed, because the gift of the Holy Spirit had been poured out on the gentiles also.*" What Paul says in Galatians

3:2–5 ties-in with this and helps make sense of where he is coming from in the whole letter.

> I would like to learn just one thing from you: Did you receive the Spirit by the works of the law, or by believing what you heard? Are you so foolish? After beginning by means of the Spirit, are you now trying to finish by means of the flesh? Have you experienced so much in vain—if it really was in vain? So again I ask, does God give you his Spirit and work miracles among you by the works of the law, or by your believing what you heard?
>
> (One again here, "flesh" means ethnic identity—"becoming Jewish"—and "works of the law" means practicing Torah)

God's sovereign action meant that Jewish Jesus-followers like Paul had to rethink their "theology" in relation to the place of the gentiles in this new era—and specifically, *the relationship of Torah to the gentiles*—since Torah had up until then been the only route through which anyone could be included in the people of God. It had always been expected that the gentiles would be included in the end times, but it had also been expected that Torah would be the route (why wouldn't they have thought that?).

To help everyone to grasp the validity of a gentile relationship with the God of Israel outside of Torah, Paul directs attention to Abraham, rather than Moses. It will be appreciated that what Jewish faith "looked like" at that time to both insiders and outsiders would very much have been centered in the visible markers of the Mosaic covenant, aka Torah— with circumcision, dietary requirements, and honoring the Sabbath all being prominent. However, Paul says we need to go back beyond Moses— there is a biblical point of reference for gentiles finding relationship with God outside of Torah further back in the story, located in Abraham. This was a relationship in existence before Torah and even before the nation of Israel. Abraham was a gentile who was invited into a relationship with the God of Israel through faith alone, rather than, through faith plus Torah. Hence, there is a clear precedent, further back in the story, for the gentiles to be invited in to a fully valid relationship with God without Torah, as they have now been invited in Christ.

Since we are to understand the various expressions of the covenantal relationship of God with his world as restatements and renewals of a continuing covenant, part of one Big Story, what Paul is effectively saying to his gentile audience here is "Don't go back to the covenant with Moses as the point of reference for defining your relationship with God.

Go back further, to the covenant with Abraham." Since Jewish people revered Abraham as the father of their faith, the idea that Abraham could also now be seen as the father of the gentiles' faith was profoundly helpful in explaining (to both gentiles and Jews alike) how gentiles could be included in relationship with the God of Israel without Torah needing to feature. Paul is therefore saying that the "overarching" expression of the covenant that his gentile believers should look to is the earlier (pre-Torah) covenant through Abraham, rather than the Mosaic covenant in Torah (which everyone would have assumed defined what a relationship with the God of Israel required). Paul is saying that God's invitation, into relationship with him, which he extended to Abraham the gentile, was one in which Torah did not feature—*and that is exactly what's now happened for you gentiles.* So, just "go with the flow." It is Christ who has made this possible—you don't need to figure it out, just enjoy it. Your access into relationship with the God of Israel is through Christ, not through "Christ-plus."

Implications and Action Points

At this point, some may be wondering whether this significantly rehabilitated view of the Israel and Judaism of Jesus' day and Paul's day is telling us something about the Israel and the Judaism of our day. However, it's something of a leap to identify "biblical Israel" directly with "modern Israel"—or for that matter the Judaism(s) of their day with the Judaism(s) of our day (yes, there's more than one of them, just as there's more than one "version" of Christianity). Unfortunately, that's too big a question to take on here (remember that the scope of this book is to help us read the Bible well, or at least, better). That said, at a minimum it should cause us to be more respectful towards modern Israel and Judaism, not least when we consider the unspeakable horrors of the Holocaust from which the state of Israel emerged and which (understandably) still casts its long, dark shadow over the world. We recall to our eternal shame that Nazi soldiers wore belt buckles inscribed with an old Prussian military slogan, *Gott Mit Uns* ("God is with us").

To sum up, those bullet-point assumptions about "Christianity" and "Judaism" (set out earlier in the chapter) are completely wrong! We should purge our preaching and our home group Bible studies of that language and those ways of thinking! We should cease and desist from

bad-mouthing "the Jews" or "the Pharisees," whether directly or by inference. Let's stick to talking about the specific religious leaders that Jesus
clashed with, and more importantly, why he clashed with them. The Gospels are not trying to tell us that *all* Pharisees—still less, all *Jews*—were
hypocrites. No doubt some of them were precisely that, but so too are
some Christians (perhaps you've noticed that). The point is that some of
the religious leaders with whom Jesus clashed clearly had "the cart before
the horse" in understanding what was most important to God. That is
what the Gospel stories are showing and they remain a lesson for us—one
can be very sincere in one's religious zeal and still be sincerely wrong. The
attitudes and assumptions that I hope this chapter will have weaned us off
are what we call "theological anti-Judaism."

Given that we're talking about biblical Judaism and biblical Israel in
this chapter (indeed, in the book as a whole) and that there is no direct
read across from Israel "then" to Israel "now," I am not saying that we are
not allowed to criticize the modern state of Israel for things it may say or
do as a nation, either politically or militarily. Equally, nor are we expected
to defend it simply because of a "biblical Israel" connection. We are free
to hold opinions on political and military behavior in the exact same way
(but no greater or lesser way) than if we were commenting on any other
modern nation state.

As to God's destiny for "Israel"—then and now—that is something
we need to leave in his hands. To try to define the correlation between
Israel then and Israel now is complex and beyond the scope of this book.
What we can say is that everything Scripture says about Israel, and God
having chosen Israel, and God's love for Israel, is true. Everything Scripture says about God's covenantal commitment to Israel is true. We should
therefore respect its truth and respect the Israel that it's true of.

And then finally, again for the avoidance of any doubt, there is nothing in legalism that is compatible with authentic Christian faith. The New
Perspective is not promoting legalism; it's simply saying that first-century
Judaism wasn't either. To the extent that in anything Paul wrote he was talking about legalism or legalistic attitudes in general, he was unquestionably
condemning them. The same goes for anything Jesus said in the Gospels.
Not least because legalism is entirely non-relational and legalistic attitudes
completely fail to reflect the nature and character of God. We can be perfectly clear on that. Equally, however, we should be clear that legalism is
and always was antithetical to authentic biblical Judaism as well. Were
there not religious "legalists" in the world of first-century Judaism? you

may ask—whom Jesus encountered, or Paul encountered? Undoubtedly there were. Just as they can be found in the world of twenty-first-century Christianity. But that doesn't mean that either Judaism or Christianity, properly understood, have (or ever have had) any place for them. We should never forget, whenever we are discussing "the law"—I prefer to say Torah, since it means "instruction" or "teaching"—that it was *God* who gave it to Israel and asked them to follow it. To speak of the "law of Moses" as if to imply that it was Moses' invention is to completely miss the point. Equally, when we are inclined to make statements like, "No one could keep the law," we must remember that (a) within the law itself such failure was already provided for, and (b) no good Father would ask his children to do something in full knowledge they would never be able to (that would be cruel). Inability to fulfill Torah is not something that Paul appears to have been concerned with, if Philippians 3:4–7 is anything to go by. Whatever Torah's shortcomings may have been, they were centered elsewhere.

Which brings us to something else that we need to be clear on. When the Holy Spirit spoke through Scripture to Luther and the other Reformers—revealing to them that salvation was by faith alone (a central belief in Reformed evangelicalism) over against the corrupted teachings of the church of their day—they were not misguided. The Reformers correctly perceived a divine revelation that has profoundly shaped our understanding of salvation ever since. However, what the Reformers *found meaningful* in Romans and Galatians through the revelation of the Holy Spirit—the Spirit *speaking to them meaningfully* about the wrongs of the legalistic mediaeval Catholicism of their day—is not the same thing as *the meaning* of what Paul was saying about the law in Romans and Galatians. We must never confuse *the meaning of* a text in its context with the Holy Spirit *speaking meaningfully through* that text in our context—or in this case, in the Reformers' context. (We will say more about this important distinction in chapter 11.) The point is that the Spirit was shining his revelatory light on legalistic mediaeval Catholicism—and on legalism in general—*not* on first-century Judaism. The truths that the Reformers discovered in their world were true and remain true. It's simply that they were not truths about Judaism in the world of the New Testament as well. Yes, of course there were legalists in the first century, just as there were in the sixteenth century, and just as there are in the twenty-first century! Human nature does not change. But Habakkuk 2:4 was a core truth in the world of both the Old Testament and New Testament: "The righteous shall live by faith" or, "faithfulness." The "timelessness" of Habakkuk 2:4

is why Paul the Pharisee quotes it in Romans 1:17 and Galatians 3:11, and why it's quoted by the very Jewish writer of Hebrews 10:38.

By the way, to have faith meant "to trust." It did not mean having mental certainty, or striving to keep one's mind free of doubts or questions or negative thoughts, as pernicious "word of faith" teaching would try to tell us (to know why it's heretical, I recommend Gordon Fee's excellent little booklet, *The Disease of the Health & Wealth Gospels*). Faith was always a "doing" word, just as love is a doing word; our word "faithfulness" conveys its meaning better in English. People of faith were those who lived and acted faithfully, illustrated by the commendations of the heroes of faith in Hebrews 11. If you want to know what living by faith looks like, it's "someone who lives as if what they believed was true." 2 Corinthians 5:7 calls us to live by faith and not by sight because if we can see something—whether that's God, or the future—then we don't need to trust him for it.

8

Heaven and Hell

W hen we talk about "heaven," I wonder what kind of mental images come to mind? How do you picture it? The classic imagery is of course cherubs playing harps, sitting on clouds. Doesn't sound like lots of fun to me! But it's interesting that when it comes to what the Bible has to say about both heaven and hell—two of the things that people are most interested in hearing about—those are almost entirely described in "picture-language." Because we live in an age of science, we tend to expect the Bible to give us facts and data and technical information— like a textbook would. But that wasn't the expectation of people at the time the Bible was written. That doesn't make the Bible "flawed" for that reason, it's just that it wasn't that kind of literature. People then had different "literary styles" or "genres"—different ways of explaining things—and that included using words to "paint pictures." Especially when they were communicating transcendent things. We, on the other hand, tend to think that pictures and picture language are a second-best way of communicating truth. And that's partly because we don't value the arts as much as the sciences.

But communicating truth through pictures has a lot going for it. For one thing, pictures are "timeless." However much scientists discover as time goes by and we learn more and more about life and the cosmos, pictures still "speak to us" in a "timeless" way. They engage our imagination, they're easy to remember, and quite literally they help us to keep "the big picture" in mind. Pictures also leave room for some mystery. Science is really important for human life and human well-being, but the very nature of science involves trying to get rid of mystery. And it's certainly true that none of us wants any more mystery than we have to when it comes to diseases and health risks. But we do need some space for mystery when it comes to spiritual things—when it comes to God. We can't expect to have him under control like we want to have diseases under control.

When we approach the Bible, it's important to give it the respect that it deserves and not to critique it for being something that it never intended to be. This includes respecting the original authors by taking account of what they were intending to be saying and not saying in what they wrote. Similarly, to respect their original audience, as to how they would have understood what was being said and what it would have meant to them at the time. Equally importantly, we need to consider the reasons that God himself may have had, as the ultimate divine author of the Bible, in choosing to convey truth through pictures and stories rather than a text book of scientific facts. We can readily imagine that part of his reasoning in choosing to speak through "timeless" art rather than "time-bound" science is that, whether we're reading the Bible in the first century, the sixteenth century, the twenty-first century, or even the twenty-fifth century, God can still speak to us about the same truths. It doesn't require scientific knowledge from another era in order to be grasped. Of course, this is not to say that "pictures" are picturing something that isn't real; they're simply describing realities in a different way. We shall need to keep that in mind when we look at both heaven and hell in this chapter.

Heaven and the Kingdom of God

As we saw when we looked earlier at the "Big Story" of the Bible, the starting point for us to look at heaven is the way that God intended his creation should be and then, by contrast, the way that it ended up being. That includes how God intended we should be and how we ended up being. We saw in the creation account in Genesis that at every stage—every "day"—God looked at each aspect that he "spoke" into being and said it was "good." And when he had finished creating, including humanity as the pinnacle, he looked at everything together and said that it was "very good." On the seventh day, it says God rested, which gave rise to the Jewish Sabbath—the day on which God said to Israel that they should imitate him (as indeed, they were called to do in the whole of life) by resting from their labors (see, e.g., Exodus 20:11 and elsewhere). That day of rest was not intended simply as some kind of "pyjama day" of doing nothing, but a day of enjoying God and his "very good" creation together.

For various reasons, centered on the infiltration of a cosmic enemy that we call "sin," this "very good" creation then became damaged and knocked off-kilter. It was an enemy that we humans collaborated with and allowed to become more powerful, to a point where the kind of creation that God designed—and the kind of people God designed—ended up a long way from the blueprint. We became a creation in which a holy God could not dwell in the way that he wanted to; our incompatibility with him had become too great. It would not have been surprising, given what happened, if God were to give up on this damaged creation completely and give up on us completely. But that would, of course, have meant that this cosmic enemy had won. "Sin"—and the damage and suffering and death that it leads to—would have won. God could not stand by and allow that to happen. Immediately this enemy entered the story, God declared his intention not to abandon his creation but to restore his creation. And if we then fast forward to the pivotal point in that restoration plan—God personally entering into his creation in his Son, the "turning point" when death itself goes into reverse and the power of sin is broken—we see the "future" arriving in the "present." This is described in the New Testament as the "coming of the kingdom."

People have often found it puzzling that Jesus said both that the kingdom of God had arrived in his ministry (e.g., Luke 9:2 and 11:20) and that it was still to come (e.g., Mark 9:1 and Mark 14:25). He taught his disciples to pray for the kingdom to come in what we call the Lord's Prayer (Luke 11:2 and Matthew 6:10) even though the kingdom was among them. Theologians make sense of this apparent dichotomy through what's called the "now" and the "not yet" of the kingdom—or, the "already" but not yet. In other words, *both* are true. Jesus inaugurated or "launched" the beginning of the rule and reign of God in this world in his personal earthly ministry. However, the completion of the coming of the kingdom in all of its fullness awaits his return. Until then, we are living in a period of the "now and the not yet," in which we have a *foretaste* of the way things will be, but not its *fullness*. We have the "first-fruits" of the coming harvest—the same in quality but not in quantity. Other biblical language pictures it as a "down-payment" or "guarantee," through the Holy Spirit working among us between now and then.

In both Old and New Testaments, the Bible pictures "the way things will be" in this future state when the kingdom has come in all its fullness.

This is what we call heaven for short. Bear in mind that neither heaven nor the kingdom is referring to a *place*. I remember many years ago hearing a sermon in which the lay preacher asked the rhetorical question, "How do we know that heaven is real?" and answered it with Genesis 1:1—"In the beginning, God created the heavens and the earth." It wasn't appropriate to point out to him that this Jewish phrase "the heavens and the earth" had nothing to do with a place called heaven, it was simply their way of saying "the cosmos" or the "entire created order," for which biblical Hebrew lacked a word.

In this present age, the kingdom is present wherever we see a foretaste of the rule and reign of God happening. It's wherever and whenever we see something (or someone, or someone's situation) coming into line with God's rule and reign through his divine power at work—God supernaturally changing things from what they are to what they should be. It's when the future "breaks in" to the present. Examples of this would be Jesus' healings and deliverances—as a "foretaste" of the way things will one day be in their entirety, "signposts" to the fullness of that future kingdom. This is why we do well to speak of them as "signs and wonders" rather than simply "miracles." In this present era between Jesus' first and second comings, we see the kingdom having come "now" in part but "not yet" in all its fullness. This current period has been helpfully described as being like the time between D-Day (the Normandy landings towards the end of the Second World War) that decisively broke the enemy's grip of power and through the success of which ultimate victory was then certain and VE Day ("Victory in Europe" Day) when that final victory could be declared as having been completed, in the enemy's unconditional surrender. Rather than talking about "heaven," therefore, we should really be talking about the fullness of the coming kingdom at the end of the age. It's OK for us to use heaven as shorthand in one sense, but given how easily it can conjure up images of cherubs, harps, and clouds, perhaps we should use it sparingly.

The picture of heaven that the Bible paints, through a variety of imagery (and I'm using heaven here in the kingdom-sense that we've just been discussing) has a number of features. They are all describing and reflecting a state where every enemy of human life and flourishing—everything that has invaded and infiltrated God's "very good" creation and caused this present disorder—has been removed and defeated. This includes the "personified" enemies of "Sin," "Death," and "Satan" and so too, sickness, poverty, injustice, oppression, and suffering. The imagery speaks of a "new" creation—a cosmos that has been restored in conformity to its original design. A new creation in which there will be no more predators and no more victims. This new creation includes eternal life as an intrinsic feature because death (and everything that leads to death) will no longer be present—so there is nothing left to bring an end to life.

At the same time as the removal of every *thing* that damages God's creation comes the removal of *everyone* who wants to continue to damage God's creation, since their continued presence is also totally incompatible with this new era, in which God both reigns and is present.

There is a linkage or "echo" here with the biblical concept of *shalom*, which doesn't simply mean "peace," as it's often translated. The concept has far more to do with a state of complete wholeness and well-being, "when the world's all as it should be" (per the line in the Matt Redman song, "Blessed Be Your Name").

Further biblical images, or pictures, speak of the natural world (as we would call it) also being brought into line and no longer bringing suffering and destruction in its own ways.

A Story That Starts with "Original Goodness"

The reason that this broader perspective is important is because it offers us concepts of what a restored cosmos looks like. If we simply do a Bible word-search for heaven we will miss all of this. Understanding the nature of heaven begins with God's promise, as soon as things started to go wrong, that one day he will put everything right. He will do that because what he said in Genesis is still true: "He saw all that he had made, and it was very good" (Genesis 1:31). The biblical story does not start with "original sin" but with "original goodness." That's why he believes it's worth saving and that we're worth saving. The rest of the story leads up to how he was willing to go to the ultimate lengths to make that possible, which included allowing humanity to crucify him on a pagan cross, unjustly convicted by a godless regime. God bearing the ultimate cost of entering into this world to "save it" from within, to restore and renew it, with all of the bad stuff taken out.

The outcome of that mission is invariably described in picture language, especially in the writings of the prophets as they "paint pictures" with words of what it will look like when God "puts everything right,"

in what's sometimes called the "Day of the Lord." Here are some of the
features of this new creation, in pictures drawn from Isaiah:

> They will beat their swords into ploughshares and their spears
> into pruning hooks. Nation will not take up sword against
> nation, nor will they train for war any more.
>
> Isaiah 2:4

> The wolf will live with the lamb, the leopard will lie down with
> the goat, the calf and the lion and the yearling together; and a
> little child will lead them.
>
> Isaiah 11:6

> There he will remove the cloud of gloom, the shadow of death
> that hangs over the earth. He will swallow up death forever! The
> Sovereign LORD will wipe away all tears. He will remove forever
> all insults and mockery against his land and people. The LORD
> has spoken!
>
> Isaiah 25:7–8

> Even the wilderness and desert will be glad in those days. The
> wasteland will rejoice and blossom with spring crocuses. Yes,
> there will be an abundance of flowers and singing and joy! The
> deserts will become as green as the mountains of Lebanon, as
> lovely as Mount Carmel or the plain of Sharon. There the LORD
> will display his glory, the splendor of our God. With this news,
> strengthen those who have tired hands, and encourage those who
> have weak knees. Say to those with fearful hearts, "Be strong, and
> do not fear, for your God is coming to destroy your enemies. He
> is coming to save you." And when he comes, he will open the eyes
> of the blind and unplug the ears of the deaf. The lame will leap
> like a deer, and those who cannot speak will sing for joy!
>
> Isaiah 35:1–6

These themes continue in the New Testament. The gospel is the hope we
have in Christ that everything that's been lost and harmed and damaged
in human life will be restored to how it should be. The kind of world that
God wants this world to be. The gospel is God's invitation to all who share
that desire—who'd also like to live in that kind of world—to partner with
him in it. Jesus carried on from where the Old Testament left off in painting pictures of what this new world would look like, when he described
the kingdom of God. And his favorite way of explaining it seems to have

been through stories called "parables." One of the most significant of those parables in explaining not only what heaven will be like, but also how it will come about, is one that's known as the Parable of the Wheat and the Weeds, or the Wheat and the Tares:

> Jesus told them another parable: The kingdom of heaven is like a man who sowed good seed in his field. But while everyone was sleeping, his enemy came and sowed weeds among the wheat, and went away. When the wheat sprouted and formed ears, then the weeds also appeared.
>
> The owner's servants came to him and said, "Sir, didn't you sow good seed in your field? Where then did the weeds come from?"
>
> "An enemy did this," he replied.
>
> The servants asked him, "Do you want us to go and pull them up?"
>
> "No," he answered, "because while you are pulling up the weeds, you may uproot the wheat with them. Let both grow together until the harvest. At that time I will tell the harvesters: first collect the weeds and tie them in bundles to be burned; then gather the wheat and bring it into my barn."
>
> Matthew 13:24–30

Jesus is painting a picture of how God originally made the world, which was, "very good"—he "sowed good seed"—and then what's happened to it since. He's also painting a picture of what God is one day going to do about it. To remove everything bad from that wonderful creation. To rescue it from the damage done by his enemy. The parable is describing a world in which all of the best of what it means to be human and everything that's great about creation stays in place and flourishes. But everything that's bad and wrong and evil—that damages creation and damages people—is taken out.

The Background Story to "the Rapture"

This is perhaps a good moment to briefly cover something else you may have come across, and that's the so-called "rapture." It's an idea that has come from Matthew 24, where in the context of his second coming, Jesus says this:

> Two men will be in the field; one will be taken and the other left.
> Two women will be grinding with a hand mill; one will be taken
> and the other left.
>
> Matthew 24:40–41

Once that is combined with what 1 Thessalonians 4:17 says about "meeting him in the air," some have interpreted these verses as saying that in Jesus' second coming, Christians will be snatched away to heavenly bliss, while the earth, along with the non-Christians, is left to burn.

Unfortunately for those who may rather like the sound of that kind of rapture experience, in its context Matthew 24:40–41 is almost certainly talking about the complete opposite. It's picturing the *unrighteous* (not the righteous) being snatched away, to judgement! "As in the days of Noah," says Jesus (in v. 37 preceding), the unrighteous are the ones "taken" (v. 39), while the righteous are the ones "left behind."

What Jesus is saying here is consonant with the Parable of the Wheat and the Weeds in Matthew 13 that we looked at a moment ago. God's plan is to rescue his creation by removing everything that is bad and harmful, not for all the Christians to be rescued as if from a burning building in the nick of time—going off to some disembodied state of spiritual bliss somewhere called heaven. What we now call "rapture theology" was completely unheard of in the first 1,800 years of the church's history. It came about in the 1820s in a small revival in Scotland, when a young girl called Margaret MacDonald fell into a trance and had a vision in which the second coming was split into two—Christ coming first for the righteous, who she saw "raptured" in that way, and then returning later to execute judgment on the unrighteous. Along with Edward Irving, John Nelson Darby (a founder of the Plymouth Brethren sect) was very taken by this and began teaching it; in due course, taking it to North America, where he introduced it to Dwight L. Moody. It gained traction with the fundamentalist C. I. Scofield's immensely popular *Scofield Reference Bible*, as a result of the sub-titles and study notes that he added, which appeared to show the reader that the text taught a rapture. (No word for "rapture" is found in the Bible itself.) Rapture theology is a "folk theology" that remains a quirk of fundamentalist evangelical Protestantism, widely propagated by Hal Lindsey's *Late Great Plant Earth* book and Tim LaHaye's *Left Behind* series (and more recently, the movie of that name). It can be damaging for a number of reasons, not least because it encourages Christian escapism, short-termism, and disdain for looking after the planet.

So going back to what the Bible does actually say, the picture the Bible is painting of this renewed and restored creation, with all of the bad stuff taken out and destroyed, so that only the good is left—where suffering and death will play no part, leaving us with eternal life, a place in which God himself will dwell with us—does rather sound like "heaven," does it not? It's a perfectly good word to use for a place that has those features!

But you may also say, "I just can't see how God could ever do that—how it could actually happen." Our scientific ways of thinking mean we find it hard to envisage how it could be technically possible. But then again, if you told people even 200 years ago about the internet and video and heart transplants and space travel, they'd have said: "I don't see how those could ever happen." What we personally find easy or difficult to visualize is not a perfect measure of whether something can happen or not—especially when it's *God* we're talking about!

When we turn to the very last book in the Bible, called Revelation, these themes that we see throughout the Bible are repeated in how the story ends.

> Then I saw a new heaven and a new earth, for the first heaven and the first earth had passed away. . . . And I heard a loud voice from the throne saying, "Look! God's dwelling-place is now among the people, and he will dwell with them. They will be his people, and God himself will be with them and be their God.
>
> "He will wipe every tear from their eyes. There will be no more death or mourning or crying or pain, for the old order of things has passed away."
>
> He who was seated on the throne said, "I am making everything new!" Then he said, "Write this down, for these words are trustworthy and true."
>
> Revelation 21:1–5

One of the wonderful things about this new creation is that God himself will personally be there: "God's dwelling-place is now among the people." Everything bad being removed makes it possible for a holy God to come to join us, as he was pictured in Genesis, walking in the garden in the cool of the day, once he's restored this world to a "holy" place. God himself will personally be wiping away the tears, in this intimate picture. The weeds or tares of Jesus' parable in Matthew 13 are the causes of "the old order of things" in Revelation 21—mourning, crying, pain, and death.

That's Heaven—What's Hell?

So that's heaven—God's plan to bring about a future new heaven and a new earth, as the Bible pictures it, with these features. In the coming of Jesus, "how things will be in the future" went on the attack against "how things are now." The future invaded the present and it's still coming. The reason Jesus healed the sick and raised the dead and expelled demons that were harming and tormenting people wasn't "to prove he was God." It was to demonstrate that the kingdom of God had arrived in his ministry, pointing to the fact that the change had begun. It was extending an invitation to us to be part of it, if we want to be; to start practicing what life looks like, when God is King—practicing for the future, if you like. The invitation to "become a Christian" is an invitation to join him in that kind of a world, starting now.

So . . . what about "the other place"? What about hell? We'll start with what's clear and obvious in what the Bible says about it and then look at what's not so clear and obvious.

It's rightly said that God is both a God of love and a God of justice, which must be the starting point for this question. In fact, God being a God of love is part of the reason why he is a God of justice as well. Love that ignores justice is only wishy-washy emotion, willing to turn a blind eye to victims. If for no other reason, God's love for the victims of sin and evil who do not receive justice in this life compels him to make certain that they do at the end of life—ensuring that its perpetrators do not walk away consequence-free. The fact that one day their abusers will stand before a holy and just God who is on the side of life's victims may be the only justice they will ever receive. But of course, it's not just the "really bad people" who should feel uncomfortable about facing a God of justice. The Bible says we will all give an account. In 2 Corinthians 5:10: "We must all stand before Christ to be judged. We will each receive whatever we deserve for the good or evil we have done in this earthly body." Similarly, in Romans 14:10–12: "Remember, we will all stand before the judgment seat of God . . . each of us will give a personal account to God."

Before we go on to look at the various ideas about hell, it's important to say that believing in a day of judgement (aka, a day of reckoning, or a day of accountability before God) does not directly lead us to any obvious conclusion as to what the judicial consequences (or "sentence") from God as heavenly Judge "must" look like. There is sometimes a view amongst Christians that if one has doubts about the kind of "torture in the flames of hell for eternity," which the classic imagery of mediaeval paintings and Dante's *Inferno* conjures up, it is tantamount to denying that God is a God of justice or denying a day of judgement. That linkage is inappropriate and confuses two entirely different things.

In many ways, as a church pastor I would much rather stay away from talking about hell. I want people to want to know Jesus because they're excited about receiving his love and forgiveness and being part of his family—not just because they're scared of his judgement. It would, of course, be quite wrong to neglect the truth that each of will stand before God to give an account of our lives, since that is clear in the Bible. So too, that how we have lived this life, the decisions that we have made, will have consequences, including potentially unpleasant consequences, for our eternal destiny. How we explain that and frame that, however, is very important. People do understand the need for justice and judicial consequences for evil doers. They are pleased that justice has been done when the "baddie" gets his comeuppance at the end of a movie, not least because there have usually been multiple victims along the way. However, rather than leading with hell, the starting point for the gospel is surely a story of mercy triumphing over judgement (James 2:13) and the kindness of God that leads us to repentance (Romans 2:4). It isn't required in order to be "biblical" that we preface our message gospel with phrases such as "God's wrath," "condemnation," "punishment," and "judgement"; not least because each of them requires considerable explanation. Most people do not see themselves as baddies who "obviously" deserve to "get their comeuppance." Whether they should is another matter, of course, but we're talking here about where we start from. It is not essential (and nor is it wise) to start with the negative, especially if our audience is unlikely to "get it."

From a missional perspective, fitting hell into a presentation of a loving God is problematic because of the commonplace imagery that everyone has of it, thanks to those mediaeval paintings and Dante's *Inferno*. We start behind the eight-ball, as it were. We start on the defensive. Immediately we are faced with some perfectly good questions that are inclined to set the agenda: Would God supernaturally keep someone alive for eternity just to torture them? Would he create billions of humans knowing full well that the vast majority of them are going to be tortured forever after three-score years and ten? Some will immediately respond, "Well, if that's what the Bible says, then that's what the Bible says and we just have to live with it. We aren't at liberty to pick and choose the verses we like." That would be true. But it doesn't mean those weighty questions then go away. As we said a moment ago, to believe that the Bible speaks of justice, consequences, and even, judicial sentencing, does not automatically take us to a particular kind of punishment or an obviously eternal duration for it. Looking at it from the other perspective, it's easy for evangelists to be tempted to use the stereotypical imagery of hell to get people to become Christians—playing on their fear of it, if they don't. I know that many preachers believe this to be valid and effective for evangelism. Personally, I'm not at all sure that it is. After all, according to 1 John 4:18, perfect love casts out fear; it doesn't weaponize it for evangelistic purposes. Is scaring people into the kingdom really God's agenda? Does it produce healthy Christians? The Anglican biblical scholar John Wenham says: "It seems to me to be a complete fallacy to think that the worse you paint the picture of hell the more effective your evangelism will be" (*Facing Hell*, 249).

Different Christian Understandings of Hell

Let's now turn to the various different ways of understanding hell. Although there are some variations, if we aim to keep it fairly simple the thinking of theologians boils down to two main understandings (there's a further one that we'll mention at the end). It's important to say that you are not required to believe in a particular view to be a Bible-believing Christian (since verses and passages can perfectly reasonably lead us to different conclusions), though some churches may say you have to for their own reasons.

Before we go into them, it's as well to be aware of the extent to which our views will be influenced by the beliefs that we hold (the assumptions that we make) concerning the following:

1. Whether the human soul is intrinsically eternal—an idea that originated in Greek philosophy. This would mean that, when our physical body dies, our eternal soul "has to go somewhere" (i.e., souls that don't go to heaven must go someplace else).

2. The nature and duration of after-death punishment that is warranted for the "crime" of which we are all guilty before God (living an unrepentant sinful life), in order that the requirements of divine justice are appropriately fulfilled.

3. Even if the soul is not intrinsically eternal, whether God supernaturally maintains its existence forever (or for some extended period) in order to complete that divine punishment (and by the same token, to enable those who are "saved" to experience eternal life).

4. Whether human destinies are forever fixed at the point of death. In other words, whether there is the prospect of any subsequent transfer from "hell" to "heaven"—some form of postmortem "second chance," in an intervening period or place, between death and final destiny. And finally,

5. How we read the relevant Bible verses on this subject (and, which we consider those verses to be . . .).

Eternal Conscious Torment

OK, with that in mind—understanding number one is known as "eternal conscious torment." This is the popular imagery of hell that those mediaeval paintings and Dante's *Inferno* are picturing ("popular" in the sense of widely held, not in the sense of having widespread appeal!). It contrasts heaven as the very best place imaginable, where everything is wonderful, with hell as its counterpart and antithesis, the very worst place imaginable, where everything is horrendous.

Eternal conscious torment "fits" with the soul being eternal (either by being inherently immortal by nature or by God's keeping it in existence), physical punishment that is unlimited in duration (because that is the appropriate sentence for the crime), and reading certain Bible verses to be supporting that (which we'll look at in a moment). We may also be influenced by thinking that this is the "traditional" view—or even, that it's the only view—depending on what we've previously been told.

Eternal conscious torment as it's commonly pictured depends on a particular view of what judicial divine "punishment" looks like. In bygone days—when torture and physical violence was widely practiced as judicial sentencing, before the advent of penal reform and a prison system based on custodial sentences—it was extremely easy to think of all judicial punishment in those terms, because that was what people were familiar with. It was "obvious" in worldview terms. It's far harder for people to think of it like that nowadays. What's "obviously" right and fair in terms of types of punishment has changed. This does not mean that

God has changed his mind about what divine punishment should look like, of course, but it may cause us to wonder about the extent to which past understandings of what divine punishment "obviously" looks like may have reflected an ancient-world way of thinking rather than timeless divine thinking.

Some readers may see a logical connection here between how Jesus' death on the cross saves us and the destiny of those who are not saved. In other words, whatever a person is saved *from* must be what will happen *to* an unsaved person. The narrative of eternal conscious torment fits particularly well with one understanding of the gospel that we call "penal substitution." Namely, that on the cross Jesus "took the punishment" that we deserve, the judicial sentence that would otherwise be coming our way as sinners: he was being punished in our place. It's a very prevalent understanding among evangelicals, and indeed for many Christians it's assumed to be the only one. It's commonplace for everyday Christians who believe in penal substitution as the right way of understanding the gospel to also insist on eternal conscious torment as the right way of understanding hell, because the two seem to go hand-in-glove in that way. It is felt that the one requires the other, and vice versa.

The theology concerning "how" Jesus saves us is what's called the doctrine of the atonement. The word literally means being brought into a state of being *at-one* with God (rather as "contentment" means a state of being content). Space does not permit us to discuss this in great detail, but a few brief observations may be helpful.

1. The Bible speaks of Jesus saving work in a variety of ways—a "kaleidoscope" of ways. We are not required to believe or preach a particular understanding to be a "proper" Christian. What is essential to Christian belief is that only through Jesus—his incarnation, life, death, and resurrection—are we saved. The question of *how*, exactly, that salvation came about is secondary and was never thought necessary to address by the early church fathers in the classic creeds that define Christian orthodoxy.

2. What happened to Jesus at the cross in terms of its physical violence and suffering is not a biblical picture of what will eternally happen to unrepentant sinners in hell. We should not commingle the imagery.

3. All the best biblical understandings of the atonement are "substitutionary"—that Jesus did for us what we could not do for

ourselves—but not all substitutionary atonement is "penal." It does not need to be penal to be substitutionary.

For more on the doctrine of the atonement, I recommend a book by Joel Green and Mark Baker, *Recovering the Scandal of the Cross: Atonement in New Testament & Contemporary Contexts*. Also, my own book, *Atonement and the New Perspective: The God of Israel, Covenant, and the Cross*, which was my PhD thesis and also engages with the New Perspective on Paul that we spoke about in the previous chapter.

Conditional Immortality

Understanding number two is "conditional immortality." This starts from the standpoint that the soul is not eternal. It takes its cue from verses like Romans 6:23, which says "The wages of sin is death"—with "death" understood to mean . . . death! The end! In other words, that the natural outcome and consequence of sin is that both body and soul die, unless immortality is acquired. How we may acquire immortality instead of this natural consequence of death is explained in the continuation of Romans 6:23: "The wages of sin is death, *but the free gift of God is eternal life through Christ Jesus our Lord.*" In other words, "conditional immortality" is saying that the "condition" for acquiring "immortality" is receiving it as the free gift of God through Jesus. If that condition is not fulfilled, then neither is immortality, whether in somewhere called heaven or somewhere called hell. It's perhaps worth mentioning in passing that death is still a form of "eternal" penalty—it lasts forever. It is also worth mentioning that conditional immortality need not be taken as saying that death is *the only* penalty or consequence, simply that it is not conscious punishment for eternity.

So which is it to be? One of these, or some variation on one of these? Much as we might want to simply be "biblical" on this—and just believe what "the Bible says"—as we've seen so often already, that is not as simple as it sounds and hell is an example of that. The UK Evangelical Alliance did a study called *The Nature of Hell* (it's out of print, but obtainable second-hand, somewhere like eBay. If you're interested in the subject and can get hold of a copy, it's worth reading) in which it concludes:

> The Christian doctrine of hell is ultimately a construct of sys-
> tematic theology. This is to say that it represents a programmatic
> synthesis of all relevant material from the canon of Old and New

Testament Scripture, as developed through centuries of ecclesial debate and reflection.

The Nature of Hell, 36

In other words, just believing what "the Bible says" isn't an option. A "doctrine" is a set of beliefs on a subject. "Systematic theology" (and biblical theology) looks at a subject from a top-down perspective of Scripture as a whole. "Programmatic" means following a logical method rather than picking verses from here and there. And "synthesis" means connecting everything together well, with all relevant factors taken into account—which is what we're aiming to do generally with all of the subjects we're looking at in this book.

What the Bible Says

Let's review some of the key texts that lead people to each of these understandings. To start with, the Old Testament is remarkably silent on hell. As *The Nature of Hell* points out, "The Old Testament concentrates primarily on the present life, in which God reveals himself to his people and they obey, serve, and worship him." It continues, "Most Israelites probably believed that everyone who died went down to the underworld"—remember that in the ancient world they pictured the cosmos in a tiered way, with the physical realm having different levels (hence, the "up" to the heavens and the "down" to the underworld)—"a dark, silent place of dreary half-existence. The Old Testament contains very little description of this underworld . . . ." This may explain why two of the main groups within first-century Judaism, the Pharisees and the Sadducees, held different beliefs on the resurrection of the dead (see Acts 23:8).

Our thinking today on the afterlife is mostly influenced by the New Testament. Space does not permit us to lay out every single verse and passage that has potential relevance, but a representative sampling will show that verses implying both eternal conscious torment and conditional immortality are to be found. For example, as *The Nature of Hell* helpfully summarizes: "Matthew, Mark, Luke, Jude, and Revelation refer mainly to Gehenna, Hades, and fire, and imply some duration of punishment. John, Paul, and the other letters refer mainly to perishing, destruction, and death." Helpful though that summary may be, it is not so helpful in "synthesizing" them! In Jude and Revelation we see themes of "darkness" and "exclusion." Revelation (which we need to remember belongs to a type or genre of prophetic literature called "apocalyptic," with heavy use of "picture language") uses graphic imagery of death, destruction, torment, and the "lake of fire." Paul, meanwhile, never speaks explicitly about hell, and nor does the book of Acts. None of the "evangelism" we see in Acts mentions hell as a theme. Paul talks variously about death as the "wages of sin," as an enemy that will be destroyed; of divine "wrath" against those who practice evil; and a final reckoning for all, appearing before the judgement seat of Christ. He speaks of those outside of Christ as "perishing" and headed for "destruction." 2 Thessalonians 1:9 speaks of a penalty of "eternal destruction," in which we note that eternal "destruction" is not the same thing as eternal "conscious torment." The verse also indicates a consequence of being "separated," "shut out" or "excluded" (depending on the translation), "away from the presence of the Lord." It's interesting that on every other occasion Paul uses "eternal" it's to do with the destiny of believers. The Johannine literature (i.e., John's Gospel, and letters) makes no reference to Gehenna, Hades, fire, or torment. John's Gospel contrasts "death" and "perishing" with "eternal life."

Three passages in Matthew, Mark, and Luke have been particularly influential in Christian thinking, particularly in relation to eternal conscious torment:

1. The Parable of the Sheep and the Goats and what follows it, in Matthew 25:31–46;

2. Jesus' warnings about Gehenna, as the unpleasant destiny of those who "cause one of these little ones who believe in me to stumble," or whose hand, foot or eye causes them themselves to stumble, in Mark 9:42–48; and

3. The Parable of Lazarus and the Rich Man tormented in Hades, in Luke 16:19–31.

Gehenna as Hell

It's appropriate for us to say more about both Gehenna and Hades, not least because each of them is sometimes translated as hell. We'll start by looking at the Mark passage and Gehenna:

> If anyone causes one of these little ones—those who believe in me—to stumble, it would be better for them if a large millstone were hung round their neck and they were thrown into the sea.

> If your hand causes you to stumble, cut it off. It is better for you to enter life maimed than with two hands to go into Gehenna, where the fire never goes out. And if your foot causes you to stumble, cut it off. It is better for you to enter life crippled than to have two feet and be thrown into Gehenna. And if your eye causes you to stumble, pluck it out. It is better for you to enter the kingdom of God with one eye than to have two eyes and be thrown into Gehenna, where "the worms that eat them do not die, and the fire is not quenched."
>
> Mark 9:42–48

The quotation that Jesus includes at the end comes from Isaiah 66:24, the context for which is the "new heavens and the new earth" that God will bring about (verse 22), where it says that people "will go out *and look on the dead bodies* of those who rebelled against me [the LORD]; the worms that eat them will not die, the fire that burns them will not be quenched." Note that Isaiah is not talking about a place of eternal conscious torment for living souls, but a place for *dead bodies*. It's the *worms* that do not die, not the people thrown outside the city.

Gehenna is the name of a valley outside Jerusalem. When someone translates it as "hell," that's an interpretation. The word Gehenna means Valley of Hinnom. In the Old Testament, it was notorious as the scene of idolatrous worship of the Canaanite gods Molech and Baal, in which children were sacrificed by passing them through a fire into the hands of their gods. Jeremiah prophesied that it would also be called "the Valley of the Slaughter" because of the vast number of Judeans who would be killed and thrown into it by the Babylonians (Jeremiah 7:31–32 and 19:5–6). At the time of Jesus, the Valley of Hinnom was a rubbish dump. Tom Wright (N. T. Wright, when he's writing academically) says this about it:

> The most common New Testament word sometimes translated as "hell" is *Gehenna*. Gehenna was a place, not just an idea: it was the rubbish heap outside the south-west corner of the old city of Jerusalem. There is to this day a valley at that point which bears the name *Ge Hinnom*. . . . The point is that when Jesus was warning his hearers about Gehenna he was not, as a general rule, telling them that unless they repented in this life they would burn in the next one. . . . His message to his contemporaries was . . . [that] unless they turned back from their hopeless and rebellious dreams of establishing God's kingdom in their own terms . . . Rome would turn Jerusalem into a hideous, stinking extension of its own smouldering rubbish heap.

Surprised by Hope, 188–89.

J. B. Phillips reflects this understanding in his translation: "It is better for you to go one-eyed into the kingdom of God than to keep both eyes and be thrown on to the rubbish-heap, where 'their worm does not die and the fire is not quenched.'" Wright explains that "once Christian readers had been sufficiently distanced from the original meaning" of Gehenna "alternative images would come to mind, generated not by Jesus or the New Testament, but by the stock of images, some of them extremely lurid, supplied by ancient and mediaeval folklore and imagination."

Hades as Hell

Let's now turn to that key parable of Jesus in Luke 16, which speaks about Hades. Once again we'll quote it in full:

> "There was a rich man who was dressed in purple and fine linen and lived in luxury every day. At his gate was laid a beggar named Lazarus, covered with sores and longing to eat what fell from the rich man's table. Even the dogs came and licked his sores.
>
> The time came when the beggar died and the angels carried him to Abraham's side. The rich man also died and was buried. In Hades, where he was in torment, he looked up and saw Abraham far away, with Lazarus by his side. So he called to him, "Father Abraham, have pity on me and send Lazarus to dip the tip of his finger in water and cool my tongue, because I am in agony in this fire."
>
> But Abraham replied, "Son, remember that in your lifetime you received your good things, while Lazarus received bad things, but now he is comforted here and you are in agony. And besides all this, between us and you a great chasm has been set in place, so that those who want to go from here to you cannot, nor can anyone cross over from there to us."
>
> He answered, "Then I beg you, father, send Lazarus to my family, for I have five brothers. Let him warn them, so that they will not also come to this place of torment."
>
> Abraham replied, "They have Moses and the Prophets; let them listen to them."
>
> "No, father Abraham," he said, "but if someone from the dead goes to them, they will repent."

He said to him, "If they do not listen to Moses and the Prophets, they will not be convinced even if someone rises from the dead."

Luke 16:19–31

As with Gehenna, the first matter of significance is what and where is Hades. *The Anchor Yale Bible Dictionary* helpfully explains:

> The Greek word Hades is sometimes, but misleadingly, translated "hell" in English versions of the New Testament. It refers to the place of the dead but not necessarily to a place of torment for the wicked dead. In Greek religious thought Hades was the god of the underworld; but more commonly the term referred to his realm, the underworld, where the shades or the souls of the dead led a shadowy existence, hardly conscious and without memory of their former life. In early times it seems Hades was usually conceived as a place of sadness and gloom (but not punishment) indiscriminately for all the dead. However, as early as Homer the notion existed that some individuals experienced endless punishment in Hades, and later, especially through the influence of Orphic-Pythagorean ideas, belief in post-mortem rewards and punishments in Hades became common.

"Hades," in *The Anchor Yale Bible Dictionary*, Volume 3, 14.

It would appear that Jesus is drawing on these popular notions of the time in picturing a conversation between Abraham and an unnamed rich man from this life (with Lazarus, the poor beggar from this life, at his side). Although the two are said to be far away from each other, they are clearly able to talk. It seems that Jesus pictures both as being in (parts of) Hades, the place of the dead, albeit separated by a chasm that the dead are unable to cross. Hades seems to include comfort for those like the poor beggar who is named, yet agony and torment for those like the heartless rich man who is not named. The question—from an "interpretation" standpoint—is not what does "the Bible say" here but "what does it mean by what it says?" More particularly, why is Jesus telling this parable, and to whom? What point, or points, is he wanting to make through the parable?

As always, some simple consideration of the "context" will help us. The whole of Luke 16 is about money. It begins with a parable about money that concludes with Jesus' famous statement: "No one can serve two masters. Either you will hate the one and love the other, or you will be devoted to the one and despise the other. You cannot serve both God and

Money." In the very next verse, the audience for what follows becomes clear: "The Pharisees, who loved money, heard all this and were sneering at Jesus. He said to them, 'You are the ones who justify yourselves in the eyes of others, but God knows your hearts. What people value highly is detestable in God's sight.'" Again, he's talking about money, and about attitudes and behavior in this life in which money is at the root. Interestingly, in the same discourse, Jesus continues: "Anyone who divorces his wife and marries another woman commits adultery, and the man who marries a divorced woman commits adultery." Quite likely, the linkage here is a reference to the catastrophic financial consequences that a divorced woman (especially, one divorced unfairly) would experience. What we then read in this parable about Abraham, the rich man, and the beggar is part of a continuing discourse about money in *this life*—Luke's quotation of Jesus' words (above) follows straight on.

We therefore need to make a judgement call as to whether in this parable Jesus is primarily telling us something about heaven and hell (we must remember it's a parable) or, whether he is primarily highlighting— particularly, for the Pharisees, "who loved money" according to Luke— the serious consequences in the afterlife of how one has behaved in this life. Specifically for those (represented by the "rich man") who callously ignore what is said in "Moses [i.e., the Law] and the Prophets" about how one should treat the poor (represented by the "beggar"). Of course, there is no reason Jesus can't necessarily be saying something about both. However, the picture language that the parable uses to convey its message need not be speaking of something that is literal any more than any other parable does; parables always used familiar everyday concepts and imagery, so that they could easily be identified with and grasped by the ordinary people who were the audience. In this case, the fact that Jesus used popular thinking about Hades as a vehicle for a message about the serious eternal consequences of how one has behaved in this life does not necessarily mean he was offering a doctrine of hell at the same time; still less that the parable was seeking to compare and contrast "eternal conscious torment" and "heaven," as the final fates of the two characters. This is all the more so, given that "Hades" was also used at the time to speak of the intermediate abode for all of the dead prior to final judgement. We need to distinguish the vehicle from the cargo. One thing we might well feel that this parable is warning against, however, is the idea of a "second chance" after death for those who ignore the things they should not ignore in this life and trust in that second chance instead. If nothing else, Jesus seems to be saying that this is a pretty risky, if not foolish, strategy.

And then finally, the Parable of the Sheep and the Goats in Matthew 25.

> When the Son of Man comes in his glory, and all the angels with him, he will sit on his glorious throne. All the nations will be gathered before him, and he will separate the people one from another as a shepherd separates the sheep from the goats. He will put the sheep on his right and the goats on his left.
>
> Then the King will say to those on his right, "Come, you who are blessed by my Father; take your inheritance, the kingdom prepared for you since the creation of the world. For I was hungry and you gave me something to eat, I was thirsty and you gave me something to drink, I was a stranger and you invited me in, I needed clothes and you clothed me, I was ill and you looked after me, I was in prison and you came to visit me."
>
> Then the righteous will answer him, "Lord, when did we see you hungry and feed you, or thirsty and give you something to drink? When did we see you a stranger and invite you in, or needing clothes and clothe you? When did we see you ill or in prison and go to visit you?"
>
> The King will reply, "Truly I tell you, whatever you did for one of the least of these brothers and sisters of mine, you did for me."
>
> Then he will say to those on his left, "Depart from me, you who are cursed, into the eternal fire prepared for the devil and his angels. For I was hungry and you gave me nothing to eat, I was thirsty and you gave me nothing to drink, I was a stranger and you did not invite me in, I needed clothes and you did not clothe me, I was ill and in prison and you did not look after me."
>
> They also will answer, "Lord, when did we see you hungry or thirsty or a stranger or needing clothes or ill or in prison, and did not help you?"
>
> He will reply, "Truly I tell you, whatever you did not do for one of the least of these, you did not do for me."
>
> Then they will go away to eternal punishment, but the righteous to eternal life.
>
> Matthew 25:31–46

If once again we look to the context of the passage—which really begins with Matthew 24:36, if not Matthew 24:1 before that—it clearly has to do with the end of the age. And yet, just as we saw with the passage in Luke

16, Jesus' particular concern seems to be the connection between the afterlife and how we have lived in this life. In relation to the afterlife, it can hardly be denied that there is an end-time separation spoken of between the "sheep" who are the "righteous" and the "goats" who are the "cursed." The righteous receive their kingdom inheritance and the cursed are told to "depart" into "the eternal fire prepared for the devil and his angels." Readers will make of the imagery in this parable what they will. Again, however, as with Luke 16, a valid question to ask ourselves is whether Jesus is primarily telling us something about hell or primarily telling us about the serious consequences for the afterlife of how one has behaved in this life. Specifically, in this parable, that how we were treating people is how we were treating Jesus. Again, of course, there is no reason Jesus can't be saying something about both; but the question will be (since this is a parable) how literally should the imagery be taken. Do we need to distinguish the vehicle from the cargo? The fact that it's a parable does not mean it isn't presenting a real truth—the only question is, *which truth is it presenting?*

How to Read Parables Well

At this point, it's important to say just a little bit more about the nature of parables in Jesus' day as a particular kind of genre; not least because, the Parable of the Sheep and the Goats (interpreted literally) is a key text for those believing in eternal conscious torment. A parable was like an extended metaphor, picturing something that was true in certain ways, but which became not true if the imagery was then pushed too far, or taken too literally (e.g., picturing Jesus as "the Lamb of God"). Parables were stories that had an ulterior purpose lurking beneath what was visible on the surface. Rather than simply teaching something obvious, they were designed to engage the listeners into thinking for themselves (even, debating) what that purpose might be. Characteristically, parables had "a shock factor"—they had features that would strike the hearer as atypical, unlikely, or even absurd. Hence the questions here would be, what parts are to be taken as true literally, and which would be pushing the imagery too far? What aspect or aspects are the "shock factor" (might it be, perhaps, that Jesus would use popular ideas of there being a place called "Hades" which was the intermediate place of the dead to situate his story)? Are there elements in his crafting of this story that listeners would consider atypical, unlikely, or even absurd? If so, which? Listeners would have known that what was visible on the surface in the parable was not the teaching; the teaching was lurking beneath, and they were being challenged to discover what that was.

It's interesting that this parable is the last of three that are ostensibly to do with end-of-the-age rewards and punishments. The series begins with the wicked slave in Matthew 24:45–51, followed by the wicked slave in the Parable of the Talents in Matthew 25:14–30, before moving directly into the Parable of the Sheep and the Goats from verse 31 onwards. The first two parables are punctuated by the Parable of the Ten Virgins, in which no punishment is prescribed for the five underprepared "foolish" virgins, save for the consequence of being "shut out" from the wedding celebrations and being told by the bridegroom, "I don't know you." The punishment for the first wicked slave is dramatic: to be "cut to pieces" (the text offers no suggestion that this is an unexpected or unreasonable punishment by the owner of the slave). The slave is then "put with the hypocrites" (presumably now in his dismembered state) in a place "where there will be weeping and gnashing of teeth." The punishment for the wicked slave in the second parable is less dramatic: to be "thrown outside into the darkness"—which will, again, be a place of "weeping and gnashing of teeth." Interestingly, although the Parable of the Virgins may appear to be something of a detour in the series, Jesus links it to the "wicked slave" parable that follows, with the phrase, "Again, it will be like . . ." So, immediately before the sheep and the goats, we have three previous accounts, all in parable form, all addressing the same or similar subject matter, but with somewhat different consequences and outcomes. All three of them picture great sadness and sorrow in "weeping and gnashing of teeth." Two picture the exclusion of being "shut out" or "thrown out" (one referencing being left out of the party, the other being put out into the darkness). One says it's a place for hypocrites. And one pictures brutal, physical violence leading (presumably) to death, carried out by a master on a slave. So, are all of these parables to be taken literally? Are we to give one (or more) priority over the rest? Can they all be literally true at the same time, given that, e.g., a previously dismembered slave can scarcely also be subject to "eternal punishment," in an "eternal conscious torment" sense? Or are we to read these as different ways—different stories, each using the genre of the parable—for Jesus to grab people's attention and convey an underlying truth about the serious adverse consequences at the end of life for the ways in which we have lived (consequences that his audience should not assume do not have elements of these features about them)? Finally, it should briefly be noted that biblical scholars debate the meaning of the Greek word (*aiōnios*) that's customarily translated "eternal" here (with its implication, to us, of "never-ending"). If, as it is argued, the sense in its wider classical Greek usage is more along the lines of, "lasting for an age," or for an initially undetermined period of time, "with no horizon in sight," or even, "for a lifetime," such as with a title granted to a person "in perpetuity," then this would direct us towards a different way of thinking about the verses in which the word appears, yet without undermining the overarching message of the extremely serious consequences that all of these parables are picturing in their own ways.

What I would suggest is clear, is that whether we picture these things more in terms of the imagery of Dante's *Inferno*—as an active and ongoing punishment suffered continuously for eternity—or more in terms of the everlasting finality of death, will ultimately have to be decided on grounds that go beyond a simple "the Bible says" applied to a small number of verses. Either way, though, the Bible would seem to be clear that justice would not be served by death being the only consequence before God of how we have lived this life. Death alone could be seen to be "getting away with it." Nor should we pay scant attention to the deep sadness and remorse that the Bible presents to us, as a consequence of being "left out of the party"—excluded from eternal life with God.

If we allow our understanding of biblical theology to inform our thinking—what the Bible tells us as a whole about the nature and character of God—we might find serious problems in reckoning ancient-world cultural understandings of appropriate judicial punishments to be coterminous with what God would consider appropriate. We might also feel, speaking personally, that we could not countenance having a wonderful time in heaven while some of our friends and family from this life were being tormented in hell forever.

Yes, God is undoubtedly a God of justice, but justice requires punishment that's appropriate to the crime. The question is, what does divine justice, for the way each of us has lived this life, look like? It certainly seems that "separation" from the presence of God and "exclusion" from the new heaven and new earth is part of the adverse consequences. But what would make us think that justice is (and can only be) served by unlimited divine punishment for limited human sins, as eternal conscious torment proposes? Is it really true that all of us commit sins that are so big as to warrant punishment that lasts forever?

2 Corinthians 5:10 is clear: "We must all stand before Christ to be judged. We will each receive whatever we deserve for the good or evil we have done in this earthly body." What do we "deserve"? I don't know. What will we "receive"? I don't know—only God knows. And I'm not entirely sure that he wants us to have a watertight understanding one way or the other. God surely wants us to focus on avoiding the question entirely and proclaim the free gift of God, which is eternal life through Jesus—an abundant life that begins now.

Universal Restoration

It would not be appropriate to close this chapter without a word on another understanding, which we might call "universal restoration" (or, "ultimate reconciliation"). This is to be distinguished from a kind of "liberal" universalism that works backwards from the assumption that God is so nice that he obviously just wants everyone to go to heaven—rather like my wife's reputation with our grandkids: "We love Nanna because she never says 'no.'" In contrast to that rather "woolly" approach, universal restoration (or as one author has characterized it, "evangelical universalism") does not suggest that there is no accountability before God for the way in which we have lived our lives nor any potentially negative consequences for that, but it sees the ultimate outcome as God restoring all things to himself (per Colossians 1:19–20: "For in him all the fullness of God was pleased to dwell, and through him to *reconcile to himself all things*, whether on earth or in heaven, making peace by the blood of his cross"). It does not deny a post-mortem place of judgement, but sees its primary function as a purifying process through which all will ultimately be brought to a point of repentance and reconciled to God. Those who argue for this understanding note that a number of Scriptures support it and these must be taken properly into account if one is to talk about a truly "biblical" view on the subject; for example, Romans 11:32: "For God has imprisoned all in disobedience so that he may be merciful to all."

Although universal restoration is a minority position, it deserves consideration for a number of reasons. One is that it is said to have been a prevalent view amongst some of the early church fathers, such as Gregory of Nyssa and Origen. Another is that it finds advocates amongst a number of eminent contemporary biblical scholars and theologians.

Arguably, its weaknesses include (a) downplaying the significance of mission (and a relationship to Jesus) in this present life and (b) how God would ensure/guarantee that all people will come out of that period of purifying having freely repented and received reconciliation. It may be said that when people see and encounter God in the next life and realize he is true, then they will "obviously" turn to him and want to be with him forever; but that's quite a strong "obviously," especially when we have been created as people with free will. That is not to say, of course, that those who have never heard of Jesus or properly heard the gospel in this life will not receive an opportunity post-mortem (that's a different point—I have no doubt they will). Indeed, it would surely be a violation of freewill to deny the chance of that opportunity.

Evangelical universalists make the valid observation that if unrepentant sinners are punished forever, then sin and evil have not been destroyed but perpetuated for eternity; they've just been isolated and contained in a place called hell. If, on the other hand, those sinners then realize their error and become repentant—as an ongoing life existence would presumably enable them to—would God continuing to punish them for eternity anyway be just? Is there a logical reason (based on the justice of God) that physical death "must be" the point after which salvation is "obviously" impossible? These are good questions, particularly in relation to the idea of eternal conscious torment.

Personally, based on my understanding of the nature and character of God revealed in Jesus, I would like to think that I am at the very least a "hopeful universalist." By which I mean, I would hope that whatever hell is or implies, everyone possible will be redeemed from it. I'm distinguishing "everyone possible" here from "everyone," primarily because it seems to me that there needs to be space for both human freedom and divine freedom (we can't dictate to either) and because what the Bible has to say on the subject retains a degree of ambiguity that militates against defining too much detail with too much certainty. It doesn't seem unreasonable to share Paul's hope that God "wants all people to be saved and to come to a knowledge of the truth" (1 Timothy 2:4) to the maximum extent that this is possible in God's perfect plan, which we do well to be cautious about second-guessing.

For those who wish to read more on universal restoration, a thoughtful presentation is offered in Gregory MacDonald, *The Evangelical Universalist*.

9

Was Jesus Superman?

I n this chapter, we're going to do some "Christology." That's the word theologians use for thinking about Jesus. It comes from the Greek words *Christos* and *logos*, literally, "words about Christ." So Christology is the study of Jesus—thinking theologically about who he was and who he is.

In the early church there was great debate on a number of key doctrinal questions, one of which was how Jesus could be both God and man at the same time. The answer to that question is critically important for a number of reasons that we'll go into in this chapter. (It was ultimately settled by the Chalcedonian Creed of 451 CE, but reading this chapter will be more fun than just reading that creed.)

When I first did a talk on this subject many years ago, I started by asking people this question: "Do you think that 'Superman and Clark Kent' is a good way of explaining how Jesus was both 'God' and 'man' at the same time?" I wonder how you would answer that. Of course, the question does presuppose that you know the story of Superman, at least in general terms! For anyone who may not, Superman is a comic book super-hero character whose story began in the late 1930s. Most people think of him as the original super-hero. The story goes that he was born on the planet Krypton but was sent to earth as a baby by his natural parents, in a small spaceship, just before Krypton was destroyed. The spaceship landed near a town called Smallville and he was found and adopted by an elderly farming couple, Jonathan and Martha Kent, who named him Clark. When he grows up, Clark Kent gets a job as a reporter for the *Daily Planet* newspaper in the city of Metropolis. Although he looks like any other man on the outside and he acts "mild-mannered" to conceal his true identity, he's really Superman on the inside, with super-human powers—the ability to fly, x-ray vision, unimaginable strength, and virtual indestructibility.

So, Clark Kent looked just like a normal human being—he looked just like one of us. But he wasn't really. He was actually from another planet. With super-powers. Underneath, he was really Superman. That is the background to asking: "Do you think that 'Superman and Clark Kent' is a good way of explaining how Jesus was both 'God' and 'man' at the same time?"

I did a talk about this in the US a couple of years ago, and it happened to fall on St. Thomas's Day in the church calendar, which is always the first Sunday after Easter. Thomas was one of Jesus' disciples. If you know what Thomas is most famous for, it's hard to believe the church would name any day in his honor, since he's the one we call "Doubting Thomas." The disciple who famously said he wouldn't believe Jesus had risen from the dead, unless and until he saw Jesus for himself. It's easy for us, looking back now, to be harsh on Thomas for his skepticism. But in fairness, Thomas didn't know what we know. He didn't have the benefit of the New Testament and the creeds and the Westminster Shorter Catechism and a multitude of evangelical statements of faith. It wasn't just Thomas—all of Jesus' disciples spent the whole time he was with them trying to figure out who he was. Including Judas, who presumably would not have betrayed him if he'd known then what we know now—that would be about as stupid a thing as anyone could do, would it not?

"Messiah"—Meaning What, Exactly?

It's easy for us to say now, 2,000 years later, that Jesus was "obviously" the Jewish Messiah. But even that wasn't straightforward at the time. The Messiah was a major figure for many faithful Jews in the first century—a promised "saviour" and "rescuer" figure whom they believed God was going to send. But there was no single Old Testament "picture" of who this Messiah would be and what he would be like and what exactly he would do. And for sure, no one was expecting him to be divine; not least because that wouldn't easily "fit" with one of the core tenets of Israelite faith, that there is only one true God and that God is one. The idea of a "second God" or more than one God was complete anathema. Even though Christians now understand the Holy Spirit to be a person of the

Trinity, one God in three persons, at the time he was understood simply as the manifestation of the presence and power of God. "Messiah," meanwhile, just meant "anointed one," with no implications of divinity beyond potentially being a heavenly messenger figure. Generally, the Messiah was expected to be some kind of great leader like Moses or King David, who would put the world to rights and rescue Israel from its enemies, but the detail was sketchy. There was lots of speculation about when the Messiah would come (and, why he hadn't yet come—whose fault it was), whether he'd be a king or a priest or a prophet figure, whether he'd lead a revolt against the Romans, and so on. Although the narratives of Isaiah 53 and the "redemptive suffering" of the Maccabean Martyrs (2 Maccabees 7:37–38) would have been familiar texts in first-century Israel, it was really only in hindsight, reflecting on Jesus, that the early Christians recognized a "suffering servant" portrait of the Messiah, alongside the "conquering king" one. This is hardly surprising, given that Israel was under Roman occupation. They were suffering enough already, all by themselves—they really didn't have a felt need for a Messiah to come and suffer with them.

So, we shouldn't be too hard on the disciples for taking some time to figure out who Jesus was. It was only after the resurrection—as they reflected on their experiences of Jesus and the Holy Spirit and the Old Testament Scriptures about the Messiah and they brought their experiences and their Scriptures together—that the full picture began to emerge, of Jesus the Son of God as we now understand him.

The Jesus they knew—and knew well, from spending several years in his company, day after day—was a bit of a paradox during his lifetime. Although we might think (from our twenty-first-century Christian vantage point) that the signs and wonders in his ministry should "obviously" have led them to the prompt and inevitable conclusion that "Jesus was God," signs and wonders had characterized the ministries of some of the great Old Testament characters before him; plainly, none of them were divine. And yet . . . there was clearly "something of God" about Jesus, and that "something" was clearly significant, if not also unique.

At the same time, the disciples were equally well-aware that Jesus got hungry and thirsty. He became exhausted and fell asleep. He cried when one of his friends died. He experienced temptation and pain and suffering. In the Garden of Gethsemane, he begged for there be "some other way" to avoid crucifixion, and in the agony of the cross, he felt like God had abandoned him and cried out in anguish: "My God, why have you forsaken me?" All of this is stuff that *we* feel and questions that *we* ask. These were signs of real, genuine humanity that appeared to go way above and beyond what one might expect of, say, some sort of angelic figure.

In short, while there was (what we might see now as) overwhelming evidence of Jesus' divinity, it was commingled with at least equally overwhelming evidence of his humanity—all at the same time and all in the one person.

Two Pictures of Jesus in the Gospels

As a result, when we read the story of Jesus, it's almost as if we're looking at two pictures being painted for us—a Jesus who was God and a Jesus who was human. A far better way of putting it, though, would be to say that we're looking at one Jesus from two different directions. Through two different lenses—in one pair of binoculars—both of which need to be brought into focus for us to see him clearly. The way that theologians describe this, is looking at Jesus "from above"—through the lens of "Jesus was God"—and looking at Jesus "from below"—through the lens of "Jesus was human."

It wasn't just the disciples who struggled with how these two aspects of who Jesus was come together and hold together. It was one of the questions that was most debated in the early church as well and, not surprisingly perhaps, led to some of the early heresies. One of those was called "Docetism"—from the Greek word "to seem like" something. Docetism said that Jesus only "seemed" to be human; God "dressed up" in a human body. Like Clark Kent, who also only seemed to be human. Interestingly, the early church doesn't seem to have had a problem with the idea of Jesus being God (or, at least, divine in *some* sense)—they seem to have seen that as "obvious." The questions they had seem to have been to do with his humanity.

The same thing tends to happen with Christians today, and I think there are a couple of reasons for that. Firstly, we're nervous about focusing too much on Jesus' humanity for fear of "bringing him down to our level"—making him "too human." That's probably because we feel that we have to focus our efforts on persuading people that Jesus "really was God" and "not just" an ordinary human being. Secondly, we're wanting to point people to the heavenly Jesus who is King of kings and Lord of lords, with the power to change their lives. So we "retro-fit" the eternal Jesus, ruling and reigning in heaven at the right hand of God, onto the Jesus we see in the Gospels. A bit like first-century Jews, we're more comfortable with a "conquering king" kind of Jesus who defeats our enemies than "gentle Jesus, meek and mild" (as the Charles Wesley hymn puts it).

Raymond Brown says this:

> Since opponents of Christianity deny Jesus' divinity, believing Christians are far more sensitive about limitations placed on his divinity than they are about limitations placed on his humanity. Realistically, it may well be that most Christians *tolerate* only as much humanity as they deem consonant with their view of his divinity. . . . They cannot visualize him as being like other men.

An Introduction to New Testament Christology, 27.

I wonder if any of us think a bit like that?

Many Christians assume that because God knows everything and Jesus was God then Jesus must have known everything as well. So he "must have" known about gravity, DNA, the earth being a globe revolving round the sun (as opposed to being flat and fixed in place), how to split the atom, perform open heart surgery (if called upon), and so on—scientific discoveries that would not be made for many centuries to come. In the seventeenth century, some Carmelite theologians followed this line of thinking to its logical conclusion: If Jesus was the perfect human, they said, then he must have had every perfection that is possible for a human to have. He must have been the greatest artist, the greatest musician, the greatest doctor, and so on—the best at everything. Today we might wonder, if Jesus had been a betting man, could he have won the lottery every week, if he'd wanted to? Or beaten Tiger Woods without ever having a golf lesson? I bet Superman could . . . .

Max Lucado said this—see whether some of it makes you feel a bit uncomfortable:

> Angels watched as Mary changed God's diaper. The universe watched with wonder as the Almighty learned to walk. Children played in the street with him . . . .
>
> Jesus may have had pimples. He may have been tone deaf. Perhaps a girl down the street had a crush on him or vice-versa. It could be that his knees were bony. One thing's for sure: He was, while completely divine, completely human.
>
> For thirty-three years he would feel everything you and I have ever felt. He felt weak. He grew weary. He was afraid of failure. He was susceptible to willing women.

He got colds, burped, and had body odor. His feelings got hurt. His feet got tired. And his head ached.

To think of Jesus in such a light is—well, it seems almost irreverent, doesn't it? It's not something we like to do; it's uncomfortable.

It's much easier to keep the humanity out of the incarnation.

God Came Near: God's Perfect Gift, 8.

Implications of Jesus Being "Fully Human" as Well as "Fully God"

The reason I started studying theology after being a Christian for many years was because I had more and more questions about things that weren't making sense to me. Years ago in church (or maybe it was just the kind of churches I knew?) you really weren't allowed to have questions. You were told to "just have faith" and "not let your head get in the way of your heart." And that seemed to be mainly because the church leaders I was asking didn't seem to know the answers themselves, but were too embarrassed to say so. In that vein, have you ever wondered about any of the following?

- I knew that Jesus had "won the victory" over Satan and sin and death. But then again, Jesus was the Son of God, so he was hardly going to lose, was he? Surely Jesus was always odds-on to win that one?

- Then there were the three temptations in the Wilderness, that Jesus successfully resisted. That's great, I thought, well done Jesus. But personally, I get three temptations a minute, not three in a lifetime (in the Gospels, we never seem to read about any other temptations after those). And my temptations are a bit more challenging than the three Jesus faced. They're a bit less "theological," if you know what I mean. And anyway, surely the Son of God was never going to fall for a few trick questions from Satan. He must always have known the Bible off by heart—or so I assumed. It is the Word of God, after all.

- I wondered whether Jesus cried as a baby. In the Christmas Carol, "Away in a Manger," it says "The cattle are lowing, the Baby awakes, but little Lord Jesus, no crying He makes." So maybe he didn't.

- I wondered whether Jesus ever fell over and got cuts and bruises playing a first-century version of rugby. Obviously he wouldn't have been playing American football, because America hadn't been invented yet. But if he did play sport, I wondered if he always let the other side win? That would seem to be the "nice" thing to do.

- I wondered whether being the perfect human meant he was always top of the class. Or did he pretend not to know everything, so he didn't sound like a know-all?

- I wondered if he fancied any of the girls in the village. Whether he ever felt like getting married and starting a family. Whether he was ever tempted to give up on his mission, for an easier life, especially when he faced criticism and opposition.

And then there's the cross. You might be shocked by this. Forgive me if you are. But in the back of my mind, I was always thinking: if Jesus knew that he was the Son of God, and he knew without a shadow of a doubt that he'd be coming back to life again on the third day—returning to heaven, as King of kings and Lord of lords—then surely that would have made it a lot easier. After all, lots of people die painful deaths (at least 30,000 were crucified by the Romans). And all of us have to die without having the benefit of knowing exactly what's going to happen afterwards, as I assumed Jesus must have done. We have to have faith—but if Jesus knew it all already, he wouldn't have needed faith. He would have had a distinct advantage over us.

If none of those questions have ever bothered you, then please don't worry about it; it's probably just me! But if they do bother you—or maybe, they bother you now that I've mentioned them!—then good Christology is the route to answering them.

We're going to focus on three passages, starting with Philippians 2:

> You must have the same attitude that Christ Jesus had. Though he was God, he did not think of equality with God as something to cling to. Instead, he gave up his divine privileges; he took the humble position of a slave and was born as a human being.
>
> Philippians 2:5–7

This is an example of a passage where it can be helpful to look at more than one version to get the sense of it. For example, in the phrase that the NLT translates "he did not think of equality with God as something to cling to," the NIV says he "did not consider equality with God something to be used to his own advantage." Other versions say "although he was equal with God, he did not take advantage of this equality." Where the NLT says "he gave up his divine privileges," the NASB says that he "emptied himself"—which is closer to the original than the NIV's "he made himself nothing." What the passage is telling us is that, although Jesus was truly God, in becoming truly human as well, he refused to take advantage of any aspect of what it means "to be God" that would have given him an unfair advantage over us in what it means "to be human." He voluntarily "laid down"—or "emptied himself"—of everything to do with being God that would have been incompatible with being fully human. An easy example of that is omnipresence (in other words, God being everywhere at once). For the sake of being human as we are, and to fully identify with us, Jesus had to give up that privilege—lay down that right and empty himself of that attribute. The same is true with omniscience (God knowing everything about everything). That too would be incompatible with being human like us, because we don't know everything. So Jesus laid that aside as well. He chose to limit himself in all these ways. Not because he had to, because of weakness, but because he chose to (that's very important). The theological word to describe this is *kenosis*—the Greek word for "emptying"—that we find in Philippians 2.

But why, you may ask, did Jesus have to do that? Why was it so important for him to be fully human as well as fully God? Why couldn't he have just come to earth like Superman did? For the answer to that, we need to look at our second passage, in Hebrews 2:

> Since the children have flesh and blood, he too shared in their humanity *so that* by his death he might break the power of him who holds the power of death—that is, the devil—and free those who all their lives were held in slavery by their fear of death. For surely it is not angels he helps, but Abraham's descendants. For this reason he had to be made like them, fully human in every way, in order that he might become a merciful and faithful high priest in service to God, and that he might make atonement for the sins of the people.
>
> Hebrews 2:14–17

Do you see the "so that" link between Jesus' humanity and Jesus' achievement—breaking the power of the devil? "For this reason" Jesus "had to be" "made like" us—"fully human in every way"—"in order that" "he might make atonement for the sins of the people." Atonement simply means making us "at one" with God, bringing us into relationship with God. Being "made like" us "in every way" was essential to Jesus' mission. It was essential to Jesus becoming a mediator for us, our advocate with the Father, a "merciful and faithful high priest."

Verse 18 then adds something else which is amazing: "Because he himself suffered when he was tempted, he is able to help those who are being tempted." Which is great—but cast your mind back to those questions I used to have about Jesus' humanity and divinity, and specifically the one about Jesus having just those three temptations. I used to think they were "symbolic," so that he could say "OK, I've done 'temptation'— tick box, move on." If it's just those three that are in mind here, then perhaps Jesus' identifying with us in our temptation is not so great after all. Clearly, though, it's not just those, if we look at Hebrews 4:

> For we do not have a high priest who is unable to feel sympathy for our weaknesses, but we have one who has been tempted in every way, just as we are—yet he did not sin. Let us then approach God's throne of grace with confidence, so that we may receive mercy and find grace to help us in our time of need.
>
> Hebrews 4:15–16

The reason we can approach the throne of grace with confidence is because we're approaching through Jesus, who knows exactly what it's like to be human like us. This is a Jesus who understands us from personal experience. That's why we can have "confidence" that we'll "receive mercy" and "grace to help us" in our "time of need," because Jesus is at that throne of grace and Jesus understands. It's why someone need never say to God, "You wouldn't understand. You wouldn't understand what it's like to be me and have to live my life." No other major religion believes in a god who would become directly and personally involved in a suffering creation, as one of us, and suffer alongside us in the ways that we do.

Dorothy Sayers writes this:

> For whatever reason God chose to make man as he is—limited and suffering and subject to sorrows and death—he [God] had the honesty and courage to take his own medicine. Whatever game he is playing with his creation, he has kept his own rules and played fair. He can exact nothing from man that he has not exacted from himself. He has himself gone through the whole of human experience, from the trivial irritations of family life and

the cramping restrictions of hard work and lack of money to the
worst horrors of pain and humiliation, defeat, despair, and death.

Letters to a Diminished Church, 14.

"He had to be made like them, fully human in every way"

Let's just take a moment to reflect on this idea that Jesus was tempted
"in every way as we are." Isn't that a scary thought. Not just the "little bit
naughty" kinds of temptation, but the really embarrassing ones as well.
The ones we'd rather not talk about. Who would have thought that Jesus
would be tempted like that? This is one reason why it's so important that
we understand the difference between temptation and sin. So that when
Satan whispers in our ear that "you've already thought it, so you might as
well carry on and do it"—preying on our guilt for thinking such a thing—
we can "say no," because temptation is not sin. Jesus was tempted like us
"in every way," but it never became sin in him so it needn't become sin in
us. The implications of Jesus being "made like us" in every way "except
for sin" are mind-blowing. What that means is, anything and everything
that is not sin that I experience as part of being human can also have
been experienced by Jesus as part of his humanity. And that makes sense
of what Max Lucado was saying, because it's not a sin for a baby to cry.
It's not a sin to be weary or lonely, or wonder if you've made the right
decision. It's not a sin to not know everything, or to have to live by faith
rather than by watertight certainty that what you believe is true. In fact,
to live by faith and not by sight is something that Scripture asks us to do
in 2 Corinthians 5:7. So if none of these things are sin, and all of them are
part of being authentically human, then they are all things that we can
expect to have been true of the incarnate Jesus as well: made like us in
every way apart from sin.

One aspect of being human is to have free will—to have the choice as
to whether we love God or not and whether we will do what God asks of us
or not. The significance of that is, in order to be like us "in every way" apart
from sin, Jesus had to have had free will as well. Free will is not sin, it's only
what we do with free will that can end up including sin. When Philippians
2:8 says that Jesus "humbled himself by becoming obedient to the point
of death, even death on a cross," that would hardly be saying something
meaningful if disobedience was never a possibility. A foregone conclusion

isn't called a victory, it's called "a fix." That explains why there was rejoicing in heaven at the victory Jesus won for us through his obedience.

If Jesus already knew for certain how everything was going to pan out in the end, if he'd "already watched the movie" of his earthly life, with no faith required, then the incarnate Jesus would still be someone we could admire. But he wouldn't be someone we could relate to as a role model or example for how we live our lives day-to-day, because we don't have the advantage of knowing any of that. God asks us to trust him that what we hope and believe in—but can never be absolutely sure of—is true. And I don't for one moment think that God would ask more of you and me in our humanity than he asked of Jesus his Son in his humanity. "In every way as we are" includes having to live by faith as we do.

So how did Jesus do it? How did he win the victory? The virgin birth—or more accurately stated, the virgin conception—is pointing us to Jesus not having "inherited" the human bias that draws us to sin, like a car pulling to one side of the road because something internally is out of alignment; severing the inevitability of the truths reflected in Romans 3:23 (that "all have sinned and fall short of the glory of God") and in 1 John 1:8 ("If we say we have no sin, we deceive ourselves"). However, the idea that this inevitability was severed, birthing Jesus' humanity in the place from which 'adam began, is by no means saying that Jesus could not have sinned or could not have abandoned his mission; were it otherwise, his temptations would have been merely symbolic and not real in the terms that we experience them.

If you ask anyone "How did Clark Kent do it?" the answer's obvious—it's "because he was Superman." He looked human, but wasn't really. But the answer to "How did Jesus do it?" is not "because he was God." Jesus "did it" as an authentic human being, "fully man." He could have done it like Superman, of course, but he didn't. He did what he did—he lived as he lived—by the power of the Holy Spirit. Jesus laid aside all of the advantages of being God so that in doing everything he did, he would be doing it as someone just like us.

If we are to live like Jesus and "do the stuff" that Jesus did, it will be through being human in the same way that he was; which means:

- Being born of the Spirit, as Jesus was (in our case, *born again* of the Spirit, in the John 3 sense);

- Being anointed by the Spirit, as Jesus was; and

- Being continually filled with the Spirit, as Jesus was.

In chapters 3 and 4 of Luke's Gospel, we see a series of anointings, fillings, and empowerings, one after the other.

- Jesus was anointed by the Spirit on his baptism (Luke 3:22), when his mission began;

- He was "full of the Spirit" when he returned from the Jordan (Luke 4:1);

- He "returned to Galilee in the power of the Spirit" after his temptation (Luke 4:14); and then finally-

- In his first sermon—quoting from Isaiah 61, as his mission statement—Jesus says: "The Spirit of the Lord is upon me" because he's "anointed" him to bring good news to the poor, proclaim that captives will be released, the blind will see, the oppressed will be set free, and the time of the Lord's favor has come (Luke 4:18–19).

The reason the Holy Spirit anoints us is not just so we feel good, or get charismatic goosebumps. It's to empower us to live as Jesus did and "do the stuff" that Jesus did, in the same way that Jesus did. Raymond Brown says this:

> Unless we understand that Jesus was truly human with no exception but sin, we cannot comprehend the depth of God's love.
>
> A Jesus who walked through the world with unlimited knowledge, knowing exactly what tomorrow would bring, knowing with certainty that three days after his death his Father would raise him up, would be a Jesus who could arouse our admiration, but a Jesus still far from us.
>
> He would be a Jesus far from a humankind that can only hope in the future and believe in God's goodness, far from a humankind that must face the supreme uncertainty of death with faith but without knowledge of what is beyond.
>
> On the other hand, a Jesus for whom the detailed future had elements of mystery, dread, and hope as it has for us and yet, at the same time, a Jesus who would say "Not my will, but yours"—this would be a Jesus who could effectively teach us how to live, for this Jesus would have gone through life's real trials.
>
> An Introduction to New Testament Christology, 151.

A proper understanding of the humanity of Jesus—a good "Christology"—is essential not only for understanding everything that the Bible says about Jesus but also for our relationship with Jesus.

The Vital Significance of Jesus' Humanity

So to return to our question, in closing: "Do you think that 'Superman and Clark Kent' is a good way of explaining how Jesus was both 'God' and 'man' at the same time?" Answer? No! It's a *terrible* way of explaining it! In Jesus, we not only see "God translated into terms that we can understand" (Raymond Brown's phrase, in *Introduction to New Testament Christology*, 150)—which is wonderful in itself—but we also see God as someone who can perfectly understand us from first-hand experience.

Evangelicals understandably focus on the role of the cross in our redemption, but it should never be at the expense of the significance of Jesus' becoming human like us, living life like us, and experiencing the resurrection that we are destined for, as the "first-born from the dead" (Colossians 1:18; Romans 8:29). The incarnation, the life, the cross, and the resurrection are all essential to our salvation. Properly understanding the significance of Jesus' humanity alongside his divinity is fundamental not simply for our theology of Jesus but for our relationship with Jesus.

The resurrected Jesus who is our advocate with the Father (1 John 2:1)—who is at the right hand of God interceding for us (Romans 8:34)—is the same Jesus who became fully human in every way (Hebrews 2:17). No wonder, then, that we can approach God's throne of grace with confidence, to receive mercy and find grace to help us in our time of need (Hebrews 4:16). Finally, the anointing, filling, and empowering of the human Jesus by the Holy Spirit becomes the model for Christians from a charismatic tradition to understand and practice spiritual gifts and prayer ministry, including healing.

— 10 —

Why Is There Evil and Suffering in the World?

Why is there evil and suffering in the world? Strictly speaking, there are two questions here, but they are often linked together in people's minds, so they're worth addressing together. Time and again in surveys of big questions about the Bible, this one keeps coming up—if the Bible is the Word of God, then it must have things to say to us about that question from God. It is also, of course, a major stumbling block for many people in relation to Christianity in general, especially those who have suffered badly themselves, or seen terrible suffering. If there is a loving God, why does he allow bad things to happen? And especially, why do bad things happen to good people?

Disclaimer first: you may well find my answer less than perfect—and that might be a charitable way of putting it! However, I would prefer to offer an inadequate or partial answer than a glib answer. Anyone who is painfully familiar with evil and suffering will see right through that, and rightly so. Christians who present "the" answer in simplistic terms are doing themselves no favors and Christian faith no favors. Such a complex question that has affected so many people's lives in so many devastating ways is not advanced by offering explanations that fly in the face of their lived reality. It's undoubtedly meant well, but overreaching for answers is at least partly driven by thinking that, for Christianity to be credible, we "have to have" an answer to everything. Because we honor the Bible as the Word of God, it "must have" God's answer to every question (we just need to find it). But to a large extent, the reason we think like that is down

181

to living in the era of modernity, in an age of science, where everything to do with "how things work" and "why things happen" is assumed to be knowable and hence, should be explainable. Many modern Christians instinctively feel that to allow for any element of mystery is undermining Christian faith. If God knows everything, and the Bible is God's Word, then it must have all the answers. Mystery sounds like a euphemism for a flaw in our knowledge; an excuse for not knowing things that as Christians we ought to know. But maybe we unwittingly do more harm for the gospel by saying that we have an answer on this question that ought to be fully persuasive, than by admitting we don't.

So in this chapter, I am not intending to present "the" answer, because I don't believe there is one; rather, I just wish to offer some thoughts that for me personally are part of an answer; aspects of how we might think about it that I have found helpful and I hope others might find helpful. It's undoubtedly a difficult question, but just because we can't say everything about it doesn't mean we can't say anything. Ultimately, though, to whatever we say, we will need to add in a large dollop of personal trust (aka, faith) in the nature and character of God. We will need to echo the father of the sick boy who said to Jesus, "I do believe; help me overcome my unbelief" (Mark 9:24).

It's worth just saying that questions and doubts are not the opposite of faith and trust; the opposite of faith and trust is deliberate unbelief. We are allowed to have questions and we are allowed to have doubts; God made us to have enquiring minds. If we never had questions or doubts to be explored, we would never learn anything or discover anything. As we said in the introduction, Christianity is never under threat from good people asking good questions with good attitudes.

If God Is "in Control," Why Do Bad Things Happen?

Now, we can kind of understand how bad things might happen to bad people because, to some extent, it fits with our ideas of justice. Most movies have goodies and baddies, and we all feel that "justice is done" when the baddies get their comeuppance, even if they meet a gruesome end. But the opposite is true when we see bad things happening to good people. And that's because we tend to think that bad things must happen to bad people *for a reason*—that there's some kind of cause-and-effect going on. The bad people deserve it in some way. However, notions of "justice" and "fairness" seem to suggest that only good things should happen to good people. If we claim to have a good God—who is or should be the very epitome of justice and fairness—and bad things happen "unjustly" and "unfairly," this surely must mean either (a) that there is no God after all, or (b) that he is not as just and fair as we have made out. I have seen many people struggle with their faith and even lose their faith over exactly that.

Another element of this, when bad things happen, is that it can make people wonder whether they've done something to deserve it. In a "cause-and-effect" universe, it's assumed that every effect must have a cause; everything must happen for a reason. If God is the ultimate cause of everything—if God is ultimately "in control" and all-powerful—then surely he must either have caused it, or at least he could have stopped it. Either way, this must mean he doesn't love me, because if he did love me, it wouldn't have happened. Surely, if there is a God, and he loves us, and he is omnipotent (he can "do anything") then he could have stopped it, and he should have stopped it. If God is the God of love that Christians present him to be (a loving heavenly Father who delights in giving good gifts to his children) then it feels like, by definition, this bad thing ought not to have happened. However, if God is indeed like that, then in some way it must be my fault (or someone's fault); it must be divine punishment or divinely initiated consequences.

As Christians we can sometimes tie ourselves up in knots on this when we talk about God being "in control." What we intend to be a statement instilling faith and comfort can lead us into some awkward territory, because it's pretty difficult to claim that God causes good things to happen but that he doesn't cause any of the bad things. If we take being "in control" to be defined per the age of the machine—with God flicking all the switches and pulling all the levers in the universe, making everything happen—then that's the only logical conclusion. There is of course a strong sense in which we believe that God is indeed in control of the cosmos (albeit, not in a "micro-management" sense), not least because of his promise to redeem it and renew it, as we discussed in chapter 8, and his commitment that at the end of this life there will be a day of reckoning for evil, and justice for life's victims. The question is how much control God retains and how much he releases, in how he has intentionally designed his creation to be, in the present.

This leads us to identify a "tension" between God being in control and creation being given freedom, including human freewill. We need only think for a moment about what allowing personal freedom involves, to see that retaining control at the same time is an impossibility. Any parent who has ever grappled with the extent to which their teenagers should be allowed personal freedom will immediately appreciate the risks involved. By the same token, that parent will also appreciate—at least on paper—its necessity and ultimate desirability.

In relation to the question of evil, then, this tension between human freewill and divine control is a major factor. If, in a general sense, evil is the opposite or absence of good, then evil is the opposite or absence of God. As we discussed in chapter 3, if human love for God (and choosing God) was to be real and genuine, there had to be an alternative story to choose to live in. A story had to be allowed that was the opposite to God's story, in which God was absent through humanity having excluded him. Otherwise, we would simply be robots, if God was "in control" to that extent and we had no choice. Again, however, as with the teenager analogy, the risks involved are obvious.

Self-evidently, we live in a broken and damaged world, where not everything is as it should be and people are not as they should be. We're part of a world that's been "knocked off-kilter." Look that up in a dictionary and it means: a bit askew; not in perfect balance; out of order; and, not working as it was supposed to. In other words, something's "not right." To greater and lesser extents, we are all broken people living in a broken world. Sometimes we're victims of that and sometimes we're part of the cause of that. When we ask God why bad things happen we have to accept that sometimes *we* are part of the problem. For example, we shouldn't blame God for that fact that millions are starving, when the world God made is easily able to produce more than enough food to feed everyone. We shouldn't blame God that in our western world we have chosen a capitalist economic system, because we believe that on balance that is for the best, when we know full well that will inevitably not end up as the best for everyone. Having "winners" means having "losers," especially when capitalism tells us that wanting "more for me" is an inherently good motivation. This is exacerbated when it's allied with an insufficiently compassionate view towards those who suffer from that model. One of the downsides of God having created us with freewill— the freedom to make choices—is that it allows us to make bad choices, including the choice to live our lives selfishly; to be unfair and unjust in how we treat others. As we said earlier, freedom for the pike can be death for the minnow.

If we're looking for another, less-religious-sounding word for sin, *selfishness* is not a bad starting point. The very worst sins are forms of hyper-selfishness. Sin is selfishness with no conscience and no borders: living life to "serve me" and my interests, with scant if any regard for those who may be harmed in the process. The outcome of our human choices includes many things that we then "blame God" for, or wonder why he doesn't prevent. Without wanting to sound over-dramatic, one of the reasons that there is evil in the world is that there are *people* in the world— people with *choices*. The only way to prevent evil is to prevent choices.

The Bible Invites Us to Ask These Questions

When we turn to the Bible, we find that these "why?" questions are not new ones. Many, many people in the Bible asked the same. If the Bible says it's OK to have questions about why bad things happen—why God allows them and where he is when they do—then clearly we're allowed to ask as well. One of the longest books in the Bible, the book of Job, is about nothing but those questions. About one third of the Psalms is cries of the heart that come from anguish and pain, asking God "why?" They're called "laments." There's even a book in the Bible called Lamentations. Here's an example of a lament:

> Be merciful to me, LORD, for I am in distress; my eyes grow weak with sorrow, my soul and body with grief. My life is consumed by anguish and my years by groaning; my strength fails because of my affliction; . . . I am the utter contempt of my neighbors; . . . I am forgotten as though I were dead; I have become like broken pottery.

> Psalm 31:9–12

The person who's saying this is presented in the psalm's title as the mighty King David, who slew Goliath. The David whose story we use as a metaphor for overcoming giants in our lives. Similarly, the prophet Jeremiah wrote: "My sorrow is beyond healing, my heart is faint within me" (Jeremiah 8:18).

So it's OK to respond to what happens in life with normal, human emotions. We're not supposed to deny the reality. Feeling grief and responding emotionally is in no way a lack of spirituality. We're not letting God down, and we're not a bad person or a bad Christian, when we feel that way. It's part of being authentically human. Jesus is our example in that, because as well as being fully God, Jesus was also fully human. In the lead-up to the cross, the Bible says he was "deeply distressed," "troubled," and "overwhelmed with sorrow" (Mark 14:33–34; Matthew 26:38). The shortest verse in the Bible is John 11:35: "Jesus wept." The reason he wept was because his friend had died. On the cross, he cried out: "My God, why have you forsaken me?" (Matthew 27:46). God hadn't of course, because God has never forsaken anyone; but it *felt* like that, because Jesus was authentically human, as well as authentically God. It's natural for us to feel like that ourselves at times. "My God, why have you forsaken me?" is something that David felt, in Psalm 22:1 (see too the other references to this psalm in the Gospels' crucifixion narratives). The message of the Bible is not to deny the reality of our feelings and experiences, it's to find Jesus in the reality of our feelings and experiences, because he understands.

A further thought that I find helpful is that even though bad things are never good and they're never God, he can make them work together for good. There's a big difference between saying "God causes bad things" and "God can turn bad things around and cause good to come out of them." Romans 8:28 says: "We know that in all things God works for the good of those who love him, who've been called according to his purpose." Note that it doesn't say all things are good in themselves; rather, that *in all things God is working for our good*. So, however hard it may be (which God completely understands), our response to bad things happening should be rooted in trust—not just trusting in Romans 8:28 as a proof-text, but trusting in the nature and character of God. We keep on loving him, keep on inviting him, and keep on trusting him to do that. To respond authentically but also faithfully, saying "Come, Holy Spirit into my hurt and my suffering and my wondering 'why?' and even, my doubting." Ecclesiastes 3:4 says there's a time for everything: "A time to weep and a time to laugh, a time to mourn and a time to dance . . . ," so when bad things happen, we're allowed to weep, and mourn—there's a time for it. Allow your tears to come; but, at the same time, allow God to come, and turn things around. Psalm 30:11 says: "You've turned my mourning into joyful dancing. You've taken away my clothes of mourning and clothed me with joy." That's what he wants to do for us—but give it time.

Responding Relationally When Bad Things Happen

We have a choice as to how we respond when bad things happen. It's like reaching a junction in the road and having to decide which way to turn. Do we turn to bitterness and anger, and turn away from Jesus at that point, because "he allowed this" to happen? Or do we turn *to* him? Do we fill in the gaps in what we don't understand—those "why?" questions—with trust and faith in who God is and what he's like? Trusting that he loves us and cares for us and feels our pain?

In that verse we just read—Romans 8:28—the apostle Paul is saying "I know that in all things God is working for my good." But, how does he know that? The answer is: he doesn't! He knows it only by faith. He's chosen to believe it and to cling on to it when bad things happen.

My wife Lyn and I really like detective dramas. To a fault, in fact—we spend far too much time on box sets. . . . Anyway, there's a typical story in which the detective is investigating something really bad that's happened and she's faced with a dilemma. All the evidence so far leads everyone to assume that a certain person must have been responsible. But the detective knows that person. She knows him so well that she's convinced in her heart that her friend couldn't possibly have done it—there must be more to it, other information that she hasn't yet discovered. So, she keeps asking questions, keeps working the case, but also keeps faith in what she knows her friend is really like. She just needs time to find the answers. And eventually, as the story plays out, what happened and why all comes to light and starts to make sense. That friend, who she always wanted to believe the best of from the very start, is proven not to have done it. When bad things happen, do we approach them like that? Do we feel we know our friend Jesus that well? Well enough to say: "We don't have all the information yet and probably never will have in this life. But we do know in our hearts that he couldn't possibly have done this thing, because that's not what he's like"?

No analogy or metaphor is perfect, and this one only works to a point. For example, the detective must be professional enough to retain an open mind in her investigation and not overlook or suppress crucial evidence just because it might implicate her friend. The analogy I'm making here is not to encourage blind faith (or to copy the three wise monkeys), but to encourage a fundamental trust in the goodness of God—to allow the entirety of the biblical account of who God is and what he's like to be the foundation for our response when bad things happen. Even although we do not presently know why, and may never know why, in this life.

Viewing the Present from the Future

Which brings us neatly on to my next thought in relation to evil and suffering: we need to "work backwards" from the future to the present. What I mean by that is, we have to look to the end of the story to make sense of the place in the story that we're at right now. That's called an "eschatological" perspective. Eschatology is to do with "the end times," so it simply means looking backwards from how everything is going to end, in order to make sense of what's happening now; looking at the present from the perspective of the future. In 2 Corinthians 4:17, Paul says: "Our light and momentary troubles are achieving for us an eternal glory that far outweighs them all." He's not trivializing our suffering when he says that. He can only say that because he's looking backwards from the perspective of eternity. Revelation 21:1–4 offers us a prophetic glimpse—painting a picture with words—as to how things will be in the future:

> Then I saw a new heaven and a new earth, for the first heaven and the first earth had passed away. . . .
> And I heard a loud voice from the throne saying, "Look! God's dwelling-place is now among the people, and he will dwell with them. . . . He will wipe every tear from their eyes. There will be no more death or mourning or crying or pain, for the old order of things has passed away."

The "old order" of things is characterized by death and mourning and crying and pain. It's hard to see God in the old order of things, except with eyes of faith. In the old order of things, he's invisible (as it were). But in the new order of things, we will see him. God will dwell with us. And he will personally wipe every tear from our eyes. It's an intimate and relational picture, in which God is palpably present rather than seemingly absent, as he is now. With all eternity to look forward to, our short life here on earth pales into insignificance, even though it's currently all we can see. So it's understandable that it fills our thoughts. But only the future makes complete sense of the present.

Jesus—Suffering with Us

Perhaps the greatest statement—the greatest possible evidence—of the goodness of God is the incarnation. Namely, that in Jesus God himself came to personally experience the bad things that happen in our world. He is not a distant God, impassive and unmoved by what's going on in his creation, just sending instructions from afar through human messengers. He is a God who got his hands dirty, by becoming as one of us, living life as we do. Why would he do that, apart from an overwhelming love and a passionate desire to redeem it? No other religion believes in a god who would "lower himself" and become involved in a fallible and corrupt world in that way (indeed, for many other religions, the very idea is enough to put Christianity beyond the pale). It completely rewrites the rule-book on what "holiness" means and on the presumed separateness of God and creation.

Jesus didn't just come into our world as a generous gesture, he came into our world as a sacrificial commitment. If you'll forgive the slightly crude analogy, it's like the egg and bacon breakfast: the chicken is involved, but the pig is committed. God chose to redeem his creation from the inside. To experience first-hand what human life was really like, so that no one need ever say: "You wouldn't know what it's like to be me." He came not just to be involved but to be *committed*. Jesus was also realistic as to the challenges of living in this broken world. He said that in this world we would have trouble (John 16:33). The reason we should not worry about tomorrow, he said, is because today has enough troubles of its own (Matthew 6:34). Can't get much more realistic than that! So much for religion being escapist!

Israel was experiencing a lot of suffering in Jesus' time, not least because it was under occupation by the Roman Legions. Everyone was asking, "What have we done to deserve this? Why doesn't God do something about it? Doesn't he love us?" All the kinds of questions that we ask; these are perennial questions. The people's natural hope, which became their expectation, was for the promised Messiah to be like King David—who would lead an army and deliver them from the Romans. But that wasn't the kind of Messiah that Jesus came to be. Rather, he became a Messiah like the servant of the LORD graphically described by Second Isaiah, in Isaiah 53: "Despised and rejected by mankind, a man of suffering, and familiar with pain. Like one from whom people hide their faces, he was despised, and we held him in low esteem. Surely he took up our pain and bore our suffering . . . and by his wounds we are healed."

The Gospels are not so much telling us the kind of things to believe as showing us the kind of God we believe in. One who took our pain and bore our suffering. Somehow, the suffering of the cross is a place of healing: our healing comes from his wounding. In the Christmas story, it says that one of the names Jesus would be given is "Immanuel," which means "God with us." He is not a God who's just "up there" somewhere—he's the God who came to be God "down here." One who experienced first-hand some of the worst that human life has to offer: falsely accused; wrongfully convicted; abandoned by his friends; tortured and nailed to a cross.

Paul and Suffering

If we are to look to someone else in Scripture besides Jesus who can help us in dealing with suffering, who better than the apostle Paul. Paul is arguably the central character of the New Testament after Jesus himself. The man to whom half the books in the New Testament are traditionally credited. Not only the great theologian of the New Testament era but also a great church-planter. The man from whom we get most of our Christian doctrine and most of our teaching about the Holy Spirit and spiritual gifts—including, the gift of healing. If anyone was close to God, before or since, you'd think it would be him. The man who taught us what it means to "live by faith."

If "health and wealth" prosperity-gospel teaching is right—which says that, if you've got enough faith, you should never be sick and you should never be in need because (they say) health and prosperity are the birthright of every believer: you just need to "name it and claim it"—then we should expect the great apostle to be the perfect example of that theology in action. The perfect example of what faith will deliver for us, in terms of results, when we put that into practice, in the way that prosperity-gospel teachers say we should. So let's have a look through Paul's story, to see how that works out.

We first come across Paul in Acts 7 and 8, and when we first meet him, we'd probably call him a religious fundamentalist. He was part of the conspiracy to kill one of the early believers called Stephen. Paul went to the high priest to get a letter of authority to go to Damascus, to arrest the Jesus-followers and bring them back to Jerusalem for trial. It's when he's on that journey that Paul has a dramatic encounter with the risen Jesus. He sees a blinding light from heaven and falls to the ground—and a voice says "Why are you persecuting me?" And Paul says "Who are you, Lord?" And the voice says, "I am Jesus, the one you are persecuting! Now get up and go into the city, and you will be told what you must do." When he picks himself up off the ground, he's blind. So his companions lead him by the hand to Damascus. It says that Paul remained there, blind, for three days.

So there's some good news and some bad news here. Paul's had this dramatic experience of Jesus, but he's blind as a result. And for some reason, Jesus hasn't told him whether he's going to get his sight back. While all this is happening, Jesus appears in a vision to one of the believers in Damascus, called Ananias, and tells him what's happening with Paul: that he's to go to a particular house and pray for him so that he'll get his sight back and be filled with the Holy Spirit. Jesus tells Ananias that Paul is "my chosen instrument to take my message to the gentiles and to kings, as well as to the people of Israel." And that's what happens. Paul gets this amazing calling and he's instantly healed. How great is that? Wouldn't we like to see ourselves in Paul's story? Wouldn't we like to be Paul? A dramatic experience of Jesus, an amazing calling and a miraculous healing. Just the kind of stories we like to hear from the stage at Christian conferences. It doesn't get much better than that, does it? Soon after that, it says Paul's preaching became more and more powerful. I like the sound of that too.

But there's a couple of things that weren't going quite so well for Paul, alongside all this amazing stuff. The first is, some people in Damascus were planning to murder him. They were watching for him day and night at the city gate. So the believers had to lower him down the city wall in a basket so he could escape back to Jerusalem. That's a bit humiliating for "God's man of faith and power for the hour." And when he gets to Jerusalem, people there want to murder him as well. So again he has to run away—this time, back to his home town of Tarsus. So much for living "the believer's life of victory." So in the midst of all this blessing and calling and miraculous healing and moving of the Holy Spirit . . . Paul's life is constantly in danger. People want to kill him—and just because he was called and chosen and anointed as a follower of Jesus, he couldn't be sure that it wasn't going to happen. After all, so too had been Stephen, who'd just recently been murdered by a mob that Paul himself had been part of. Stephen was a pretty amazing Christian as well. It says in Acts 6 that he was "full of faith and the Holy Spirit . . . full of God's grace and power, [and] performed amazing miracles and signs among the people." But none of that—including, being "full of faith"—stopped Stephen being killed.

Further on in Paul's story, in Acts 14, it says that God "confirmed his message" through Paul and Barnabas by "enabling them to perform signs and wonders." In Acts 19, "God did extraordinary miracles through Paul, so that even handkerchiefs that had touched him were taken to those who were ill, and their illnesses were cured and evil spirits left them." Wonderful stuff. But, once again, not everything went quite so well. In Acts 20, verse 7, it says "Paul spoke to the people and, because he intended to leave the next day, he kept on talking until midnight." We don't know whether this happened in a morning service or an evening service—think about that for a moment—but I do like the biblical precedent here for long sermons. Our congregation think they're suffering when we're approaching 25 minutes. Then verse 9 says: "Seated in a window was a young man named Eutychus, who was sinking into a deep sleep as Paul talked on and on" (by implication, on and on and on . . .). If you're a young person reading this—or even a not-so-young person—you may well be thinking "I know exactly how he feels . . . ."

I'm embarrassed to say this story always reminds me of something that happened many years ago when I was speaking in church. I could see an elderly lady sitting right in the middle of the auditorium, who looked like she'd nodded-off. You can imagine how off-putting that was—mainly because I was worried sick that she might be dead. It's one thing sending people to sleep, it's something else entirely to kill them off. Not the sort of thing that your reputation as a preacher ever really recovers from. Should I call the medics, or finish my rather excellent third point? (Thankfully, she was just taking a nap.)

Anyway, so Eutychus is sitting on the window ledge, he falls asleep, it's a third-floor window and he falls backward, hits the ground, and dies. Fortunately, God is good to Paul and even more so to Eutychus: Paul prays for him and he comes back to life. Another miraculous healing in Paul's ministry. God definitely bailed him out of that one.

Paul—God's Man of "Faith and Power for the Hour"?

So at this point, despite the occasional set-back, things are looking pretty good. Yes, the odd person falls asleep and dies in his sermons, but at least God heals them and brings them back to life. Yes, a few people in a few places are trying to kill him, but basically things are good. If Paul was drafting his résumé for his personal website at this point—looking for how many superlatives he can fit in without sounding too immodest (always a fine balance)—it would probably have said: "Paul of Tarsus: internationally renowned, gifted, anointed, prophetic, apostolic, signs-and-wonders, supernatural healing ministry. Evening services by appointment—ground floor only, please."

But not everything goes so swimmingly well. In 2 Corinthians, Paul is trying to deal with the fact that his opponents—some so-called "super apostles"—are trying to take over the church he planted and discredit him and his ministry. Their two basic arguments are: number one, that Paul himself is not a very impressive person, and number two, that he's suffered too much to be a real apostle. Insinuation? If God was really with him—if God was right behind his ministry—then so many things wouldn't have gone wrong in his life, would they? So Paul writes to the church at Corinth and he feels the need to defend himself: to lay out his qualifications compared to these so-called "super apostles" that the Corinthians think look so impressive, compared to him. His opponents have been boasting about their accomplishments. (I guess the church had been reading their website résumés.) So Paul says, "OK folks, it's time for me to do a bit of boasting of my own." And he says this—here's how he "defends himself," in 2 Corinthians 11.

> When I was with you and didn't have enough to live on, I didn't become a financial burden to anyone. . . . I have worked harder, been put in prison more often, been whipped times without number, and faced death again and again. Five different times the Jewish leaders gave me thirty-nine lashes. Three times I was beaten with rods. Once I was stoned. Three times I was shipwrecked. Once I spent a whole night and a day adrift at sea. I have travelled on many long journeys. I have faced danger from rivers and from robbers. I have faced danger from my own people, the Jews, as well as from the gentiles. I have faced danger in the cities, in the deserts, and on the seas. And I have faced danger from men who claim to be believers but are not. I have worked hard and long, enduring many sleepless nights. I have been hungry and thirsty and have often gone without food. And I have shivered in the cold, without enough clothing to keep me warm.

I wonder how many of these things you and I would have to experience before we decided that God didn't love us. That he clearly wasn't behind our ministry. That we obviously didn't have enough "faith," because otherwise these things wouldn't have happened. Would it have been the first time we were shipwrecked? The second time? The third time? The first time we went without food and didn't have enough to live on? That's what the people who teach a "health and wealth" gospel would be telling Paul: "You need to sort out your theology, mate—and start living in the victory that's the destiny of all believers. We don't want your kind of testimony at our conferences, thank you very much." But Paul is turning the accepted wisdom—in this "super-spiritual" Corinthian church—upside down. He's saying that the very things you think are evidence that God isn't with me and hasn't called me are nothing of the sort. It's just "life"—in which bad stuff sometimes happens. Sometimes God miraculously rescues us and intervenes and sometimes he doesn't. Or, he doesn't seem to: not in the way that we'd like him to.

So the $64,000 questions—both for Paul, then, and for me, now—are: What am I going to do about it if God doesn't intervene? When life doesn't deal me the hand I would like it to. Will I only love God when what happens in life is good? Or will I also love him in spite of what happens in life, when bad things happen as well? Am I going to let it come between me and God? This is what some Christians do. They feel like God has broken his side of a deal, which is: I become a Christian and you make life good in return. Which may well be because they've been "sold" the wrong kind of gospel in the first place. And when they feel that God's reneged on the deal, they "get their own back," by stopping coming to church, to show him their displeasure. To make a point.

Anyway, back to Paul. If this catalogue of suffering wasn't enough, Paul then starts talking about something else he has to live with. Something else that's embarrassing and that his opponents are also using to undermine his credibility and his ministry. It's something that's very well-known, because it's become a catchphrase: what we call Paul's "thorn in the flesh." Some kind of physical infirmity or illness. This is what Paul himself says about it, in 2 Corinthians 12:

> I was given a thorn in my flesh, a messenger from Satan to torment me and keep me from becoming proud. Three different times I begged the Lord to take it away. Each time he said, "My grace is all you need. My power works best in weakness." So now I am glad to boast about my weaknesses, so that the power of Christ can work

through me. That's why I take pleasure in my weaknesses, and in the insults, hardships, persecutions, and troubles that I suffer for Christ. For when I am weak, then I am strong.

When he says "three different times" I don't think he means three quick prayers at bedtime and then he gave up. I think he probably means some pretty intense times of intercession, and maybe fasting as well, over a long period. Maybe prayer ministry from a number of other leaders. Maybe calling the elders to pray, as James said to do:

> Is anyone among you ill? Let them call the elders of the church to pray over them and anoint them with oil in the name of the Lord. And the prayer offered in faith will make the sick person well; the Lord will raise them up.
>
> James 5:14–15

In any event, Paul didn't get what he asked for, even though he'd seen many healings in his own ministry. Paul was ministering healing to people while he was in grave need of healing himself. He was praying for the Holy Spirit to powerfully intervene in people's lives and situations when he had a track record of personal suffering as long as your arm. Maybe that's an encouragement for us to do the same. Rather than boast about his powerful Spirit-filled ministry and offer up a selection of spectacular "success stories" to share at his conferences, to "build faith" in the audience, I love the fact that Paul says: "If I must boast, I would rather boast about the things that show how weak I am" (2 Corinthians 11:30) rather than the things that show how powerful I am. No wonder his opponents said he was unimpressive. How many of us would buy the books of someone like that? How many of us would join the church of someone like that?

This, would you believe, is the man from whom we get our understanding of faith. This is the man from whom we get our understanding of the gifts of the Spirit, including, the gift of healing. And, in addition to all the other stuff that goes wrong in his life, he's got a chronic illness that isn't responding to prayer. We don't know what it was. It was probably an eye condition, or maybe a speech defect. Either way, it just adds to the evidence that Paul didn't look very impressive or sound very impressive by human standards. He probably wouldn't have been the kind of main-platform conference speaker who would put "bums on seats." At best he might get a breakout session in a side room. Frankly, not a good enough advert for the victorious Christian life. One look at Paul and the donations would probably stop coming in. Didn't he believe James 5:14–15 . . . ?

I said a moment ago that God didn't answer Paul's prayer those "three times" he prayed. But actually, that isn't quite correct: Paul says that God did answer. Each time, the same answer was the same: "My grace is all you need. My power works best in weakness" (2 Corinthians 12:9).

"Name it and claim it" didn't work for Paul. If healing in this present-life is available to all believers now, if only they have enough faith, as word-of-faith preachers claim, then clearly God forgot to tell Paul that. The Vineyard founder, John Wimber, used to say: "Never trust a leader who doesn't walk with a limp"—alluding to Jacob, in Genesis 32, but he could just as easily have been talking about Paul.

I don't know about you, but I think I'd rather listen to someone like Paul than those so-called "super apostles." I think I prefer Paul's kind of boasting to their kind of boasting. The reason that I'd rather listen to Paul is because his experience of life is more like my experience of life. When I'm asking God the question "Why?"—"Why has this bad thing happened?"—there's no point me listening to what the "super apostles" have to say. I want to know what Paul has to say, because he's been there, done that, and got the first-century equivalent of the proverbial T-shirt. I know that Paul won't just quote proof-texts at me, making me feel bad for my "lack of faith," with overblown expectations that don't match life's realities.

All of the thoughts I've shared in this chapter have something in common. They're all inviting us to make a decision; to choose to trust God rather than blame God. When we can't see God in our circumstances, they invite us to live by faith and not by sight (2 Corinthians 5:7). When bad things happen, that's more than ever the time to live by faithfulness to what we believe and by faithfulness to the one in whom we believe; in spite of what we see.

— 11 —

Original Context and the Boundaries of Biblical Interpretation

One of the critical factors in reading the Bible well, that we've touched on already, is starting with the "original meaning" of a verse or passage in its original context. What we have in mind by that is how the human authors and their original audiences would have understood what it was saying (as best we can determine it). It means allowing where, when, why, and by whom it was written to play their full part in informing how we ourselves should understand it. Stated the other way around, it means resisting the temptation to read a verse or passage in a decontextualized way: plucking it from where it sits, looking at it in isolation from its surroundings, and treating its meaning as something that can be determined just from those few, extracted English words all on their own. That is not by definition a "plain meaning." Even if we have "guessed right," we will gain a fuller and richer understanding when we factor in the original setting.

Whatever else we may go on to say about the meaning and application of a verse or passage, it should always start with knowing (as best we can) what that original meaning would have been and ensuring that what we say "it means" is not inconsistent with that. We should not say that a verse or passage means something "now" that it could not possibly

197

have meant "then"—in other words, our interpretations should not be
ones that would cause the original author and audience to look at us with
incredulity (if not fall about laughing).

In this chapter, we're going to look at some of the hazards of failing
to take the original meaning as seriously as we should. Many of these can
be grouped under the heading of "context." Then we'll explore some ways
in which it is not inappropriate to move beyond the "original meaning"
in its original context, along with safeguards that will stop us going to
extremes in our interpretations—"to infinity and beyond," as Buzz Light-
year (star of the *Toy Story* movie series) might say.

The Importance of the Original Context

Property experts say that the three most important things for residential
real estate investment are location, location, location. Similarly, the three
most important things for biblical interpretation are context, context,
context. First-year theology students are always warned that "a text without a context is just a pretext" for whatever meaning someone wants to
give it: take "text" out of "context" and all we have left is "con."

Ignoring context in interpreting a verse or passage greatly adds to
the risk of unwittingly doing *eis*egesis (meaning, "reading *into*" the text
things that aren't there, that we ourselves are putting into it), rather than,
what we ought to be doing, which is *ex*egesis ("reading *out of*" the text
what is already there). One potential cause of that is failing to look at
a verse in more than one translation, such that we wrongly pick up a
meaning that the text does not intend, because we've misunderstood it.
The KJV is particularly at-risk in that because its "Olde English" language
can sometimes make it appear to be saying something that it's not. "Word
of faith" and "prosperity gospel" teaching, which typically uses the King
James, can be an example of that.

Ignoring context lies behind another poor practice, called "proof-
texting." This involves quoting a verse, stand-alone, as "proof" of something—i.e., asserting that something is "biblically" true on the basis of
those extracted words. Once any verse is taken out of its context like that,
there's a clear danger of interpreting and applying it in ways that may bear
no relationship to what the words originally meant within their context. It
may still qualify as "the Bible says"—insofar as the Bible is the place those
words came from—but the *way* in which they are being used may be

quite different from what they originally meant (not least because they're also being read in modern English, with potential for anachronism to come into play). If someone then aims to "teach" something based upon that—probably combined with a few other selected proof-texts—it simply aggravates the problem.

By this point in the book, readers will appreciate that to use the word "biblical" as a stand-alone adjective can be problematic. To speak of being "a biblical church," or offering "biblical teaching," or having "the biblical perspective" on something sounds comforting at face value, but it very soon becomes apparent that it can't be divorced from the opinions and interpretations that come with it. Let's be honest, it's hard to see any church advertising itself as unbiblical, or *not* offering biblical teaching. Claiming something is "biblical" sounds impressive, given the implication that "it's what God thinks," but without further substantiation (not just a few "proof-texts" thrown in!) it's somewhat meaningless. To speak of something as authentically biblical requires rather more.

In the same vein, we should be careful about compiling a list of individual verses from here, there, and everywhere and thinking that this is giving us a "biblical" perspective on a subject (simply because they all feature a particular word, for example). The results of a Bible "word-search" will not necessarily give us a biblical theology of a subject; what they will give us is a list of verses which include that English word in that translation. For example—if we're wanting to teach on love, or grace, or mercy, or forgiveness, the search results won't include the story of the Prodigal Son in Luke 15 because none of those words are mentioned. Even though, we'd surely be hard pressed to find a better biblical presentation of God's love and grace and mercy and forgiveness.

What We Mean by Context

Context will include a number of things. The ones that are most relevant from an interpretation perspective will depend to some extent on the particular verse or passage. A helpful clue as to the kind of things we're interested in is to be found in looking at synonyms for the word *context*: namely, setting, background, situation, framework, environment, perspective, and circumstances. We should start by asking ourselves what we know about each of those in relation to the passage, the people, the events, the author, and his audience.

Although some of the detail in this passage would be debated by biblical scholars, the following gives a good general feel for the wide variety of factors involved:

> The Bible is an exceptional and unique document. It was written during a period of approximately 1500 years (forty to sixty generations). The first books of the Old Testament were written approximately 1425 BC, and the last book of the New Testament was written in AD 95. There are more than forty authors who composed the sixty-six books of Scripture. Not only were the authors separated from one another by hundreds of miles and years, but were quite diverse in their occupations. The writers of Scripture include a lawgiver, military general, shepherd, king, cupbearer, priest, prophet, prime minister, tax collector, fishermen, doctor, and rabbi. The heroes of the Bible are presented with all their faults and weaknesses. Scripture is written in several literary genres, such as historical narrative, legal literature, wisdom literature, poetry, prophetic, gospels, parables, and epistles. The Bible was written on three different continents (Africa, Asia, and Europe) and in three different languages (Hebrew, Aramaic, and Greek). Scripture was written during various circumstances, such as in the wilderness, during a military campaign, a dungeon, in captivity, during travel, in a Roman prison, and in exile; it was composed during times of peace, war, and exile.
>
> Ron J. Bigalke, "Editorial," *Journal of Dispensationalist Theology* (December 2010)

We read all that and ignore "context" at our peril! Before Scripture ever has meaning for us, now—and before it ever had meaning for Martin Luther, John Calvin, Charles Wesley, Billy Graham, or N. T. Wright—it first had meaning for its original authors and audiences. Good interpretation always starts with the latter: what meaning did it have for them, and why? Context means taking the time and trouble to ask ourselves good questions about the background to what we're reading, including, at times, perhaps, some uncomfortable questions, and finding the answers. We need to know, *"why* it says it," not just *"what* it says."

Taking, as an example, how context functions in reading Paul's letters:

- What do we know of the Greco-Roman cultural context in the cities in which these small, minority, Jesus-following communities were located?

- What was happening at the time in the church(es) that he was writing to? To what extent was what he said to a particular church being triggered by that? Paul wasn't writing a textbook for theology students, then or now, he was writing pastoral advice and encouragement to real-life congregations.

- How do we make good judgments on the extent to which what Paul said was specific to a church and its cultural situation, rather than things he thought would be universally true for all Christians in all times and places forever?

- Even if Paul himself would have thought something would be universally true for all Christians in all times and places forever, does that necessarily mean that it is, once we take into account worldview and the humanity that God has allowed to remain present within the text?

- Was Paul writing to a gentile audience, a Jewish audience, or a combination of both? Many Pauline scholars today would say that all of his letters were written to a primarily gentile audience. How might that impact on how Galatians is to be understood, for example, if he wasn't talking to Jews (or to "people in general")?

- How does the worldview of the time as to "the way things are" which sits behind the text—and at times will be visible within the text— impact on our interpretation and application of what Paul wrote?

Where, then, to start, to try to address those kinds of questions? The first thing to say is that we will not necessarily be able to answer them all (some are easier than others). The main thing is for us to have an awareness that such questions exist and that they're important. We need to avoid saying things or concluding things—and still less, "teaching" things—which patently ignore them! We need to do some hard yards in background reading and research, and not just be lazy by reading the words alone and drawing our assumptions as to meaning from that. We can start with a good commentary. Personally, in our church I recommend the Zondervan New International Version Application series. These commentaries structure their content in sections on (i) "original meaning," then (ii) "bridging contexts," and (iii) "contemporary significance." They also include overview materials on a book's background. To my mind, they are usually strongest in part (i) and weakest in part (iii); I prefer to handle the part (iii) aspects for myself. Also important is a good Bible dictionary, which will of course be subject-based rather than passage-based. Here I would recommend the IVP series (which includes titles such as *Dictionary of Jesus and the Gospels*, and *Dictionary of Paul and His Letters*). I'm also very fond of the *Anchor Yale Bible Dictionary*, volume 1 through 6, but be warned that this is more academic.

Beware Googling! Trained theologians can use internet searches, sparingly, but only because they know what they're looking for and how to evaluate what comes up in the search results. There is frankly too much rubbish out there for internet searches to be reliable. If you must Google, always check carefully who the person is who is writing something or saying something, and their scholarly credentials (what qualifications, which academic institution, etc.), before trusting it. Also check where they are coming from, so to speak, theologically, since that will impact on how a person is reading a text.

The Impact of Our Own Context

Last but not least in relation to context is *our context*—the context from within which we are reading. Theologians speak of there being "two horizons" affecting biblical interpretation—(1) the horizon of the original author and audience, and (2) our horizon as current readers. How we understand "meaning" will be impacted as much by the latter as the former. To read the meaning of something in the Bible well is to bring these two horizons into conversation.

It's widely recognized that the idea of a pure, objective Bible reading, unaffected by the context of the place, time, and cultural setting of the reader, is a practical impossibility. All we can do is to be aware of that and try to identify the various ways in which our standpoint impacts on how we are reading and understanding—for example, to be aware of the various "obvious-es" that we bring with us, the things that we think are "common sense," that unavoidably color the lenses through which we're reading. We need to recognize that a reader's lenses may not simply be colored by a *secular* cultural context; they may equally be colored by a *religious* cultural context—our prior Christian experience, things we've been told, and things we've assumed.

Amongst other risks, the presuppositions of our context place us in danger of "confirmation bias"—namely, that when we read the Bible, we are unwittingly biased towards seeing things that confirm (that are consistent with) what we already think. It's not a bad exercise to occasionally ask ourselves, as John Goldingay suggests, when it was that we last changed our opinion on something (or even more so, changed our behavior) as a direct result of something that we've read in the Bible. This is not, of course, to say that all of our presuppositions are inherently wrong, or unhelpful; it's simply to be aware of them and try to make allowance for them where appropriate. It's the presuppositions of our worldview speaking, when we use phrases like "it's obvious" or "it's common sense" or "everybody knows;" when we say that something "must be," or "can't be."

Having established the importance of these core principles, we can now look at the extent to which we can legitimately move beyond them, and in the process, perhaps answer some questions that you've been wondering about.

The New Testament Writers' Use of the Old Testament

The first and perhaps most obvious question is this one: can we really say that these core principles of original meaning and original context—that we're saying should be the start point for understanding (and teaching) what a verse or passage means—were always being followed by the New Testament authors in their use and application of the Old Testament? This is important because, if they were not, then there are obvious questions as to why we necessarily need to.

On its face, it would appear they were not being followed! For example, if we were able to ask Isaiah whether he meant Isaiah 7:14 to be speaking of the Messiah—"The LORD himself will give you a sign: The virgin will conceive and give birth to a son, and will call him Immanuel"— it seems highly unlikely from its context that he did. However, Matthew still seems to think so (Matthew 1:23). Even more so, perhaps, if we were to ask Hosea whether Hosea 11:1—"Out of Egypt I called my son"—was talking about Mary, Joseph, and Jesus returning home after the death of King Herod. Again, Matthew seems to think so (Matthew 2:15), even though Hosea 11:1 specifically says that he was talking about *Israel*. Matthew appears to have blatantly ignored the first part of the verse: "When Israel was a child, I loved him, and out of Egypt I called my son." In these and other instances, the meaning offered by a New Testament writer seems inconsistent with what the Old Testament writer intended.

Indeed, they appear to directly fall foul of some of things we've said are bad practices, such as "proof-texting."

A lengthy discussion of the various ways in which theologians view the New Testament use of the Old Testament is beyond our scope. For those interested in exploring it further, I suggest *Three Views on the New Testament Use of the Old Testament*, edited by Kenneth Berding and Jonathan Lunde, in which the editors' introduction and closing remarks offer a useful summary of the issues and viewpoints. Here, I will simply present the perspective that make most sense to me.

The first element takes its cue from the dual authorship of Scripture; that embedded within the apparent meaning (intended by the human author) there lay an additional and deeper meaning (intended by the divine author). This is known as *sensus plenior*—Latin, for the "fuller sense"—and is supported by the concept that Jesus the Messiah is the end purpose or goal of the entire scriptural story; in Greek, the *telos* (see e.g., Romans 10:4). Hence, in the light of Jesus, earlier texts necessarily took on additional and new meaning, through the involvement of the divine author, that could not have been foreseen at the earlier time by the human author. That extended meaning was always present, just not previously apparent. This ties in with the notion that only in retrospect, looking backwards from the vantage point of the future, can we (with our finite human limitations) ever understand the full significance of any current events.

A second element is that the approach of the New Testament writers appears to reflect a way of reading Old Testament passages that was practiced by Jesus himself, who regularly shed new interpretive light on old texts in that kind of fuller or deeper sense in his teachings and his dialogue with religious leaders. Furthermore, on the road to Emmaus, in Luke 24:27, it says that "beginning with Moses and all the Prophets, he [Jesus] explained to them what was said in all the Scriptures concerning himself." Unfortunately, Luke does not offer us more detail as to which particular passages, exactly, but by way of example it would seem feasible that Isaiah 53 was amongst them, not least because of the immediate context of verse 26 preceding: "Did not the Messiah have to suffer these things and then enter his glory?" In a similar vein, the apostle Paul seems to have found a fuller or deeper sense in certain Old Testament Scriptures in relation to Jesus: "what I received I passed on to you as of first importance: that Christ died for our sins according to the Scriptures, that he was buried, that he was raised on the third day according to the

Scriptures . . ." (1 Corinthians 15:3–5), although again he doesn't tell us which particular Old Testament Scriptures he's thinking of.

A third element is that the things the New Testament authors wrote citing Old Testament Scriptures are, of course, canonical Scripture in their own right. Hence, we might simplistically say that these New Testament verses are allowed to metaphorically "break the rules" (of our day) in how they draw forward Old Testament verses, because of their own canonical status. Under the inspiration of the Holy Spirit, the New Testament writers were perceiving extended and expanded meanings, centered in Jesus. They're not ignoring the "original meanings" in a cavalier fashion—it's not "anything goes." Rather, it's a case of "more than" the original meanings. There is a uniqueness to the circumstances surrounding those fuller or deeper meanings, given that Jesus the Son is the pivot or fulcrum for the entire story—the "Big Story" of God and his creation, as we've been calling it. Jesus, uniquely, made sense of everything that had happened before in the Old Testament, and everything that was happening then, in the New Testament writers' day. Viewing the New Testament authors' readings in a canonical perspective cautions us against automatically granting ourselves the right to be finding "fuller or deeper meanings" in the Bible in the same kinds of ways that they did.

A fourth and final element is that the New Testament writers were not, in fact, "breaking the rules" in their interpretive approaches. Rather, they were simply applying the methods of good Jewish rabbinical scholarship from their own time. For instance, midrash, pesher, and allegory. The term midrash is applied to a range of practices, but it includes reflective interpretation or commentary on a text with relevance to the present situation. According to Richard Longenecker, the basic maxim of midrash is *"that* has relevance to *this"* (quoted in *Three Views on the New Testament Use of the Old Testament*, 26). Pesher, however, goes beyond "that has relevance to this," to say, *"this* is *in fact that."* It has a sense of prophetic fulfilment about it. Examples are found in, e.g., Matthew 1:22; 21:4; Acts 2:16.

It would not be appropriate for us to try to directly copy these rabbinical approaches now, since (1) we do not live in their world, immersed in the principles and boundaries that governed those interpretive methods (which would have averted the risk of unduly imaginative, extravagant construals), and (2), their use and application of the Old Testament in the New Testament has canonical status; patently ours would not.

To Infinity and Beyond in Our Interpretations?

This leaves us with one final, important question. To what extent is it feasible to see an ongoing place today, for the Holy Spirit to reveal to us a *sensus plenior*—a "fuller sense" of deeper meaning, present in other scriptural passages—as well? What we might call a controlled biblical theological extension of what the New Testaments authors were doing?

I confess to being slightly torn on this. On the one hand, simply because the canon is closed by no means closes the possibility that the Holy Spirit might have embedded such deeper meanings in other texts in a similar manner (albeit not with the intention of them being granted anything remotely approaching canonical status, of course). Moreover, we know that we are invited to engage with the text dynamically, not merely statically, with a God who is alive and active and "speaks." And yet . . . perhaps because we see the Bible misused in some Christian circles in what is called "the prophetic" (not a biblical word, by the way), or in overly imaginative "teaching" from a verse or passage (which may amount to no more than "using" a verse or story as a tool to support what they want to say, suggesting that it's something the Bible itself is saying), I am in two minds about it. I wouldn't want anything I say here to be taken as an implied endorsement of those kinds of misuses.

There's certainly a place for thoughtful allegorical-style readings (a lot of contemporary preaching from the Old Testament is actually doing that—using a character or a story as a vehicle to deliver a broader message about something relevant to the Christian life today, such as David and Goliath in relation to "conquering the giants in our life," or such like), but we would do better to think of that (and present it) as metaphorical, or analogous—that "this" is a bit like "that"—rather than claiming it as a deeper, hidden meaning that God previously placed there.

Bottom line, I think my answer to the question would be three-fold: (a) we should not rule it out, but (b) we should proceed with discretion and caution, and (c) we are best to begin by applying the criteria that I am about to suggest in relation to element four below (since, if it passes that test well, then job done anyway). Modesty on our part, in not "over-claiming," and being careful in our choice of language, will help a lot, too!

In summary, then, we have so far proposed three elements to identifying "meaning" in a verse or passage:

1. What it "meant then."

2. An extended interpretive approach by the New Testament writers—drawing out a "fuller sense" (a *sensus plenior*) that the divine author intended in various Old Testament Scriptures, centered on Jesus.

3. The potential for a carefully controlled extension of that, in the present day.

To which we now need to add a fourth:

4. The distinction between *the meaning of* a verse or passage and *something we find meaningful in* that verse or passage—the difference between "meaning" and "significance."

Moving beyond the Original Meaning

Many reading this will have been part of a home group Bible study in which a passage or story is read, and the host then suggests, "Let's go round the room and each say what this means to us." The host does not have in mind what it means in the way that she would if those present were all distinguished biblical scholars. Her interest is not the meaning in that sense, but rather, what each person has found meaningful—what they have found to be *significant* in the passage. Another way of putting that—with a bit more of a "spiritual gloss" to it—is what they feel *the Holy Spirit is saying through it* to them, personally or corporately.

Although the meaning of a verse or passage in the "original" meaning sense (the first sense above) will always be vitally important, and especially if we want to "teach" things about it, Christians reading the Bible will quite rightly be wanting to ask the Holy Spirit, "What might you be saying to me through this verse or passage in my life today?" Preachers will want to extend that to what the Holy Spirit might be saying to their congregations. These questions reflect the belief that God "speaks" dynamically through Scripture now, in the present tense, as well as having "spoken" historically in Scripture in the past tense. However, these are very different kinds of questions to the question of what it meant originally.

It's not uncommon in Sunday sermons, Bible studies, and the like to hear someone talking about a verse or passage using language like "This is saying" (or, "Jesus is saying," or, "Paul is saying"), when what they *really mean* is "This is what I feel God is saying to me/us through it." What's happening is that the person concerned is mixing up two different things, by being insufficiently careful with the language they're using to describe it. Each is valid in its own terms, but it's the difference between "what it means" and "what I'm finding meaningful." It's the difference between what the biblical author and their audience would have found significant in it and what someone today is finding significant in it.

We've said a lot already about good interpretive approaches that target reading the Bible well in terms of its original meaning. What, then, constitutes "reading well" when it comes to this fourth approach—how do we go about validating what God may (or may not) be saying through a verse or passage when something does not correspond to its original meaning? How do we avoid "anything goes" interpretations claiming to be what God is saying, or claiming that God has placed them there, waiting for us to find them?

Postmodern scholars would likely say that these questions are moot, since the very idea of an "original meaning" is a fallacy: whether one existed "originally" or not, the world of the author and original audience is clearly lost to us now. Hence, the very idea is an impossibility. As a result, all we have to work with, they would say, is the meaning that we ourselves find in it as today's readers. This is sometimes called a "reader-response" way of looking at the Bible—in other words, "the meaning" is simply what I find in it as a reader "responding" to the text. Hence, its meaning is not "fixed" or limited in the first instance.

As with so much in postmodernity, one can see here an understandable reaction against modernity's belief in sure and certain objectivity in its quest for a single, inherent, foundational "meaning." However, it's unnecessary to polarize, with modernity's claimed objectivity seen as inherently "right" (and "biblical") and postmodernity's supposed subjectivity as "wrong" (just the "spirit of the age" talking). It's more a case of "both-and," rather than "either-or," since we're actually talking about two different things, each of which is appropriate in its own situation. How, then, are we to distinguish between them?

The Difference between "Meaning" and "Meaningful"

The first thing we need to do is to make sure that the language we're using to speak of each is clear, and that we don't merge the categories of meaning and meaningful together. Everything is fine provided that we treat each on its own terms and appreciate that we're talking about two different things that require different vocabulary. For example, we should always make clear that us finding something *meaningful* through the biblical text does not make that an *authoritative* reading (it is not what "the Bible says," in the sense of something the Bible is teaching).

We recognize that there is, indeed, something called an "original meaning," which reflects what the original author and audience would have understood that text to have been saying, with full account having been taken of its context. Just because we may not have a perfect grasp of that, because of our distance from the text, is not the point; we can at least try, with our best scholarly endeavors. Just because we can't say *everything* doesn't mean we can't say *anything*. That, then, is its meaning, and it remains "what it means."

However, we then separately affirm the potential for Scripture to be the vehicle for the Holy Spirit to speaking meaningfully to us in ways that do not necessarily comport with that original meaning and need take no necessary account of its context. The function of the original meaning of the verse or passage is *not* to control and limit the meaningfulness that the Holy Spirit might want to bring out of it, speaking to us today. The obvious question then, is what guidelines, rules, or controls *are* appropriate to this, so that we do not lapse into unbridled postmodern subjectivism and "anything goes"?

The way I suggest we respond to that is by analogy to a classic Reformed evangelical approach to Scripture. Chapter one of the Westminster Confession tells us that the "infallible rule" for interpretation is to allow Scripture to interpret Scripture. In other words, what the Bible says in general should be our guide to what a part of it is saying in particular; that which it says most plainly should guide us in what it says more obscurely. In the Confession's words:

> The infallible rule of interpretation of Scripture is the Scripture itself: and therefore, when there is a question about the true and full sense of any Scripture (which is not manifold, but one), it must be searched and known by other places that speak more clearly.

When we think about the meaning of a text, in its "original meaning" sense, we tend to look at it "bottom up," through the individual verse or passage itself. Inevitably that places quite strict constraints on what can be considered reasonable interpretations of what that verse or passage was saying—it can only be in line with what it was saying "there, then." However, when we're looking at what the Holy Spirit may be saying meaningfully to us through a verse or passage now (which is a different question), we should look at that "top down," instead. Rather than the original meaning being controlling here, Scripture as a whole is controlling. We reference our "testing" of what the Spirit is saying within the "big picture" of Scripture as a whole, which the Westminster Confession calls "the whole counsel of God" (drawing from Acts 20:27). And given the development that we see in Scripture as the Big Story progresses—and especially, as it reaches its zenith—we prioritize a testing that is informed by the New Testament and most especially by the nature and character of God that we see perfectly revealed in Jesus.

A Biblical-Theology-Based Approach

A more technical way of expressing this might be to say that we look to a biblical-theological approach to guide us. In case you're not familiar with that term, definitions inevitably vary, but mine would be along these lines:

"Biblical theology" is how we understand the nature, character, and purposes of God through what is revealed in Scripture as a whole, centered in the person of Jesus Christ, whose ministry and message serves as the hermeneutical key to Scripture's grand narrative and its overarching themes. Biblical theology is more than selected individual verses. It encompasses the values, emphases, and priorities in the heart of God that are reflected in Scripture read holistically, including its narratives as well as its propositions. Biblical theology invites a communal reading within our faith community rather than licensing individualistic interpretations.

Approached in this way, the original meaning of a text need not necessarily be controlling of how the Spirit may wish to speak meaningfully through that text. There is no need to suppose that the Spirit cannot speak meaningfully through a text today in ways that the text's original meaning cannot support, so long as what we perceive the Spirit to be saying is not inconsistent with Scripture as a whole. The closer that something we perceive the Holy Spirit may be saying (or that someone wants to tell us the Holy Spirit is saying) conforms to our biblical theology, the more confidence we may have in its authenticity—and vice versa. Testing something in this way is to compare against what the Bible tells us holistically concerning the nature and character and plans and purposes and ways of God; which, for the avoidance of doubt, is not simply looking to a few extracted verses as proof-texts.

Since Father, Son, and Spirit are one in heart, mind, and purposes, it is also not unreasonable to ask whether it is the Spirit saying (or doing) something if we cannot envisage Jesus saying or doing it. He is not called the Spirit of Jesus for nothing (Acts 16:7). Our familiarity with Scripture from a biblical theological perspective will assist us greatly in discerning what the Spirit is and is not saying (for example, in prayer ministry and prophetic ministry, as practiced in movements such as the Vineyard).

Clearly, this kind of biblical theological approach will not answer all questions concerning what the Holy Spirit may or may not be saying, not least in relation to highly specific questions on guidance and individual circumstances, but it will certainly assist us in bringing biblical wisdom to bear. It will help us to be discriminating in identifying the kinds of things that God does and does not say or ask us to do. Since we are focused on the centrality of Jesus in our discernment process, we will also give far greater priority to asking, "what would Jesus do?" than "what might Isaiah do?" (such as, running round naked for three years—Isaiah 20:2–4). It will allow discernment to be a conversation between spiritual wisdom and spiritual revelation (rather than, as charismatics often do, prioritizing revelation over wisdom—even though, both are equally gifts of the Spirit). It grants authority to the Bible in practice. It rewards a good understanding of the Bible, informed by the kinds of interpretive methods that we've discussed in this book.

Notice that, in my proposed definition of biblical theology, I included the phrase "within our faith community." We know from looking earlier at how the biblical writers saw their world, the thinking was group-centric, not individual-centric. In making wise decisions in Acts 15:28, they were guided by what "seemed good to the Holy Spirit *and to us*" (whereas charismatic Christians today tend to think in terms of what seems good to the Holy Spirit *and to me*). When Paul said "we have the mind of Christ" in 1 Corinthians 2:16, I think he meant that *we together* have the mind of Christ rather than each and every one of us individually. To think more collectively and collaboratively about what the Spirit may be saying and doing mitigates against rampant individualism and the spiritual one-upmanship of "God has told me." Pastors know how awkward it is to be faced with that, with the only options being docile acquiescence or responding with "Well, he hasn't told me."

A biblical-theology centered methodology that looks to Scripture as a whole can also serve us well when we're seeking to discern what the Holy Spirit may be saying today, on matters about which the Bible itself is silent, because its human authors never encountered them at the time. Along with other relevant factors, the choice of the verses and passages we look to, in order to wisely discern those things, is of course . . . an act of biblical interpretation!

— APPENDIX —

Bible Versions

I t's self-evident from wandering around any Christian bookstore, or
doing a quick online search, that a vast array of different versions of
the Bible is available to us today. How, then to choose one? Is there such a
thing as "the best" one? And if the answer is "it depends" then what does
it depend on? To respond to these questions, we need to start with a little
bit about the theory of translation.

To state the obvious, the Bible wasn't written in English, it was written in Greek (the New Testament), Aramaic (half of Daniel and two passages in Ezra), and Hebrew (the rest of the Old Testament). A further
factor is the Septuagint, or "LXX," which is the Greek translation of the
Old Testament, dating to about 250–150 BCE. It's called Septuagint from
the Latin *septuaginta*, seventy (hence, LXX), based on a legend that it
was the work of seventy Jewish elders. The Septuagint is relevant to our
questions for two main reasons: one is because almost all of the available
Hebrew manuscripts date only to the mediaeval period. The other is that
the Septuagint was the most widely used version of the Old Testament
in New Testament times. In the Mediterranean region, Greek (or, *koine*
Greek, "common" Greek), was the *lingua franca* of its time, rather as
English is today. Every version of the Bible that we read in our own language (which I'm assuming for the purposes of this discussion is English)
comes to us through translators, who have several challenges to address,
including:

- The meaning of original words in the original language—what was being "signified," what they were "pointing to"—in that culture and time period.

- What English word now most closely corresponds to that—does such a word even exist?

- How to deal with idiomatic slang, jargon, and compound words, where the way the word is used may not reflect either its literal meaning or the meanings of the individual parts (e.g., the newly-coined compound term "social distancing," where the individual words have meanings that do not tell us what the combination envisages in how it's being used).

- To what extent to apply cultural equivalence, where societal practices have changed and the original sense is now obscure (e.g., does one change "betrothed" to "engaged" in the nativity story?).

- Whether an English word that may previously have been used to translate something has changed its meaning over time. The word "gay" (which used to mean happy, carefree, and frivolous) is a classic example—the word no longer "signifies" or "points to" what it used to.

- And finally, how to treat concepts that are no longer culturally acceptable, and whether/when to be gender neutral or gender inclusive.

This is even before the translator decides which English words and phrases will be most suitable in a translation intended for the ordinary reader.

When translators are turning ancient texts into modern English, there are different options available to them in terms of how they go about achieving their aims and many judgment calls to be made along the way. The most basic distinctions are between what's called a "literal" translation, a "dynamic equivalent" translation, and a "free" translation (which is more properly called a "paraphrase").

A "literal" translation is closer to a "word-for-word" translation, or "formal-equivalence." The translator is trying to render each word of the original language into English preserving the original sentence structure, grammatical construction, and idioms (turns of phrase) as much as possible. That last phrase, "as much as possible," obviously carries some considerable weight, which is why translations that have the same objectives don't read identically. All translators want their end-product to be in readable, understandable modern English, which a "pure" "word-for-word" or "literal" approach wouldn't always achieve.

A "dynamic equivalent" translation is a "thought-for-thought" or "functional-equivalent" translation. This takes the goal of translating into readable, understandable modern English one step further. It's also called a "meaning-based" translation. It's aiming to produce the closest "natural equivalent" of the message of the original language text. So its main objective is conveying the message and the meaning of the original in today's English.

Those who prefer a so-called "literal" or "word-for-word" approach will point to the fact that a "meaning-based" or "message-based" approach inevitably includes more scope for interpretation on the part of the translators, and that will be true. However, in both approaches, this is really only a question of degree. All scholarly translations are aiming to be faithful to the original and still eminently readable. And yet, the choice of an English word or phrase to achieve that is not always easy, especially when one is writing for an audience that does not have specialized background knowledge of ancient culture and customs and will be at risk of "reading-in" meanings from today's usage of an English word, i.e., what it's pointing to now, rather than what it would have been pointing to then. A simple example would be whether to render the Greek and Hebrew words for "slave" as "slave," "servant," or "bondservant." "Slave" is in danger of conjuring up images of the transatlantic slave trade rather than ancient Israel; "servant" is in danger of diminishing the impact by visualizing modern domestic staff roles; and "bondservant" will have people asking, "What's a bondservant"? The same is true in decisions about weights and measures, money, idioms, metaphors, and so on. If those are still clear enough today in a "word-for-word" approach, all well and good—"word-for-word" and "thought-for-thought" approaches can treat them much the same. But if they are not—if the message or the meaning would then be unclear—then a "thought-for-thought" or "dynamic equivalent" translation will change them into something directly comparable that the modern reader will be better able to grasp without specialized knowledge.

Finally, there is the "free" translation approach (or, "paraphrase"), which goes still further. Perhaps the best current example of that, and one which is extremely popular, is Eugene Peterson's *The Message*. Compare some passages in *The Message* with those same passages in translations and they may be unrecognizable! Peterson's stated goal is to try to capture the "spirit" of the original, offering not a "study Bible" but a "reading Bible." In its own descriptive words, "*The Message* tries to recapture the Word in the words we use today." This includes a great deal of modern vernacular, creative reimagining, and "street language," all of which is fine so long as we are perfectly clear as to what it is and what it isn't (in particular that we do not use it for study).

So going back to the original question—which is "best"? The "best answer" to that will depend on one's objectives. My personal view as a "professional user" would be to read a good dynamic-equivalent translation (such as the NLT) for devotions and start with a formal-equivalent translation (such as the NIV) for study. I say "start with" because it is sensible to compare and contrast more than one translation. For preaching, I tend to use a variety of both types, and a range of different versions. Personally, however, I rarely if ever use a free translation like *The Message*. To my mind, a good dynamic equivalent like the NLT works well enough and further explanation of the text's intentions is the preacher's job. What that approach looks like in practice is that I will usually start by looking at the NIV, which I feel generally gets the balance right. I will also look at the NLT, which often reads more comfortably for a typical congregation (my passages will often be drawn half from the NIV and half from the NLT). If I need to go closer to the word-for-word of the original, I will look to the NASB. Very, very occasionally I may quote something from *The Message*. For example, I rather like how it treats John 1:14: "The Word became flesh and blood, and moved into the neighborhood." I will invariably make clear that *The Message* is a paraphrase, though.

Just a couple more things to mention. The first is that all of the best translations are produced by large teams of perhaps 100 or more eminent scholars. This is true of the NIV, NLT, and NASB, as well as many others. The advantages of that are obvious. Equally, some translations are the work of an individual. Years ago, the best known was by J. B. Phillips. More recently, N. T. Wright and David Bentley Hart have produced their own New Testament translations. By all means do read them, but keep in mind that however highly we may regard and respect the individuals, the potential weaknesses of a single-author version are obvious. Finally, I would personally steer away from versions produced by a single individual with a particular agenda, such as the so-called *Passion Translation*, which the publisher describes as "a heart-level translation, from the passion of God's heart to the passion of your heart." Always check any individual's academic credentials and peer reviews.

A website such as biblegateway.com has a wide range of available translations. It includes information on the background and objectives in the versions' production. Verses can be compared across all English translations.

The last thing to say is why biblical scholars do not recommend the King James Version. The reason has nothing to do with its old-fashioned language of "thees" and "thous" and such like (after all, some would say it is endearingly poetic) but rather, its many inaccuracies. When the KJV was produced, knowledge of Hebrew was not so well advanced and the New Testament Greek text that they used dated from the tenth to the thirteenth centuries. Since then, many much earlier manuscripts have been discovered dating back to the second and third centuries, which are significantly more accurate, and our knowledge of language and culture of the period from recently discovered literature is far greater. Although it's easy to think that it must be closer to the original because it sounds so old-fashioned—the old joke is that the KJV is "the version Paul used"—it absolutely isn't. Whatever majesty of language it may possess is entirely down to cultural fondness.

Bibliography

Bauckham, Richard. "Hades, Hell." In *The Anchor Yale Bible Dictionary*, Volume 3, edited by David Noel Freedman, 14–15. New Haven, CT: Yale University Press, 2009.

Berding, Kenneth, and Jonathan Lunde, eds. *Three Views on the New Testament Use of the Old Testament*. Grand Rapids: Zondervan, 2008.

Bigalke, Ron J. "Editorial." *Journal of Dispensationalist Theology* 14.43 (2010) 5. Available at https://tyndale.edu/wp-content/uploads/JODT-Vol14-No43-Dec10.pdf (accessed January 11, 2021).

Boswell, John. *Christianity, Social Tolerance, and Homosexuality: Gay People in Western Europe from the Beginning of the Christian Era to the Fourteenth Century*. Chicago: University of Chicago Press, 1980.

Brown, Raymond E. *An Introduction to New Testament Christology*. Mahwah, NJ: Paulist, 1994.

Brownson, James V. *Bible, Gender, Sexuality: Reframing the Church's Debate on Same-Sex Relationships*. Grand Rapids: Eerdmans, 2013.

Burnhope, Stephen. *Atonement and the New Perspective: The God of Israel, Covenant, and the Cross*. Eugene: Pickwick, 2018.

Dawkins, Richard. *The God Delusion*. London: Bantam Press, 2006.

Fee, Gordon D., and Douglas Stuart. *How to Read the Bible for All Its Worth: A Guide to Understanding the Bible*. Grand Rapids: Zondervan, 1982.

———. *The Disease of the Health & Wealth Gospels*. Vancouver: Regent College, 2006.

Gagnon, Robert A. J. *The Bible and Homosexual Practice: Texts and Hermeneutics*. Nashville: Abingdon, 2002.

Goldingay, John. *Models for Interpretation of Scripture*. Grand Rapids: Eerdmans, 1995.

Green, Joel B., and Mark D. Baker. *Recovering the Scandal of the Cross: Atonement in New Testament & Contemporary Contexts*. Downers Grove, IL: IVP, 2000.

Hilborn, David, ed. *The Nature of Hell: A Report by the Evangelical Alliance Commission on Unity and Truth among Evangelicals (ACUTE)*. Carlisle, UK: Paternoster, 2000.

Johnson, Luke Timothy. "The New Testament's Anti-Jewish Slander and the Convention of Ancient Polemic." *Journal of Biblical Literature* 108 (1989) 419–41.

Loader, William. *Sexuality in the New Testament: Understanding the Key Texts*. Louisville: Westminster John Knox, 2010.

Longman, Tremper, and John H. Walton. *The Lost World of the Flood: Mythology, Theology, and the Deluge Debate*. Downers Grove, IL: IVP, 2018.

Lucado, Max. *God Came Near: God's Perfect Gift*. Nashville: Thomas Nelson, 2004.

Lyotard, Jean-Francois. *The Postmodern Condition: A Report on Knowledge*. Manchester: University of Manchester Press, 1984.

MacDonald, Gregory. *The Evangelical Universalist*. 2nd ed. Eugene, OR: Cascade, 2012.

McKnight, Scot. *The Blue Parakeet: Rethinking How You Read the Bible*. Grand Rapids: Zondervan, 2008.

McLaren, Brian D. *The Story We Find Ourselves In: Further Adventures of a New Kind of Christian*. London: SPCK, 2013.

Paul, Ian. *Same-Sex Unions: The Key Biblical Texts*. Cambridge: Grove Books, 2014.

Pearse, Meic. *Why the Rest Hates the West*. London: SPCK, 2003.

Piper, John. "What Made It Okay for God to Kill Women and Children in the Old Testament?"; available at https://www.desiringgod.org/interviews/what-made-it-okay-for-god-to-kill-women-and-children-in-the-old-testament (accessed January 11, 2021).

Sayers, Dorothy. *Letters to a Diminished Church: Passionate Arguments for the Relevance of Christian Doctrine*. Nashville: Thomas Nelson, 2004.

Scroggs, Robin. *The New Testament and Homosexuality: Contextual Background for Contemporary Debate*. Philadelphia: Fortress, 1983.

Skarsaune, Oskar. *In the Shadow of the Temple: Jewish Influences on Early Christianity*. Downers Grove, IL: IVP, 2002.

Stein, Robert H. *A Basic Guide to Interpreting the Bible: Playing by the Rules*. 2nd ed. Grand Rapids: Baker Academic, 2011.

Thackway, J. P. "The Spirit of the Age and the Church in Our Day"; available at https://www.bibleleaguetrust.org/the-spirit-of-the-age-and-the-church-in-our-day (accessed January 11, 2021).

Tinker, Michael. "John Calvin's Concept of Divine Accommodation." *Churchman* 118.4 (2004) 325–58.

Trible, Phyllis. *Texts of Terror: Literary-Feminist Readings of Biblical Narratives*. Philadelphia: Fortress, 1984.

Walton, John H., and D. Brent Sandy. *The Lost World of Scripture: Ancient Literary Culture and Biblical Authority*. Downers Grove. IL: IVP, 2013.

Wenham, John W. *Facing Hell: The Story of a Nobody, an Autobiography 1913–1996*. Carlisle, UK: Paternoster, 1998.

Wright, N. T. "How Can the Bible Be Authoritative?" *Vox Evangelica* (1991) 7–32; available at https://ntwrightpage.com/2016/07/12/how-can-the-bible-be-authoritative (accessed January 11, 2021).

———. *The New Testament and the People of God*. London: SPCK, 1992.

———. *Surprised by Hope: Rethinking Heaven, the Resurrection, and the Mission of the Church*. London: SPCK, 2008.

CPSIA information can be obtained
at www.ICGtesting.com
Printed in the USA
LVHW111403070521
686781LV00003B/99